Y0-BSW-110

14

3 0700 10087 5086

WITHDRAWN

PROPAGANDA, POLITICS AND FILM, 1918–45

PROPAGANDA, POLITICS AND FILM, 1918-45

Edited by
Nicholas Pronay
and
D.W. Spring

© Nicholas Pronay and D.W. Spring 1982

All rights reserved. No part of this publication may be
reproduced or transmitted, in any form or by any means,
without permission

First published 1982 by
THE MACMILLAN PRESS LTD
London and Basingstoke
Companies and representatives
throughout the world

ISBN 0 333 30939 1

Printed in Hong Kong

Contents

Notes on the Contributors

Nicholas Pronay is Senior Lecturer in Modern History at the University of Leeds. His publications include (with Frances Thorpe) *British Official Films in the Second World War. A Descriptive Catalogue* (Clio Press, 1980) and articles and a BBC Further Education television series on various aspects of the political impact of the cinema in the 1930s and 1940s and on the problems of teaching and research in this area. He is currently Chairman of the InterUniversity History Film Consortium and Director of Television and Film for the Historical Association.

Philip M. Taylor is Lecturer in International History at the University of Leeds. He is the author of *The Projection of Britain: British Overseas Publicity and Propaganda 1919-39* (Cambridge University Press, 1981), of several articles on British propaganda and (with M. L. Sanders) of *British propaganda in the First World War* (Macmillan, 1982).

D. W. Ellwood is Lecturer in Contemporary British and International History at the University of Bologna. His publications include *Europe and America in Cultural Diplomacy* (1973) and *L'alleato nemico: la politica dell'occupazione anglo-americana dell'Italia*, 1943-6 (Milan, 1977).

Peter Stead is Lecturer in History at the University College of Swansea and has been Visiting Lecturer at Wellesley College, Mass. His publications include a history of *Coleg Harlech* (University of Wales Press, 1978) and 'Hollywood's message to the world: the British response to the 1930s' in the *Historical Journal for Film, Radio and Television* (1981). He is currently Executive Secretary of the InterUniversity History Film Consortium for whom he made *The Great Depression*, Historical Studies in Film, No. 5.

J. A. Ramsden is Lecturer in the Department of History at Queen Mary College, University of London. His publications include *The Age of Balfour and Baldwin 1902–40* (Longman, 1978) and *The Making of Conservative Party Policy* (Longman, 1980) and he has produced the film, *Stanley Baldwin*, in the Archive Series of the InterUniversity History Film Consortium.

Bert Hogenkamp studied at the University of Amsterdam and is a freelance journalist and historian. He has published several articles on film and the labour movement in *Sight and Sound* and the Dutch film journal, *Skrien.*

Elizabeth Grottle Strebel is a Lecturer in the Cinema Department of the State University of New York. Her publications include *French Social Cinema of the Nineteen Thirties* (New York: Arno Press, 1980) and several articles on French film and politics in the historical and film journals, including the *Journal of Contemporary History.*

Ian Dalrymple was head of the Crown Film Unit, 1940–3 and was responsible for the inception of many wartime propaganda classics such as *Fires Were Started, Western Approaches, London Can Take It* etc. His post-war films include *The Royal Heritage, A Hill in Korea* and the series, *The Changing Face of Europe.* He was Chairman of the British Film Academy, 1957-8.

Helen Forman (*née* de Mouilpied) worked in the non-theatrical distribution organisation of the Documentary Movement at the Imperial Institute before the Second World War. She transferred to the Ministry of Information where she became deputy director of the non-theatrical distribution section of the Films Division and later Chief Film Production Officer. After the war she was active as a governor of the British Film Institute.

Tom Harrisson (d. 1975), anthropologist and co-founder of Mass-Observation. He served in the Ministry of Information, 1940–2 and as a parachute officer behind the Japanese lines in Borneo and Sarawak. Visiting professor at several universities, his publications include *Savage Civilisation* (1937), *Britain by Mass-Observation* (1939), *Home Propaganda* (1941) and 22 other books. He produced with Hugh Gibbs the award winning film series *The Borneo Story.*

Sergei Drobashenko is Deputy Director of the Film Art Institute of the State Film Archive of the USSR. He has written extensively about Soviet film, in particular documentary film, including an introduction to his edition of Dziga Vertov, *Stat'i, dnevniki, zamysly* (Articles, diaries, thoughts), (Moscow, 1966), *Fenomen dostovernosti. Ocherki teorii dokumental'nogo fil'ma* (The phenomenon of truth. Studies in the theory of documentary film), (Moscow, 1972) and *Istoriya sovetskogo dokumental'nogo fil'ma* (The History of Soviet documentary film), (Moscow, 1980).

D. W. Spring is Senior Lecturer in Russian and East European History at the University of Nottingham. He has been Executive Secretary of the InterUniversity History Film Consortium for whom he produced *The Winter War and its European Context*, Historical Studies in Film, No. 4. He has published articles on various aspects of Russian foreign policy before 1917, and with his wife on the Finnish Communist Party, and is currently completing a book on Russian foreign policy, 1870–1917.

Introduction

NICHOLAS PRONAY

The articles comprising this volume have been prepared at the invitation of the InterUniversity History Film Consortium for delivery at two conferences held at the Imperial War Museum. With one exception they have been revised or extended in the light of subsequent discussions. The majority of the articles are the work of historians, based upon the record material which has become increasingly available in recent years. They thus represent the perspectives of current historical thinking. By contrast the contributions by Mr Ian Dalrymple and Lady (Helen) Forman, dealing respectively with the Crown Film Unit and the non-theatrical film distribution scheme of the Ministry of Information, are based on the personal experiences of two contemporaries who served, in a distinguished capacity, in the departments which they discuss. Tom Harrisson's contribution is in a category of its own. He founded and directed Mass-Observation which provided the Ministry of Information with independent assessments of the impact of its film propaganda. His contribution printed here was, however, based on research which he and his assistants carried out 25 years later in the archives of Mass-Observation and which led to his important book on British attitudes during the Blitz.

Tom Harrisson's contribution to this volume is also the only one which is printed here in the form in which he actually delivered it: he died in tragic circumstances before he could prepare the paper for publication.

The InterUniversity History Film Consortium comprises, at the time of writing, the history departments of the Universities of Leeds, Nottingham, Reading, Birmingham, Edinburgh, Sussex, Wales, Queen Mary College, London, and the London School of Economics and Political Science. Its formation was proposed by

J. A. S. Grenville and it was established in 1967–9 by a group of senior historians, under his own chairmanship, which included G. F. A. Best, Alun Davies, W. R. Fryer, H. Hearder, J. C. Holt, J. B. Joll, C. L. Mowat and D. C. Watt. The overall purpose was to overcome the financial and institutional obstacles which then lay in the path of historians wanting to work with film for academic purposes. The Consortium's first practical objective was to facilitate the making of films for use in undergraduate courses by historians interested in exploring the contribution which films and sound-recordings could make to historical understanding.

Films and sound-recordings as historical record material were then highly unfamiliar territory for historians. Their training, in analysing and classifying records in terms of historical evidence and familiarity with the processes which created them, had not extended to films or recorded sounds. The approach of the Consortium was based on the belief that, rather than theoretical debate, the first essential was for as many historians as possible to be given the opportunity of exploring their nature and problems at first hand, by actually working with them. The Consortium believed that an understanding of the evidentiary problems inherent in the medium of film, of the primary or secondary nature of different kinds of film and of the contribution which they could make to different branches of historical enquiry, would result most effectively from a practical understanding on the part of historians working in various branches of history of the way an audio-visual medium communicates information and views. In the case of such a complex and interactive process of communications, we believe, the most effective way of learning is by doing. The Consortium therefore provides the financial and technical means by which historians can make studies of major topics of twentieth-century history actually in the medium of film and which blend the different kinds of source materials, including archival film, with the historian's interpretation and analysis of the subject as a whole. The film-studies are designed for use in undergraduate history courses and intended to be discussed with colleagues and students alike.

From the beginning we believed that a corpus of evidentiary rules and a conceptual framework was more likely to emerge from personal experience in grappling with these 'media records', from trying to use the medium for conveying one's own views, from the reactions and questions of undergraduates and from discussions between historians belonging to different branches of the subject after they have had such experience, than from *a priori* debates about 'film as evidence'. The emphasis of the Consortium was therefore placed on giving an opportunity to as many historians as possible to work on one extended film study even if that meant that each 'film' as a first attempt was likely to be less polished than if it were the result of increasing experience. Historians who have taken the opportunity offered by the Consortium for exploring film records include: Paul Addison, Peter C. Boyle, D. N. Dilks, J. A. S. Grenville, Antony Polonsky, John Ramsden, Malcolm Smith, D. W. Spring and Peter Stead.

It was also hoped that the use of these film-studies within the member universities as well as in others which purchased them would not only add variety to teaching history, raise new questions and extend the empathetic understanding of the history of the twentieth century amongst students, but would generate interest for postgraduate research into the political context and impact of the new media of communications. In order to encourage the exploration of the connections between developments in communications and developments in politics or international relations, the Consortium decided in 1972, on the initiative of its Executive Secretary Nicholas Pronay, to organise conferences and sponsor research and publication in that area. The first conference topic chosen was the Ministry of Information with the focus on its film-propaganda work in the context of the broader issues of propaganda policy and censorship.

The conference, which was held at the Imperial War Museum in 1973, was well attended by historians from Britain and abroad and also by many contemporaries of the Ministry of Information. It created considerable interest, which extended also to the general public unusually for an historical conference and it led to publishing interest in the subject of propaganda. It also led to new research work and publications, including Professor M. L. G. Balfour's important work *Propaganda in War, 1939–1945*, and a comprehensive and descriptive catalogue of *British Official Films in the Second World War*.

In organising its 1979 conference, the Consortium sought to bring together some of the results of the considerable volume of research work, which had developed since 1973, on various aspects of the impact of modern communications during the period between 1918 and 1945.

In reading the studies contained in this volume one should bear in mind the general thesis which has been arrived at by those working in this area because, concerned as each article is with a particular aspect, it is implicit in them rather than being presented as a general conclusion in its own right. Yet it makes a significant contribution in itself to our understanding of the interwar period, in addition to placing these particular studies in a fuller interpretative context. This thesis is that between 1918 and 1945 the new media and new techniques of 'communications' were perceived as having a fundamentally important *political* role. And, because this belief was acted upon by governments and communicators alike, 'politics and communications' came indeed to be inextricably linked, to a much greater and much more conscious extent than ever before, both in domestic politics and to a slightly lesser extent perhaps, in international relations. Whether the new forms of communications – including both mass-communications media such as film or radio and the international telecommunications media – would have had such a significance for the politics of the period had there been a cooler and more dismissive attitude adopted towards them is impossible to answer from the available evidence. It is in fact the same sort of tantalising question as that which arises in the mind of the historian when reading the political records of the sixteenth and seventeenth centuries in respect of 'religion and politics'. Men act according to their perceptions. What politicians believe to be prime political factors and therefore prime concerns for them, become important factors in the making of political decisions while the perception lasts – whether it be 'religion' or 'unemployment'. So it was in the interwar period with 'propaganda'.

In Britain, at least, this particular perception arose in essence because certain far-reaching political developments coincided over the same brief period of time with a range of technological inventions. In themselves these inventions would have had a major social and political impact, whenever they might have occurred. However, coming as they did in the same brief period of time they gave men who were fundamentally out of sympathy with both the new political developments and the results of the new technologies, a sense of being beleaguered by it all. From the perspective of today, when both the political changes and the technological developments have run more of their course, it is probably reasonable to conclude that they over-reacted. But, the new technological media of mass-communications appeared, *prima facie*, to be tailor-made for either accelerating or controlling those very processes of change in outlook and expectations amongst the urban working masses on which rested those new political ideologies which were threatening, in Mr Baldwin's phrase, to 'blow the system into fragments'. They reacted to the appearance of this combination, a new kind of alienation amongst the industrial workers and the invention of infinitely more effective means of spreading ideas amongst them, as could be expected of men who were tough and able politicians, but whose age, social background and education predisposed them against taking a confident and optimistic view of the likely impact of these new phenomena. They simply dared not take the risk of failing to act on the claims of their young advisers about the effectiveness of new techniques of propaganda and counter-subversion operations of all kinds made possible by the new technologies. Moreover, these techniques appeared to have been tested successfully during the First World War, when some of their advisers had served in various branches of the new dark art of psychological warfare. Faced with frighteningly real political developments appearing to be coming to a head, in the immediate postwar years, it was their conservatism and caution, their 'safety first' mentality which, paradoxically, led them to back those of their 'young men' who wanted to use radically new techniques of political persuasion which had been originally developed for the political warfare campaign against the Central Powers. The initial decisions about how to respond to the availability of new communications and counter-propaganda techniques were all taken during the 1918–24 period when political developments in Britain appeared to be most directly menacing. It is against this background that we can understand the surprising willingness of this generation of leaders to go so very far in incorporating 'propaganda', in its fullest twentieth-century sense, into politics.

The first of the political changes which so deeply worried and affected the political leadership concerned the electoral basis of the political system. Before the First World War Britain possessed a political system based on long-established and still vital liberal traditions. It was in fact the most genuinely liberal-minded political system in the world. But while liberal, the British political system was not a democracy and neither had it taken 'the decisive steps' towards becoming a democracy by the end of the nineteenth century – in contrast with the view commonly found in many 'textbooks'. Beyond all the technicalities in which the issue was not altogether unwittingly wrapped, there stood the indisputable fact that the first British government of the twentieth century (elected 1900) rested on 1.8 million votes including those of the pluralists and the whole Mother of Parliaments on the votes of 3½ million people out of a population of 41 million. A gradual extension of the franchise *eventually* to encompass all was certainly an aim honestly held by most of the political leaders of the period, but so was the conviction that the arrival of the mass-electorate within the immediate future would cause a disaster. The arrival of the mass-male-electorate, with a startling suddenness in 1918 and its then inevitable extension to women was, at best, thought to open the door to demagogues and Press-power. More likely, it was feared, it would overwhelm the party-political system and, at worst, break up the whole political and social structure owing to the simple fact that practically all of that mass of people who had not been able to vote before were working men, their wives and daughters, or the unemployed.

If the franchise suddenly brought the prospect of an electorate susceptible to demagoguery and without education or balance, a more unexpected and in a sense deeper impact came from the realisation by 1916, that conscription had finally become unavoidable. No Englishman, unlike continentals, could have previously been compelled to die for the foreign policies pursued by his governments, unless he chose to transform himself into a soldier and accepted that he was paid to fight and 'not to reason why'.

The exciting game of foreign affairs particularly in the sense of acquiring and ruling, of gaining and maintaining possession of vast overseas territories in competition alike with other European powers and with the kings and emperors of the distant parts of the globe, could therefore remain substantially the cherished pre-serve of the ruling group, still very largely aristocratic/gentry based. The political equilibrium and easy temper of late Victorian Britain and the perception of foreign affairs as the stuff of 'high politics' rested on the tacit understanding that ordinary Englishmen would not have their normal lives interrupted, nor would they be heavily taxed and above all, would not have to die as a consequence of the ruling groups' pursuits in their 'sport of kings'. Since Empires are neither created nor maintained by diplomacy alone, (indeed in the 50 years before 1914 British forces fought more battles than the conscript armies of the Central Powers put together) the concomitant wars would be fought by well-drilled professional soldiers who asked no questions, were officered by the aristocracy and gentry, garrisoned abroad for much of the time and paid for in part by the revenues of the empire. Accordingly, the ruling group did not constantly have to look over their shoulders at the masses and wonder whether the foreign-policy objective of the moment was worth the risk not only of forcing them into uniform but also of putting weapons into their hands. On the contrary, they had a body of men detached from the concerns of the classes they left for the forces, were proud to be the kind of soldiers who did not ask 'why are we here?' and who could put on splendid displays to warm the hearts and bring out the cheers. And also, it provided a force which could be relied upon to act with disciplined obedience in case of 'civil troubles'. The freedom which this system gave to politicians for conducting rational, pragmatic and indeed effective foreign policies was one of the formative experiences of those who were to become leaders in the interwar period. It kept out ignorant if popular opinions, it allowed policy to be backed by instantly available force and by limited and controlled wars.

Apart from hampering the conduct of a rational and effective foreign policy, by the admission of the feelings of those who would provide the rank and file of the conscript army in place of the views of a well-informed and closely-knit circle, conscription, it was fully realised in the prolonged debate about it before and during the war, would strike a particularly fundamental blow at the whole political-social system of Britain. This was due to the large number of officers required by a mass-army. As the experience after 1916 proved in practice, they would have to come from the lower professional middle classes, the backbone of methodism and non-conformity, from groups which in Britain had particularly strong traditions of independent judgment and of a moral and ethical outlook on politics: men only too willing to reason why. The certain knowledge that henceforth any major war would have to be fought with both conscript men and conscript officers from the start, together with the effects of a mass-electorate, helped to create a gloomy perception of the future in which government policies and actions, however urgent, would have to wait upon the persuasion of masses of people without either the time or the education to be remotely as well-informed as the groups whose opinions were important before the war.

The third political development, which at times pushed the anxieties of the political leadership of the interwar period close to panic, was the growth of the labour movement and their perception of it as a political and ideological force in addition to being an organisation of labour for wage-bargaining. They saw this development as essentially a process of politicisation, whereby working people were being gradually persuaded that the daily problems which they experienced, such as inadequate wages and the insecurity of their jobs, must not be seen as the consequence of personal misfortune, or the actions of particular owners or of the economic problems of the firms they worked for. Rather, these problems should be seen as the consequences of government policies and indeed of the political system itself. Politically caused, the problems dominating their lives as individuals could thus only be remedied by political action taken by themselves acting as the working class.

It was in the concept of the 'General Strike' that the politicisation of the industrial and economic grievances of working people culminated. The General Strike, it was recognised by both sides, was a weapon for breaking the political system of a highly industrialised and urbanised country through the vulnerability of its vast conurbations in which life itself depended, for food, water, heating and sanitation, on an intricate system of transport and municipal services. The extent and temper of the strikes of 1910-13 and the even greater strikes threatened for the autumn of 1914 appeared to give a menacing air of reality to the idea of a General Strike as a means of destroying the whole political system.

The crowded events in the year following the Armistice seemed to confirm these perceptions while at the same time appeared to link the various elements into a frightening whole. The most significant of these events for conditioning the minds of the postwar political leaders were the disaffection and mutinies in the conscript army beginning in the summer of 1918; the politically conscious labour disturbances, particularly in the 'Red Clyde', and the failure of the attempted intervention in Russia which demonstrated that the army could no longer be employed for any purpose which the government thought fit on the assumption that 'the soldier' was not paid to think. The police strikes of 1919 then deepened the impression made by these events for, like the soldiers of the regular army, policemen were also recruited substantially from the working class.

Thus the opinions and perceptions of working people in Britain, who had always been the majority but who had now become by far the largest part of the new mass-electorate and who also formed the rank and file of the army and the police, came to be seen as vitally important. To gain control, therefore, over the formation of their opinions and perceptions came to be seen by the political leaders of postwar Britain as the most essential step upon which everything else depended, including survival for the political system itself. Moreover, by the early 1920s, they became conscious that the domestic impact of mass opinion replacing that of the educated and experienced minority was likely to be compounded by the same process occurring in foreign countries. If anything, this was believed to have even worse consequences for rational policies because the war had brought about changes abroad even more dramatically and, in many cases, much more comprehensively than in Britain. Looking back at this period in 1939, in one of his moods of 'appalling frankness', Stanley Baldwin encapsulated the perceptions of the interwar political leadership of which he was himself perhaps the single most influential member:

> ... it was evident that in political status vast masses of the people of Europe had advanced during those four years further than they might have in a generation, and the question was whether their status had progressed beyond their education or their power to utilise it fruitfully. In England we for the first time adopted universal suffrage, enfranchising also a large number of women, for whom a full franchise followed a few years later. In England also, largely owing to an active propaganda, there had been in the years immediately preceding the war a growing feeling of class consciousness, and there was now a certain amount of inflammable material at hand. Voices were heard towards the end of the war: 'Let us bring this war to an end and get on with the only war that really matters.' ... We were then, more than at any time in

my recollection, a divided nation . . . there was a bitter feeling running through the workshops, north and south, east and west: we were antagonistic and non co-operative. Industrial difficulties were made more difficult by the introduction of politics into the struggle. . . . The storm broke in the General Strike of 1926. The struggle had to come and the Government had to accept the challenge.

The far-reaching and extremely rapid changes in communications technology and organisation, which Lord Briggs argued were a 'communications revolution' standing alongside the industrial revolution and the Russian revolution as an equal partner in importance, coincided almost exactly in time with these political developments. By the end of the nineteenth century international communications were transformed by the laying of electric telegraph cables which linked all parts of the globe in instantaneous contact. The quick and far-sighted recognition on the part of the British Government of the strategic and political importance of cable communications led to the building of the remarkable 'Red Network' of undersea cables under British control which, as is well-known, gave the British Empire secret and secure channels of command and information of great strategic importance. Less well-known, though from the political perspective at least as important, was the development of a world-wide network of international *news*-communications by the news-agencies led by Reuters and also from Britain. By the last decade of the nineteenth century news gathering offices employing many thousands of skilled reporters had been established and were linked by international telegraph companies. The flow of information was processed by large and efficient new distribution systems which, at a remarkably low cost, made it available to any newspaper and indeed to anyone with the money for subscription and which provided a news gathering and distribution system rivalling those of the foreign ministries of the world. Lord Salisbury was not exaggerating when he complained to his officials that he, the Foreign Secretary served by the finest Foreign Office in the world, was as likely, or sometimes more likely, to find out what had happened the previous day from opening his newspapers at breakfast as he was from opening the boxes brought to him by the Foreign Office messengers. The significance of the news-agencies lay in the fact that they broke the age-old monopoly of governments to possess alone the information necessary for formulating policies, at the time when decisions need to be taken. Before the development of news-agencies the role of the general public was confined to passing judgment upon the results of actions already taken and even then relying largely on the information divulged by the government itself. The breaking of the governments' and ruling groups' privilege to know by the vast network of agency reporters spread around the globe was given particular significance by the next development, coming in 1896, that of the mass-circulation newspaper which could communicate to a large new class of people who had been hitherto outside the reach of politics.

The news-agencies were world-wide organisations. Particularly in countries with a more or less democratic political system, such as France and especially the United States, they helped to make public opinion an active and important force with which British foreign policy had to reckon. News-control therefore became an increasingly vital ingredient in the conduct of foreign policy. Britain led the way in giving practical consideration to the importance of influencing news-flow. Through secret subsidies and other means cable companies were encouraged to route their cables so that cable *termini* were established on British territories and the security services were permitted to monitor cable communications. When in the course of the Boer War the results of these policies were utilised for immediately political purposes and undesirable dispatches and telegrams actually censored or stopped, the recognition of the predominant position achieved by Britain sent a shockwave around the capitals of the world. Perhaps the preamble to the French Telegraph Act of 1900, by which a large sum was allocated in a vain attempt to create a cable network not under British control, and which was followed by similar attempts by other powers, states most concisely how the change brought by cables and news-agencies was perceived:

England owes her influence in the world perhaps more to her cable communications than to her navy. She controls the news and makes it serve her policy and commerce in a marvellous manner.

From 1882 onwards defence committees frequently considered various aspects of the strategic significance of cable-communications for Britain and their reports regularly impressed on the mind of the political leadership the significance of modern communications. It symbolised the extent to which Britain's leadership became conscious of the significance of modern communications, that the first act of war on the part of the British Empire in 1914, within a few hours of the expiry of the British ultimatum to Berlin, was the cutting of Germany's undersea cables which linked her with the Americas. It was a technological feat which astounded the Germans who had believed it to be impossible and it was achieved by permanently stationing, from 1911 onwards, specially equipped admiralty vessels close to the points where German cables were nearest to the surface. The cutting of their cables debilitated German diplomacy owing to the time it took for instructions to reach their embassies through other channels. It also secured in the American Press the dominance of the British version of the news about the war, its causes, atrocities and aims. Through the concomitant development of Britain's Postal and Telegraphic Censorship Bureau the cutting of their cables also made possible what German planners had equally assumed to be impossible, namely the hunting down of Germany's suppliers in neutral countries on which depended vital parts of the German industrial capacity for war. Germany was forced to communicate through encoded wireless messages which could be picked up and the codes broken.

The possibilities inherent in the combination of cable control which allowed the monitoring of the world's traffic, the vast extension of the scope of intelligence work into the area of communications and news manipulation were brilliantly demonstrated by the director of Naval Intelligence, Admiral Hall, in the Zimmerman telegram operation. It left a lasting impression on those who were in the know about it, such as J. C. C. Davidson, who together with Admiral Hall himself, and of course Baldwin, came to devise after the end of the war the new strategies needed to combat 'Bolshevist subversion', as well as to seek the means for building a new populist basis for the Conservative party. Symbolically again, the conversion in 1925 of HMS *Hood*, then the most formidable battle-cruiser in the world, into what was probably the most powerful wireless transmitter in the world, in order to jam the transmissions coming from outside Leningrad through which, it was believed by both sides, the

General Strike could be directed into a Russian-style revolution, encapsulated one aspect of the multi-level interaction between 'communications and politics' in this period.

As a result the next invention, broadcasting, was instantly recognised as having, as the CID Imperial Communications Sub-Committee put it in 1921, 'incalculable significance for political stability'. And, as soon as it was demonstrated that voice transmissions (as distinct from morse-code) were a practical possibility it was determined that, notwithstanding the hallowed traditions of Speakers' Corner, Wilkes and Liberty or the Freedom of the Press, broadcasting in Britain was not to be permitted to any individual lest it should become an 'engine of propaganda', in the words of Baldwin's famous description of the mass circulation newspaper after Northcliffe. The 'great power and utility of broadcasting for good or evil' derived from the fact that unlike the Press a single source could instantaneously and simultaneously reach any individual; it could do so without any intermedial organisation or group of people, such as the Post Office, printers or transport, and do it in spoken words intelligible to anyone, however uneducated, as long as he possessed a receiver. Moreover, receivers were so simple to build that, as the Imperial Communications Committee had to recognise after exploring the practicability of the idea which initially much attracted it, to enforce the possession of sets only tuned to predetermined wavelengths would be quite impossible. Broadcasting to the mass of the people by anyone who could raise the money required, on the pattern of the Press, was therefore, given the political situation as perceived at the time, a risk which it was felt impossible to take. On the other hand, the use of broadcasting during the General Strike appeared to prove that, in the hands of experts but under firm political control, radio could give the government (as represented by Parliament and not of course the party of government) a most powerful weapon in the crusade for what Conservative Central Office liked to call, the 'Soul of the Nation'.

In 1896, the *annus mirabilis* of the history of political communications, the same year in which appeared the mass-circulation newspaper and when the theory of wireless transmission reached practicability, the cinema was invented. But while the wireless required another 20 years before it could become a practical device for *mass* communications and therefore came to be born as such in the bitter, worried and infinitely propaganda-conscious atmosphere which followed the First World War, the cinema grew and developed during the Indian summer of liberal optimism. During its first decade it was therefore allowed to grow in a totally uncontrolled way and it grew at a phenomenal rate. The result was that when its real political significance was recognised, it was no longer possible to introduce any tidy and simple system for its control and utilisation in 'the national interest' as in the case of broadcasting. By the interwar years the cinema came to be perceived as being both the most powerful of the new communications media and the most difficult to control.

As a medium, film operates through images and stereotypes, through a non-verbalised intuitive identification between the individual in the darkened auditorium and the stereotypes projected on the screen. It works by drawing together into a personal whole images assumed to be photographic reality with elements of the viewer's own personal experiences, dreams and wish-fulfilment. Above all, it creates vicarious self- and group-recognition in the persons and situations portrayed on the screen. It operates precisely at that level of perceptions about oneself and one's relationship with others – work mates, bosses, police, soldiers, clergymen, parents and so on – through which people perceive their situation in the society in which they live, or alternatively, that of other persons and their situations in other countries and other social environments. The cinema therefore operates on that particular level of individual perception where personal experience is generalised and stereotyped. Moreover, in the interwar period it encompassed, most commonly, just the kind of social stereotypes which were thought to be at the heart of the political/social/economic divide.

For persons of real literacy, the drama and the novel acted in the same way. But irrespective of what census returns might show, a very considerable part of those working men, their wives and children whose perceptions were at issue, lacked either the education, ability, leisure or opportunity for the level of literacy and the amount of reading time they required. The perculiar power and danger of the cinema lay in the fact that unlike literature, the film called for no literacy, no education and no effort, provided the maker of the film knew his business.

Since a film once made could be copied at no great cost in

virtually limitless numbers and each print projected
simultaneously for a large number of people, needing premises
and staff incomparably less expensive than running a theatre,
technology had also created a medium which, for the first time,
possessed all the qualities needed for a universal mass medium,
and particularly a medium for the mass of urban working people.
Film, particularly sound-film, as a medium of communications
and the cinema as a technological/economic system thus became
the first mass medium. They crossed over the inner frontiers of
education and class, frontiers which previously only the medium
of oratory (and preaching) could cross but without the capacity of
mass distribution.

The phenomenal growth of the cinema in working-class
districts, and its remarkably slow acceptance by the educated
classes, testify to the capacity of the cinema to reach working
people and especially the vitally important younger, most
vigorous and potentially dangerous section of it. By 1900, within
4 years of the very first 'moving pictures' demonstration as a
scientific curiosity at the North London Polytechnic, the War
Office recognised its impact amongst the young working class and
engaged its English inventor to produce a series on the British
Empire for encouraging recruitment. By 1911, within 5 years of
the opening of the first custom-built cinema, the Home Secretary
was conducting extended negotiations with the distributors of
film in order to find the most effective, acceptable and
apparently non-governmental way for establishing a censorship
over the cinema. In the winter of 1911, coinciding almost exactly
with the establishment of the War Office Admiralty Press
Committee (the 'D' Notice system), the British Board of Film
Censors was set up. Almost its very first action, in that period of
extensive strikes, was to secure the suppression of films showing
the strikes also going on in South Africa and Central Europe.
Before long, by the final years of the war, an elaborate set of
censorship rules had evolved. Amongst other subjects, the
'relationship between capital and labour' was banned. There had
also grown up during the war many organisations partly within
and partly outside the official information services, which were
eventually amalgamated in a Ministry of Information for the
production and distribution of propaganda films, both at home
and abroad.

But the problems presented by the cinema, greatly highlighted during the First World War, appeared to grow rather than diminish once the war was over and the feeling of fighting a more subtle and dangerous war at home and world-wide settled in during the course of 1919. The cinema, by this time, was manifestly *the* medium of the urban working masses and it was recognised as inherent in the medium that it operated over the way individuals perceived their own relationship to the world in which they lived and its capacity to envision different worlds. Given the political leaders' own perception of the existence of a deep and fundamental difference of outlook dividing society as the root cause of the dangers they believed they were facing, the cinema could hardly make a film which would not be perceived as propaganda. If it was set in the contemporary world and in British society it would either confirm and uphold or question and 'subvert' perceptions of authority, wealth distribution, social or working relationships, and so forth, in the context of which its story took place, however trivial or fanciful that might be. If it was set in the past, it would do the same for the history and thus the very traditions of England which were perceived to be at stake and the interpretation of which was thought to be a crucial part of those political perceptions about which there was so much concern.

It is immaterial, and impossible to decide on the evidence available, if right was on the side of the minority, who believed with George Strauss MP that it was nonsense to operate on the assumption that if Londoners kept seeing films about the October Revolution they would eventually storm Buckingham Palace or, to put it more fairly perhaps, those who believed that the great majority of working-class people were nowhere near as 'politicised' as was feared by their rulers and were more likely therefore to 'live out' through the films their sexual and family-peer group traumas instead of politicising them. The fact is that the majority of the political leaders of the interwar period in Britain saw the cinema as a singularly powerful medium for propaganda – just as Lenin, Stalin, Hitler, Mussolini and the Japanese government did. Consequently, an ever more elaborate and wide-ranging system for controlling what the mass of young working-class people should see continued to develop and become more sophisticated all through the interwar years.

By the end of the First World War knowledge of the secret operations of Wellington House, conducting propaganda towards the United States, directing the political warfare offensive against Austria and Germany and of the Postal and Telegraphic Censorship, which was ruefully described by a German Intelligence officer as 'the terrible net which strangulated Germany' came to enter the consciousness of the political leaders. They were themselves aware of the scale and extent of these operations, only a part of which could be publicly admitted, but were largely without the means for assessing what they had actually achieved. A belief in mass persuasion or 'propaganda' as a particular new technical expertise, involving essentially the manipulation of the new media of communications, coupled with a refurbished concept and scope for intelligence operations, came to be accepted by the political leadership as one of the many new, disagreeable but unavoidable, facts of postwar political life, alongside others such as an 'immature' mass-electorate and incipient class war fuelled by 'Bolshevik agitation'.

The rise of right-wing totalitarian mass movements, equally based on 'propaganda', in competition and in addition to 'Bolshevism', the onset of the Depression and the incipient or actual civil wars in many European countries, most notably in France, Austria and Spain, kept alive the identification between 'propaganda and politics' even after the immediate danger in Britain had passed in 1926. In fact the 1930s saw an increase in the link between 'propaganda and politics' when the issue of rearmament and preparations for another European war entered. The rate at which rearmament was possible was perceived to be dependent upon the pace of what Mr Baldwin called 'the education of the public'. With the spectre of facing Germany with a nation disunited along class lines, watching anxiously the progress of those who, like Sir Stafford Cripps, harangued workers of munition factories to seize the arms and turn them against the capitalist imperialist Tory Government, realising from intelligence reports the existence of pockets of ideological treason, the identification between politics and propaganda and more broadly between communications and politics was very strong indeed. After 1934, in addition to the plethora of private/semi-private organisations in the British manner, MacDonald, then Prime Minister, and Baldwin decided to establish a 'National Publicity Bureau'. This was under the effective direction of Major Sir Joseph Ball who came to Central Office soon after the war, like Admiral Hall before him, from the

Intelligence Services (in his case MI6) to build up the new kind of propaganda organisation which it was believed the age required. The significance attached to the work of the National Publicity Bureau and the scale of its operations may be gauged from the fact that its annual expenditure, which was additional to and separate from that of Central Office, reached at times £300,000, perhaps 9 times as much as Crewe House then the world's largest war-propaganda organisation cost in 1918.

There can be little doubt that in their perception of the political conditions and needs which had come into being after 1918, the political leaders of the period saw a direct link between politics and propaganda, and that they acted on their perceptions. This is a fact which the historian needs to take into account like other facts. Moreover, if the essence of political democracy is that it leaves political power and the responsibility for its use ultimately in the hands of the people, then communications and propaganda are a rather more essential part of the workings, and therefore of the history, of a democratic than of a totalitarian state. Although the word 'propaganda', as Mr Baldwin was always the first to emphasise, is indeed surrounded by an 'unattractive ambience', and doubly so in the conditions created by modern communications technology when it involves much else besides 'putting out bumph', the historian need not condemn him and his colleagues out of hand for employing it on such a scale.

Despite many gloomy predictions to the contrary, it can be argued, the counter-insurgency contingency plans first prepared in 1919 and annually revised until the late 1930s never had to be put into operation. Neither physical force, nor the weight of the law, nor social bribery on a large scale with all its consequences of inflation and economic distortion, had to be used to any significant extent to see Britain through essentially the same crises which shook and in some cases broke the liberal and democratic governments of many European countries. How great was the role, in that story of success, of the sustained effort to communicate, to persuade and to dissuade by all the means available and thus fight political battles in people's minds instead of in the streets?

The evidence is complex and requires careful balancing. Much of the wealth of the record material on the subject has yet to be fully explored. It is clear already, however, that 'propaganda', whether positive or negative in the sense of censorship, formed a significant part of the history of the interwar period. It provides an important subject for the historian seeking to understand and explain the events of that complex period when the political processes of Britain – and of course not only of Britain – had to adjust to those new expectations and technologies which set the twentieth century apart from previous ages.

PART I
The projection of Britain

1 British official attitudes towards propaganda abroad, 1918–39

PHILIP M. TAYLOR

'Propaganda' was not a word which most educated Englishmen chose to discuss freely during the inter-war years. Angus Fletcher, Director of the British Library of Information at New York, wrote in 1928 that it was 'a good word gone wrong – debauched by the late Lord Northcliffe' and he appealed for its complete removal from the diplomatic vocabulary.[1] Nor was propaganda an activity with which British officials generally felt comfortable. Sir Horace Wilson, for example, writing nearly 20 years after the dismemberment of Britain's elaborate First World War propaganda machinery, expressed the view that,

> Having been old fashioned for many years, I find myself unable to show enthusiasm for propaganda by this country and I still cannot bring myself to believe that it is a good substitute for calmly getting on with the business of Government, including a rational foreign policy.[2]

Another Treasury official, Edward Hale, who was becoming increasingly alarmed at the rapidly growing expenditure devoted to such work by foreign governments, warned in 1938 that 'a sort of armament race in propaganda is developing, to which it is no easier to see finality than the armament race itself'.[3] He continued:

> Armaments may be infinitely more expensive than propaganda but they, at least, have the virtue of being dumb and do not

cause the same ill-will. From the point of view of appeasement, the propaganda race seems to me the more serious danger.[4]

Apart from the somewhat dubious assumption that words spoke louder than even silent guns, views such as these were by no means uncommon in the late 1930s, and reveal the degree of prejudice and suspicion which still surrounded the use of propaganda as an instrument of national policy.

However, such opinions were based upon a misunderstanding of both the nature and the extent of Britain's involvement in conducting propaganda abroad. From the Treasury's point of view, familiarity with continuous requests for more money may well have served to breed contempt, but as Anthony Eden recognised during his first term as Foreign Secretary, propaganda had become an unavoidable fact of peacetime diplomatic life. He wrote in late 1937:

> It is perfectly true, of course, that good . . . propaganda cannot remedy the damage done by a bad foreign policy, but it is no exaggeration to say that even the best of diplomatic policies may fail if it neglects the tasks of interpretation and persuasion which modern conditions impose. We have daily experience of what we may expect to suffer if we leave the field of foreign public opinion to our antagonists, and we must face the fact that these misinterpretations can only be countered by equally energetic actions on our part on behalf of the truth.[5]

This statement reveals three of the basic assumptions on which the conduct of British overseas propaganda was based. In the first place, propaganda was designed to serve as an adjunct to normal diplomacy and not, as Sir Horace Wilson seemed to believe, as a 'substitute' for it, which was more often the case in the totalitarian regimes.[6] Secondly, the British Government, or more specifically the Foreign Office, embarked upon such work as a response to the anti-British propaganda activities of other countries. It was rather a reaction to external stimuli than the consequence of any desire to extend the responsibilities of the Foreign Office. And thirdly, Eden's statement reveals the basic conviction in the value of 'propaganda with facts' within which, as Sir John Reith later put it, news was considered to be 'the shocktroops of propaganda'.[7] It might further be added that the

Foreign Office believed in the value of qualitative rather than quantitative propaganda, and that the financial costs involved were slight when compared with the enormous expenditures of rival powers.

Nevertheless, it is also true to say that the depth of prejudice and suspicion was decidedly less deep-rooted in the late 1930s than it had been at the end of the First World War. A simple illustration of the change which had taken place, at least in Parliamentary opinion, can be found in the contrast between the virtually unanimous hostility of the House of Commons towards the work of Lord Beaverbrook's Ministry of Information in 1918[8] and the equally unanimous support given by all parties to the propaganda work being done by various new British organisations during major debates on the subject in 1938[9] and 1939.[10] This was largely because the evidence and arguments which had first prompted the creation of the British Council in 1934[11] continued to gather force and wider currency during the remaining years of peace. Indeed, it was during this quinquennium that, both within official circles and beyond, the subject of propaganda received a measure of consideration unprecedented since the Armistice. The issue was kept alive not only by the continuation of anti-British propaganda, and the steps taken by the government to counter it, but also by questions and debates in the House of Commons, regular attention in the Press, numerous articles published in learned journals,[12] and by the appearance of several influential books.[13] Nor was it a question of concern merely confined to the lower and middle levels of government administration. Quite the contrary, in fact, for, by the late 1930s, propaganda became a recurring topic of top-level and even Cabinet consideration. 'This generation', observed one author in 1938, 'is witnessing a boom in propaganda'.[14]

In order to examine the transformation in official attitudes from general antipathy towards propaganda at the close of the First World War to its gradual acceptance as an essential ingredient of British peacetime diplomacy, it will be convenient to divide the process into three basic parts. First, it is important to recognise at the outset that although British propaganda was drastically reduced on the return of peace, it nonetheless did not cease entirely, even though it was to remain a constant victim of financial retrenchment and prejudice throughout the 1920s. Secondly, it will emerge from an examination of the arguments for and against the continuation of propaganda that it was, perhaps surprisingly, the Foreign Office which led that body of opinion which maintained that the virtual amputation of the 'fifth arm of defence' (as Wickham Steed called it)[15] had been a disastrous and short-sighted mistake, and argued that Britain must take positive steps to make herself more widely known and understood abroad. The most articulate exponent of this concept was Sir Stephen Tallents who first coined the phrase 'the Projection of England' in an influential pamphlet published under that title in 1932.[16] Thirdly, it is necessary to examine how the work begun as the projection of Britain gave way soon after its formal inception to a new phase described as 'psychological rearmament' with the growing conviction that Britain might soon find herself involved in another major war.

I

Such a prospect seemed inconceivable in 1918. Propaganda, it was believed, had helped to win the war, emerging in the process as a fully integrated wartime activity of government. This, in itself, was a remarkable achievement. Having entered the war almost completely unprepared for the control and influence of public opinion abroad, the necessary machinery was hurriedly improvised culminating in the establishment of a Ministry of Information under Lord Beaverbrook and of Lord Northcliffe's Department of Enemy Propaganda at Crewe House for conducting psychological warfare. Whereas the exact contribution made by British propaganda towards the achievement of Allied victory is perhaps impossible to measure, its role was nonetheless believed at the time to have been such that its use in any future war seemed guaranteed. Many people would have agreed with Christopher Addison who wrote that 'this kind of thing is repugnant to the British spirit, but surely it is a weapon we ought to use in a struggle such as this'.[17] If proof was needed, it was soon to manifest itself in the form of testimonies by prominent enemy personalities,[18] including Ludendorff and later, of course, Adolf Hitler. However, the value and, even more, the acceptability of propaganda as an instrument of peacetime diplomacy remained open to considerable doubt.

On the return of peace, the automatic reaction of most

politicians and officials was to abandon altogether the system of propaganda, though this was not the inclination of those with most direct experience of it. In October 1918, for example, Lord Beaverbrook devised a scheme for the continuation of his ministry to carry on its work at least until a peace treaty was signed because, he argued, 'the policy of the British Government at the Peace Conference will have to be explained to the world day by day if the solidarity of Allied opinion is to be maintained'.[19] While accepting that the aims and content of British propaganda would necessarily have to change, he recognised a 'golden opportunity' for securing 'public support in all foreign countries for the view of the Imperial Government and to give the reason why the Imperial Government is justified in adopting a certain attitude towards the problems before the Conference'.[20]

Similar proposals were formulated at Crewe House where Sir Campbell Stuart, Northcliffe's assistant, considered that the maintenance of British prestige 'demanded that our position in regard to the peace should be explained and justified by the widespread dissemination of news and views'.[21] Wickham Steed, then Foreign Editor of *The Times*, suggested that Crewe House be converted into an 'agency of enlightenment on both sides'.[22] Northcliffe himself considered that the work could be used as a means of 'enabling the German people gradually to see why Germany had lost the war, and to understand the force of the moral ideals which had ranged practically the whole world against her'.[23]

These various schemes came to nothing. Relations between Northcliffe and Lloyd George, always erratic, were fast deteriorating, and the question of the future role of propaganda became submerged beneath more immediate problems.[24] Lloyd George, fearful of the additional influence Northcliffe would gain, thought his proposal 'dangerous in the extreme' and, he wrote, 'I curtly told him to go to Hades'.[25] Northcliffe resigned on 12 November. On the following day, Beaverbrook's scheme was hurriedly dismissed by the Cabinet,[26] although the Minister of Information had already effectively abandoned his plan by resigning a fortnight earlier. The 'golden opportunity' of which he had written was gone. John Buchan (later Lord Tweedsmuir) was given the unenviable task of liquidating the wartime organisation, which he chose to dismantle almost in its entirety. The responsibility for any remaining work, about which he was either uncertain or which he considered it desirable to maintain, was transferred into the hands of the Foreign Office, complete with staff and duties.[27] The Ministry of Information and Crewe House were officially closed down on 31 December 1918, but the process of liquidation took less time than originally anticipated, and the Foreign Office did, in fact, assume responsibility some weeks earlier.[28]

During the winter of 1918–19, there existed much confusion within the Foreign Office concerning the inherited remnants of the ministry. It might be assumed that transference into Foreign Office care would mean instant termination. This was not the case. The Foreign Office had effectively been in charge of British overseas propaganda during the first three years of the war, and a 'Propaganda Department' had already been envisaged in at least one scheme of post-war reconstruction.[29] Although the precise details of his decision remain vague, Foreign Secretary Balfour decided in December 1918 to reconstruct a smaller version of the Foreign Office News Department, itself a wartime creation, in order to carry on such work of the Ministry of Information as was considered desirable to maintain in peacetime.[30] Thus there began a salvage operation on the wreckage of the wartime machinery in order to construct 'a skeleton organisation at home and abroad which can be clothed with flesh and blood at short notice in case of need'.[31] This decision to retain a department for the supervision of publicity and propaganda overseas within the overall diplomatic apparatus marked a significant departure from established pre-war tradition.

Nevertheless, opinions within the Foreign Office concerning the desirability of continuing such work varied greatly. Lord Robert Cecil, who had been involved in propaganda in one way or another since 1915, said that he now 'disliked the idea of propaganda in foreign countries on general principles, apart from commercial propaganda which was the real line to follow'.[32] On the other hand, the advocates of continuation, particularly former wartime propagandists, presented their case forcefully and with great perception. George Beak, for example, who, as Consul General in Zurich had played a key role in distributing material into Germany through neutral Switzerland, argued that 'because the masses will now demand to know much more than previously of what is going on . . . it would probably not only be futile but dangerous to attempt to keep knowledge from them'.

'The great thing', he continued, 'is to protect them from half-truths by letting them know as much as possible ... [and] it is, therefore, of the highest importance that only accurate news should get abroad'.[33] Furthermore, he wrote,

> It need hardly be said ... that the spirit of British propaganda would differ wholly and entirely from the German, in that it would not be aggressive in character. Germany's aim was to secure an Empire and dominate Europe; our aim is, presumably, to preserve and develop what we already have. The object of our propaganda, therefore, would be chiefly to make our institutions, mode of Government, arts and sciences, known and understood.[34]

Similar views were held by another official, S. A. Guest, who believed that propaganda was not merely desirable in the post-war world, but essential. His argument is worthy of lengthy quotation:

> One of the chief lessons to be drawn from the experience of the war, and the events leading up to it, is that Diplomacy by itself is not enough for the maintenance of satisfactory international relations ... The fault lies in our lack of foresight in having to provide something further than diplomacy. Now that nations are taking a much larger share than hitherto in their own government, and international relations are being influenced by interests other than those of dynasties, we should be living in a Fools' Paradise if we were to expect that we should be able to maintain international equilibrium by means of a service which was originally designed to work under conditions which no longer exist. Commercial, financial, labour organisations and the Press, to which the officially accredited diplomat, as such, cannot obtain direct access may, at any given moment, exercise a far more powerful influence on international politics than that which can be exerted by any Foreign Office, and unless we have means of directly observing and affecting these and other agencies, we shall not be in a position either to obtain knowledge of the drift of affairs, or to intervene in time to forestall injurious tendencies. For this purpose we require a permanent organisation for Political Intelligence and 'Propaganda'.[35]

Guest maintained that because the return of peace had been accompanied by an increase in the use of propaganda by foreign governments to further their national interests, often at the expense of British prestige, it had become essential for the British Government to counter the false and malevolent claims of others, and substitute for them a more accurate and representative picture of its aims and policies. He continued:

> It would be the most puerile folly on our part to expect that henceforth a true version as to the policy, either internal or external, or the resources of the British Empire, will permeate everywhere and will be maintained intact, and [that]erroneous and dangerous misconceptions will be obviated, without continuous effort on our part.[36]

The views of Guest and Beak were representative of a growing body of opinion not confined solely to the Foreign Office which regarded publicity and propaganda as a necessary response to the new demands of twentieth-century diplomacy, and one which could play a genuinely constructive role in promoting international understanding.

The various arguments were considered at a departmental conference held on 20 March 1919. Lord Curzon, Acting Foreign Secretary in Balfour's absence, found it necessary to lay down two fundamental principles in order to avoid further dispute, namely '(1) that propaganda should continue, and (2) that it should continue strictly in connexion with, or under the control of, the Foreign Office'.[37] Curzon was determined to ensure that any propaganda conducted abroad would go hand in hand with British foreign policy, which had not always been the case following the transference of responsibility for the work into the hands of Beaverbrook and Northcliffe early in 1918.[38] Accordingly, a circular despatch was transmitted to all diplomatic missions, with the exception of the Embassy in Washington,[39] informing them that 'British propaganda in Foreign Countries shall, in future, be regarded as part of the[ir] regular work'. The despatch, signed by Curzon, ended with the following note:

> I do not doubt that, from the experience of the past four years, you will have learned what forms of propaganda to encourage and what to avoid ... British interests would be ill-served by a

blatant publicity of the kind associated with German agents abroad, official and unofficial, before and during the war. On the other hand, a complete and contemptuous silence, however gratifying to our self-respect, is no longer a profitable policy in times when advertisement – whether of past achievement or future aims – is, perhaps unfortunately, almost a universal practice of nations as of individuals.[40]

Although the Foreign Office had disclaimed 'all intention of conducting propaganda of the "Corpse Factory" type',[41] the Treasury proved reluctant to support the work. While acknowledging that it was not 'at the present moment practicable to terminate altogether the [remaining] system of propaganda' it nonetheless expected the Foreign Office 'to discontinue any type of propaganda as soon as experience shows that it is not productive of valuable results'.[42] Moreover, cultural propaganda was completely forbidden while the Treasury took note of the policy of 'gradually converting British propaganda from a purely political aspect to largely commercial line and assume that, as a corollary, the work will pass to a great extent to the Department of Overseas Trade'.[43]

The general reluctance of the Treasury to authorise large-scale expenditure on propaganda stemmed, it was claimed, from an inability to justify or defend continuation in peacetime to a Parliament mindful of the need for financial retrenchement and sensitive to the widespread suspicion concerning the use of official propaganda. This opposition had undoubtedly originated during 1918 when the Ministry of Information had been publicly discussed. From a political point of view, the ministry had been disliked because of its direct accountability to the Prime Minister, and not to Parliament or the Treasury. Indeed, given the nature of the Lloyd George government and of the premier's notorious flirtations with the publicity world, it was not beyond the imagination of many contemporaries to envisage the use of official propaganda by an unscrupulous government as a means of sustaining political power. This fear had largely motivated Austen Chamberlain's attack on the appointments of Beaverbrook and Northcliffe in February 1918.[44] The Ministry of Information had even been accused of putting out propaganda based on policy which had not previously been discussed in Parliament.[45] Hence, 'the manner of its creation the appearance of an extra-Parliamentary power, and the fear that its propaganda activities might survive the war, had obviously combined to inspire a mood of deep suspicion'.[46] All propaganda, irrespective of the form it took, or the differences between its political, cultural or, to a lesser degree, economic variations was viewed with distaste, as an 'un-English' wartime expedient associated with secrecy, subversion and the activities of other governments. As one observer wrote:

> That the State should advertise itself was an idea which occurred to few before the war and which, had it been brought before the notice of the general public, would have seemed to them repellent; advertisement, apart from commercial advertisement, which through lapse of time had acquired respectability, was thought to be the work of the vulgarian: it was also thought useless.[47]

If propaganda was to continue at all, it was natural for the Treasury to express a preference for commercial propaganda, given its vocation and the economic pre-occupation which characterised most contemporary political thought. It was far more acceptable to undertake, in effect, an advertising campaign on behalf of British trade and commerce than an uncharacteristic form of national self-glorification. A lasting peace, safeguarded by the League of Nations, would remain as a more than adequate testimony to the merits and achievements of British ideals and civilisation.

Whereas S. A. Guest had considered that it would be the 'most puerile folly' to expect the League of Nations to function successfully in an atmosphere which had not first been cleansed of all mutual suspicion by propaganda serving as an instrument of international understanding, the prevailing opinion was that international harmony would be achieved in the halls of Geneva. In other words, the League, not propaganda, was a more acceptable method of securing international understanding and mutual respect. The result was that British overseas propaganda was severely reduced, and the reconstructed News Department was forced to operate under the constant threat of reductions. However, this was not simply a question of economics as undoubtedly the nature of the Foreign Office's work was frequently misunderstood. As one official explained:

In reference to the work being done, the word 'propaganda' is a
misnomer and the aim which we have put before us is rather
that of correcting misapprehensions which arise abroad either
through ignorance or as a result of the aggressive propaganda
of other nations.[48]

Despite such assurances, suspicion remained. In the quest for
normalcy, the carnage of the war with all its related nightmares
haunted the national consciousness. Britain disarmed in the
weapon of words as she did in other more conventional forms of
armaments. Yet it meant that the British case went largely un-
stated and left open to misinterpretation. Although the Foreign
Office laboured hard to correct such false impressions as were
created by state-subsidised foreign agencies, it had neither the
financial resources nor the staff necessary for continuous effort.
On receiving a request from Lord Allenby for permission to
inaugurate British propaganda in Egypt, the News Department
was unable to support the scheme on financial grounds,
prompting one of its officials to reflect: 'We shall have to rely on
successful administration for propaganda in Eygpt'.[49] That this
was applicable to most areas of the world was a sorry reflection on
the limited scope of Britain's overseas propaganda in the
immediate post-war years. Nevertheless, the fact remains that
there was a department, however straitjacketed, specifically concerned with information and propaganda, and that diplomats
serving abroad, not just the Press Attachés, were instructed to
regard propaganda as part of their normal duties. The wartime
experiment had created not only an awareness of the power of
propaganda but also an appreciation, at least in the circles which
had experience of it, of the role it could play in pursuit of
national interests. The basic groundrules of British propaganda,
such as the importance of news content, its dependence on clear
policy and the effectiveness of the non-retaliatory approach, were
thus appreciated long before they were really put to the test in the
late 1930s and early 1940s.

II

The arguments and ideals which had led to the reduction of
propaganda work in 1918–19 were soon to be exposed as illusory.

If, on the return of peace, it was widely believed that British overseas propaganda was unnecessary, the subsequent growth in its
use by rival governments made a reappraisal inevitable.
Ironically, the governments of France, the Soviet Union, Italy
and later Nazi Germany utilised the lessons of the British wartime
experience and combined them with technological advancements
in such areas as broadcasting and the cinema in order to mould
propaganda into a powerful weapon of ideological and political
expansion, while Britain meanwhile remained a helpless and
disarmed bystander. The area in which British interests initially
suffered as a result was commerce. The challenge to Britain's
domination of world markets, begun in earnest during the final
decades of the nineteenth century, intensified with the search for
post-war economic recovery. The Foreign Office argued that not
only was Britain's somewhat limited commercial propaganda
insufficient to counter the large-scale programmes of rivals, but
also that commercial and cultural propaganda were mutually
complementary. As foreign governments were proving at Britain's
expense, the one was dependent on the success of the other.
Trade no longer followed merely the flag but now also followed
the teaching of the English language, the school teacher and the
text book. This was a long-term strategy which, it was argued,
could be designed to create an atmosphere of mutual respect and
understanding which would in turn benefit not only Britain's
commercial interests and prosperity, but would also serve to
produce a background favourable to the peaceful conduct of
diplomatic relations. To a more critical Treasury, however, such
innovative ideas appeared to be an expensive substitute for good
government and healthy competition. Even the short-term visible
returns promised by commercial propaganda alone proved
insufficient to prompt, say, greater official involvement in international exhibitions.[50] Rather, supreme acts of faith, such as the
insertion of clauses relating to propaganda in the Anglo-Russian
Trade Agreements of 1921 and 1930,[51] were indicative of general
British reluctance to involve themselves in propaganda to any
large degree.

   By the late 1920s, both the Foreign Office and the Department
of Overseas trade were becoming increasingly alarmed at the
frequency of disquieting reports received from overseas missions
which generally made it clear that British interests and prestige
were suffering from a lack of adequate explanation and

representation abroad. Foreign propaganda was assuming an increasingly anti-British flavour and the limited scale of Britain's counter-activities was proving wholly inadequate. The battle for influence in neutral countries, ably fought by Wellington House during the First World War, was being gradually lost in peacetime. Sir Roderick Jones, himself a former Director of Neutral Propaganda during the war, warned that Reuters, of which he was Managing Director, was finding it difficult to compete successfully with the state-subsidised continental news agencies, with the result that British news was not gaining adequate publicity abroad.[52] Reinforced by such decisive evidence as that provided by the Report of the British Economic Mission to South America in 1929, which emphasised the inter-dependence of cultural and commercial propaganda,[53] the Foreign Office redoubled its efforts and in 1930, Foreign Secretary Arthur Henderson succeeded in persuading the Treasury to reverse its embargo of 1919 preventing the conduct of cultural propaganda,[54] thus beginning the process which finally led to the British Council in 1934.[55]

Meanwhile, it was to the newly established Travel and Indus-trial Development Association of Great Britain and Northern Ireland, founded in December 1928, that the Department of Overseas Trade looked for help in rectifying the deficiencies in commercial propaganda. This body, which evolved from the privately sponsored 'Come to Britain Movement', was the initiative of several influential businessmen who managed to secure a small government grant to aid their efforts. Lord Derby, President of the Association, conceived a dual role for its work namely, he wrote, 'the promotion of international understanding through personal contacts and – let us be honest about it – business'.[56] However, it was the former aim which attracted Derby's, and indeed the Government's, interest. In a speech which epitomised the mood of the early pioneers of national pro-jection, Derby explained:

> We believe that people who visit these islands and see John Bull at home will discover that he is really a good natured person of simple tastes, who never harbours malice and only wishes to be friends with all the world. Having discovered this they will be slow to believe that John Bull is actuated by base motives such as are imputed to him, sometimes by his enemies, and

sometimes through ignorance of his character. Similarly, it cannot but be good for John Bull at home to learn that there may be another point of view than his own, and that the stranger is a fellow much like himself. If at the same time the country is benefited by the expenditure of our visitors – well John Bull is a practical person and business is business.[57]

The Travel Association operated on two different, albeit related, levels. The first may be described as tourist information and publicity – providing details and advice concerning the various beauty spots and holiday resorts in the British Isles. 'Travel', it was claimed, 'is world-wide, a great common idea'.[58] By utilising publicity to promote the British tourist industry, the Travel Association aimed to capture a proportion of the world's tourist market and thereby 'exert what may be called a human tidal pull towards these shores'.[59]

On the second level was the political and international aspect of its work. As Lord Derby pointed out, the Association's publicity was not merely confined to tourist promotion, 'but has set out to develop through travel a greater knowledge of, and interest in, British culture and British goods, thus bringing about, we are confident, an increase in our export trade, visible as well as invisible'.[60] It was further argued that:

> The visitor who comes over here, reads our newspapers, shares our recreations, talks with our people and makes friends, with many of whom he keeps in touch afterwards – such a person recognises the common interests of nations ... In fact, he becomes an ambassador for this country.[61]

Motivated by such ideals, the Travel Association's publicity greatly benefited from the earlier techniques pioneered by the Empire Marketing Board in the use of posters, pamphlets and, of course, documentary films.

The formation of the Travel Association was significant for three reasons. In the first place, it provided the first real recognition in peacetime of the need to conduct a national, permanently active publicity campaign abroad in an attempt to make Britain more widely known and understood. Secondly, it was a recognition of the fact 'that the trade and commerce of any nation are enormously helped if potential customers can be persuaded to see and get to know that nation'.[62] Thirdly, and perhaps more significantly, it provided testimony to the growing realisation that public opinion was becoming a determinant factor in the making of foreign policy. As one official wrote: 'the era when it was possible either to lead opinion in foreign politics by mere authority or tradition, or to ignore it from Olympian heights, has long since vanished'.[63] It was because these factors were beginning to infiltrate influential circles, both official and in the private sector, that support for the advocates of national publicity was more readily forthcoming.

By 1930, therefore, a start had been made in the projection of Britain abroad, albeit in a limited way. Both the Travel Association and, following a decision of the Imperial Conference that year, the Empire Marketing Board recognised the value of overseas propaganda as an instrument for promoting national interests and international goodwill. The Foreign Office embarked upon a programme of cultural propaganda, beginning in Latin America.[64] Had it not been for the interruption of the Economic Crisis and the necessity for financial economies, progress may have been more dramatic. As it was, however, the recent advancements threatened to be halted, particularly after the closure of the Empire Marketing Board in 1933. Stephen Tallents, the Board's Secretary, was determined that this should not happen.

Tallents was an unusual man with an unusual career, a curious blend of diplomacy and publicity. His background was essentially diplomatic, having served as British High Commissioner in the Baltic Provinces and as Imperial Secretary for Northern Ireland before becoming Secretary of the Empire Marketing Board in 1926. His continued influence in the field of public relations and propaganda was to be reflected by his later appointments as Public Relations Officer at the GPO in 1933, and at the BBC in 1935, a post which he held simultaneously with that of Director General Designate of the nucleus Ministry of Information. In 1932, he set out his views concerning the importance of what he termed 'the Projection of England'. Essentially, his argument was that Britain no longer enjoyed that position of supremacy which had enabled her to remain aloof from world opinion for long periods in the past; her world-wide responsibilities, as a European partner and as head of a great Empire, and also as a trading power with global interests, made it essential for her to project by all means available an accurate and representative picture of herself to the peoples of other countries. 'No civilised country', he wrote, 'can today afford either to neglect the projection of its national personality, or to resign its projection to others'.[65] Britain must make a constructive effort to make herself more widely known and understood because, he believed, 'peace itself may at any time depend on a clear understanding abroad of her actions and motives'.[66] The widespread currency of the English language provided an enormous advantage for such a task, language being the natural vehicle for the communication of ideas, as the work of such private organisations as the Pilgrims, the English Speaking Union and the All Peoples Association had clearly demonstrated. Yet Tallents wanted to see the creation, as he put it, 'in the borderland which lies between Government and private enter-prise, [of] a school of national projection' which would maintain close contact with the various existing publicity bodies and with the Press, the BBC, the news agencies and the film industry. Indeed, here was the basic outline of an organisation which resembled in almost too many ways to be mere coincidence that established in late 1934 under the auspices of the Foreign Office: the British Council.

III

The decision to establish an organisation specifically designed to conduct cultural propaganda injected a new dimension into the traditional conduct of British foreign policy – that of cultural diplomacy. The man chiefly responsible for converting the ideas of Tallents into reality was Reginald Leeper, who was to become the controversial head of the Foreign Office News Department in 1935. Following the demise of the EMB, Leeper devoted his considerable energy and imagination to the question of establish-ing an organisation under Foreign Office control to promote and co-ordinate Britain's long-term cultural relations, based on the French model of the Alliance Française. He was greatly aided in this task by Sir Robert Vansittart, Permanent Under Secretary of State for Foreign Affairs since 1930, who had, on his appoint-ment, begun to take an active interest in the project.[67] An indication of the extent to which the necessity for propaganda was coming to be admitted openly was revealed in *The Times* which reassured its readers:

Those who dislike publicity may dismiss the idea [of the British Council] on the plea that it is nothing but veiled propaganda, but none need fight shy of the word 'propaganda' so long as the work associated with it is openly performed and the principles spread are honestly held and are not insinuated into the minds of readers or listeners, but are provided as a contribution to thought and experience for those who wish to learn them.[68]

However, beneath such fine words and the public emphasis on the educational and cultural aspects of the Council's work, were the more practical as well as the more immediately political considerations. As Sir Samuel Hoare, Foreign Secretary in 1935, recognised:

The commercial arguments in favour of intensifying the work of British cultural propaganda are no less strong than the political arguments. In all, the danger of German cultural and commercial penetration, which may be expected to increase as the power and wealth of Germany revive, makes it particularly desirable for British cultural propaganda to secure as firm a hold as possible on the minds and interests of the population, and particularly on the younger generation, before the counter-attraction becomes too strong.[69]

The British Council was created and developed as a democratic response to the new and urgent problems caused by the emergence of the totalitarian state in Europe. To meet these problems a new outlook was required. The totalitarian use of propaganda, powerfully and deliberately directed against British interests abroad, forced Britain onto the defensive by offering foreign audiences an alternative ideology. Hence the Council's projection of British democratic institutions and indeed all that was considered best in the British way of life.

In 1936, Lord William Tyrrell, the Council's first chairman, underlined his appeal for more funds with a significant new line of argument. He said:

We have much to learn from others, but we also have much to teach them. If we do not do the teaching ourselves, we shall be misunderstood and misinterpreted. If you will regard us as a body able and willing to do this educational work abroad, may I ask you also to regard us as people who are assisting practically in our national defence. Modern defence consists not only in arms but in removing misunderstanding.[70]

Tyrrell was in an authoritative position to make such claims. Serving as Sir Edward Grey's Private Secretary before the First World War, he had been responsible for receiving journalists who called at the Foreign Office. His experience in this work was put to good use on the return of peace when he was made the first head of the News Department. In 1925, he succeeded Sir Eyre Crowe as Permanent Under Secretary and continued his support for propaganda work until becoming Ambassador in Paris in 1928. This appointment provided him with the opportunity of studying at first hand French democratic propaganda, always more extensive than Britain's, experience which was put to good use on his retirement when he not only became Chairman of the British Council but also President of the British Board of Film Censors. Indeed, Tyrrell provides the link between the practices of the pre-war Foreign Office and the inter-war partnership of propaganda and diplomacy and it is a great pity that we do not know more about him.

The political importance of 'The Projection of Britain' gained in significance with the growing conviction that Britain might have to face another war in the near future, and one in which, it was believed, morale, both at home and abroad, would play a decisive role. It was a conviction which assumed a greater sense of urgency with the re-emergence of a powerful Germany and the estrangement of Italy following the Abyssinian crisis. As Vansittart recognised, '. . . in the business, strict business, of "making eyes at" lesser but serviceable people, we have now very keen and efficient rivals who are already getting the better of us . . .'[71] Or, as one influential Foreign Office memorandum warned in February 1937:

It is particularly important to spend now, before the danger has grown to unmanageable proportions, and we must row against the tide. It is no exaggeration to say that unless we are prepared to show our concern for the world to which modern development is binding us continually closer, we shall, when the need of them arises, find our present and potential friends the unwilling but helpless allies of those who have shown their intention of making every encroachment on our power that we can be forced, or deluded, into allowing.[72]

The Foreign Office was fully aware that, despite the start made in the long-term task, world events were moving at such a pace that there remained an urgent need to rectify the immediate deficiencies which hampered the short-term dissemination of British news and views. 'While visibility increases', wrote Leeper, 'vision lags behind'.[73] If Britain's actions and policies were to be understood, they had first to become known. It was towards this goal that he expanded the British Official News Service in 1935[74] and, in 1937, he negotiated an arrangement whereby the diplomatic correspondent of *The Times* enjoyed special privileges from the News Department.[75]

When Leeper next turned his attention to the question of broadcasting news in foreign languages, he found a sympathetic ally in Sir John Reith, the Director General of the BBC, who had long been aware of the value of overseas transmissions, even before the inauguration of the Empire Service in 1932. Leeper and Reith had worked closely together on the high-powered CID Sub-Committee to Prepare Plans for the Establishment of a Ministry of Information in Time of War, which began its work in 1935,[76] and both had urged the importance of foreign-language broadcasts to the Ullswater Committee. The report of this Committee provided a further stimulus to the cause with its statement that,

> It is all the more important that what has been called 'the projection of England' should be effectively carried out by a steadily developing Empire service of our own ... In the interests of British prestige and influence in world affairs, we think that the appropriate use of languages other than English should be encouraged.[77]

This proposal took on added significance with the escalation of anti-British propaganda in the eastern Mediterranean and the Middle East, particularly the hostile broadcasts from the Bari radio station. Preliminary negotiations between the BBC and the Foreign Office began in the summer of 1936,[78] and a year later, Foreign Secretary Anthony Eden, prompted by the continued concern of Parliament,[79] informed the Cabinet that,

> The time has come when some more positive steps should be taken than that of asking the Italians to desist. Without attempting to imitate the tone or the methods of Bari, it is

essential for His Majesty's Government to ensure the full and forcible presentation of the British view of events in a region of such vital importance.[80]

The Cabinet agreed, and decided to appoint a special committee for the purpose of examining the logistical problems,[81] and it first met in September 1937 under the chairmanship of Sir Kingsley Wood.[82] Within a month, a report was produced which recommended that the BBC should begin broadcasting in Arabic as soon as possible.[83] The Cabinet accepted the report in its entirety,[84] and broadcasting began on 3 January 1938. Three months later, the service was extended to broadcasts in Spanish and Portuguese for South American audiences. Reith was triumphant; he described these momentous decisions in his memoirs under the sub-title: 'Projection at last'.[85]

Such was the obvious need for propaganda abroad, particularly in the Mediterranean area, that by the winter of 1937–38 there were few objections to the new measures. Indeed, as Prime Minister Chamberlain announced in the House of Commons:

> His Majesty's Government fully realise that . . . the old stand-upon-your-dignity methods are no longer applicable to modern conditions and that, in the rough-and-tumble of international relations which we see today, it is absolutely necessary that we should take measures to protect ourselves from constant misrepresentation.[86]

Yet there still remained an urgent need to co-ordinate the work of the various official and semi-official organisations engaged in the projection of Britain abroad with an effective utilisation of the available media. Previous attempts had proved either unpractical, largely due to the diverse evolution of Britain's propaganda activities since the end of the First World War, or half-hearted, because the necessary motivation had been absent. By 1938, the first of these problems remained a serious one to resolve; the second, however, no longer applied.

Leeper believed that increased centralisation was an essential prerequisite to further progress. He was 'strongly opposed' to the creation of a Ministry of Information in peacetime largely because such a body, as then envisaged by the Committee of Imperial Defence, would exercise special powers on the home front,[87] and would excite widespread political opposition. The progress achieved so far had been gained largely because the question of influencing foreign public opinion was considered as being outside party politics. This became more apparent in February 1938 after a non-party debate on the subject on a motion tabled by a private member,[88] a debate which Herbert Morrison described as 'one of the most peaceful we have ever had in the House of Commons'.[89] On this occasion, the House enjoyed that rare event of unanimous support for the resolution which, in its final form, urged that, 'being of opinion that the evil effects of state propaganda of a tendentious or misleading character can best be countered, not by retaliation, but by the widespread dissemination of straightforward information and news based upon an enlightened and honest public policy', the government should devote the full weight of its moral and financial support to increasing Britain's overseas propaganda.[90]

In fact, the government had already acted. In January 1938, Leeper had proposed the creation of a Central Co-ordinating Committee under the Chairmanship of Sir Robert Vansittart who, to borrow Valentine Lawford's phrase, had recently been exiled to 'a sort of newly discovered Siberia known as Chief Diplomatic Adviser'.[91] Eden had submitted the proposal to the Prime Minister on 18 January adding that it 'seems to me . . . to be the natural outcome of the preliminary work done so far'.[92] Chamberlain agreed,[93] and the existence of the committee was announced three weeks later.[94] The announcement was received favourably by both the House of Commons and the Press. *The Times*, for example, published a lengthy explanatory article justifying the need for the committee and expressing general support for its aims.[95] The German Press, however, predictably received the news with less enthusiasm. The *Völkischer Beobachter* led the chorus of hypocritical indignation, invoking memories of British propaganda during the First World War, but with the substitution of Vansittart for Northcliffe.[96] Such comparisons were, of course, misleading. The Vansittart Committee was not a propaganda department on the Crewe House model and had no executive powers; nor did it conduct propaganda itself. Its functions were purely advisory and aimed simply at the increased efficiency and co-ordination of the existing work abroad.

British overseas propaganda was organised by reference to its variable forms rather than by reference to media. Hence, the

British Council was responsible for cultural propaganda, and the Travel Association for tourist propaganda. Vansittart's report, produced in May 1938, proposed that a major deficiency would be rectified if an organisation for trade propaganda were created,[97] but the Treasury opposed the suggestion on the grounds that such work should more properly be conducted by the private interests concerned.[98] Eventually, however, the opposition was overcome and in April 1939 an Industrial Publicity Unit was secretly established under the auspices of the Department of Overseas Trade on the condition that its propaganda would be designed 'to benefit the trade and industry of the United Kingdom as a whole and not particular trades or industries or individual concerns'.[99] Vansittart also suggested that much of the tension and rivalry which had characterised relations between the British Council and the Travel Association, despite the existence of joint committees on films and broadcasting, could be avoided if Lord Lloyd, the formidable Chairman of the Council since September 1937, also became President of the Travel Association on Lord Derby's retirement later in the year. When this occured in December 1938, a great deal of overlapping and duplication of effort was avoided. Vansittart was also successful in persuading the Treasury to appoint an additional 15 Press attachés to supervise the work 'on the spot', bringing the total number to 20 by 1939. A further proposal to establish a National Film Council to co-ordinate the activities of government with the film industry in general proved less acceptable and never really overcame the suspicion that it might also be used as an instrument for domestic film propaganda until the creation of the Crown Film Unit during the Second World War. Meanwhile, however, Lord Lloyd proved successful in securing a government grant of £160,000 for the Council's work in 1938–39 (it had been £5,000 in 1935) and Sir John Reith extended the foreign-language broadcasts to various European languages during the crisis of September 1938.

The Vansittart proposals were a major event in the evolution of Britain's involvement in peacetime propaganda abroad. They were, in many ways, the logical outcome of two decades of gradual, staggered and diversified growth in a controversial new area of governmental responsibility. They were a powerful, and not altogether unsuccessful, attempt not only to extend the existing work of national projection but also to rectify the more serious deficiencies so that the entire system would be more efficiently co-ordinated and adapted to meet the new conditions required for psychological rearmament abroad. By this, the Foreign Office meant the containment of the spread of extremist ideologies in areas vital to British interests by the substitution of democratic ideals and the dissemination of confidence in an increasingly hesitant world. It was an attempt to reinforce Britain's search for peace by supplementary methods. If that search failed, plans were well under way for the creation of a Ministry of Information and various 'black' propaganda units such as Electra House and Section D.[100]

British propaganda, unlike its totalitarian counterparts, was not aggressive in character, but attempted rather to provide an opportunity for foreigners to learn more about Britain's actions and policies without forcing them to 'think British' if they had no desire to do so. It was, by nature, more 'pro-British' than 'anti-foreign'; while engaging in self-explanation and self-justification, great care was taken to refrain from criticising the activities of other countries. Even so, propaganda continued to be regarded generally as a necessary evil rather than something positively useful. The idea that it could be used as an instrument for the promotion of international goodwill, as epitomised in the BBC's motto that 'nation shall speak peace unto nation', gradually gave way to a more realistic appraisal of its value as an instrument of defence in a world threatened by the possibility of another holocaust. By the late 1930s, propaganda had become a subject which received consideration at the highest levels of British Government. The volatile combination of a controversial activity with such controversial figures as Reith, Tallents, Lord Lloyd, Vansittart and Rex Leeper demanded no less. Yet, whatever the validity of Leeper's own explanation as to why greater official support for their work had not been more readily forthcoming, namely that 'new ideas are anathema to the official mind',[101] it would be true to say that what these men meant by propaganda was so often misunderstood by others less familiar with their work. Suspicion remained because no sooner had the word 'propaganda' escaped its dubious wartime connotations than it regained notoriety with the aggressive activities of the dictatorships. It was for this reason that Stephen Tallents went to great lengths to avoid using the word in his pamphlet *The Projection of England*. In fact, it does not appear once. But as one enlightened Member of Parliament said after a lengthy Commons debate on the subject in February 1939:

> We have heard much tonight about the projection of Britain and the British people. Well, what is that but propaganda? We may dislike the word because it has collected unpleasant associations. But the thing itself may be necessary and right. Let us not be ashamed or afraid of it.[102]

Had more people been prepared to admit this sooner, they would not have been so quick to seize upon one of the more sinister aspects of totalitarianism for their own definition.

NOTES

1   A. Fletcher to A. Willert, 10 May 1928. Public Record Office, Foreign Office News Dept FO395/437, P732/732/150.
2   Minute by H. Wilson, 18 Jan. 1938. Public Record Office, Prime Minister's Office PREM1/272.
3   Minute by E. Hale, 2 June 1938. Public Record Office, Treasury T161/933, S42850/2.
4   Ibid.
5   Eden to Sir John Simon, 23 Dec. 1937. T161/907, S35581/03/38/1.
6   Z. A. B. Zeman, *Nazi Propaganda* (London, 1973) p. 65.
7   J. C. W. Reith, *Into the Wind* (London, 1949) p. 354.
8   *Parliamentary Debates* (Commons) 5th series, vol. 109 (5 Aug. 1918) cols 947–1035.
9   *Parliamentary Debates* (Commons) 5th series, vol. 331 (16 Feb. 1938) cols 1909–69.
10 *Parliamentary Debates* (Commons) 5th series, vol. 343 (15 Feb. 1939) cols 1808–67.
11 Philip M. Taylor, 'Cultural Diplomacy and the British Council, 1934–39', *British Journal of International Studies*, 4 (1978) 244–65.
12 It would be unpractical to cite all such examples, but see: W. E. Berchtold, 'The World Propaganda War', *North American Review*, vol. 238 (1934) 421–30; M. Garnett, 'Propaganda', *The Contemporary Review*, vol. 147 (1935) 574–81; Aldous Huxley, 'Notes on Propaganda', *Harper's Magazine*, vol. 174 (1936) 32–41; A. Huxley, 'Dictators' Propaganda', *The Spectator*, 20 November 1936; A. Willert, 'British News Abroad', *The Round Table*, vol 27 (1937) 533–46; A. Willert, 'Publicity and Propaganda in International Affairs', *International Affairs*, vol. 17 (1938) 809–26; S. N. Siegel, 'Radio and Propaganda', *Air Law Review*, vol. 10 (1939); E. H. Carr, 'Propaganda in International Politics', *Oxford Pamphlets on World Affairs*, no. 16, 1939.

13 Of particular interest are: A. J. Mackenzie, *Propaganda Boom* (London, 1938); S. Rogerson, *Propaganda in the Next War* (London, 1938); A. Blanco White, *The New Propaganda* (London, 1939).

14 Mackenzie, *op. cit.*, p. 7.

15 H. Wickham Steed, *The Fifth Arm* (London, 1940).

16 S. Tallents, *The Projection of England* (London, 1932)

17 Memorandum by C. Addison, 17 Dec. 1917. Public Record Office, Cabinet office. CAB24/36, GT3031.

18 Northcliffe frequently cited such statements as a means of justifying the success of his work. See, for example, the enclosures in Northcliffe to J. T. Davies, 18 July 1918. FO800/213. *The Times History of the War*, written while Northcliffe was still at Printing House Square, also uses this approach to perpetuate the reputation for success.

19 Memorandum by Lord Beaverbrook, 'The functions of the Ministry of Information on the cessation of hostilities', 16 Oct. 1918. CAB24/67, GT6007.

20 Ibid.

21 Sir C. Stuart, *Secrets of Crewe House: The Story of a Famous Campaign* (London, 1920) p. 202.

22 Steed, op. cit., p. 41.

23 Steed, *Through Thirty Years* (2 vols, London, 1924) II, p. 248.

24 The History of The Times, *The 150th Anniversary and Beyond, 1912–48*, pt I (London, 1952) pp. 384-98.

25 D. Lloyd George, *Memoirs of the Peace Conference* (2 vols, New Haven, 1939) I, p. 176.

26 CAB23/8, 501(11) 13 Nov. 1918.

27 In January 1919 the total staff of the News Department was estimated at 223, including 44 messengers and typists and 19 charwomen, of which 118 seem to have been inherited from the Ministry of Information. 'Notes on the liquidation of the Ministry of Information'. Public Record Office INF4/1B.

28 Minute by Sir Henry Newbolt, 17 Jan. 1919. FO395/301, 00346.

29 Memorandum by V. Wellesley, 'The reconstruction of the Foreign Office', 30 Nov. 1918. FO395/297, 001377.

30 W. Tyrrell to H. Batterbee, 30 Dec. 1918. FO395/297, 0012.

31 Minute by S. Gaselee, 28 Jan. 1919. FO395/301. 00409.

32 Minute by J. Tilley, 31 Jan. 1919. FO395/301, 00409.

33 Memorandum by G. B. Beak, 'Policy and propaganda', 2 Dec. 1918. FO395/301, 00409.

34 Ibid.

35 Memorandum by S. A. Guest, 24 Jan. 1919. FO395/301, 00409.

36 Ibid.

37 Note of proceedings at a meeting held on 20 Mar. 1919 to consider the future of British propaganda abroad. FO395/297, 001377.

38 For further details see Philip M. Taylor, 'The Foreign Office and British propaganda during the First World War', in *Historical Journal*, 1980.

39 British propaganda in the United States was something of an exceptional case. For further details see Philip M. Taylor, *The Projection of Britain; British Overseas Publicity and Propaganda, 1914–39*, Leeds, PhD, 1978, chap. Four, pt. One.

40 Circular despatch signed by Curzon, 19 May 1919. FO395/304, 00848.
41 Note of proceedings of a conference held at the Treasury, 14 May 1919. FO395/297, 002006.
42 T. C. Heath to Tyrrell, 31 May 1919. FO366/787, 82638.
43 Ibid.
44 A. Chamberlain to Lords Curzon and Milner, 21 Feb. 1918. AC15/7/7. Austen Chamberlain Papers. Birmingham University Library.
45 *Parliamentary Debates* (Commons) 5th series, vol. 109, 5 Aug. 1918, cols. 947–1035.
46 K. Middlemas and J. Barnes, *Baldwin: A Biography* (London, 1969) p. 68.
47 H. O. Lee, 'British propaganda during the Great War, 1914–18', undated (probably 1919) INF 4/4A.
48 Memorandum by P. A. Koppel, 10 Feb. 1922. FO366/783, 5.
49 Minute by J. Tilley, 24 Oct. 1919. FO395/304, 00848.
50 Alfred Longden, 'British art exhibitions at home and abroad', 31 Oct. 1935. BT60/44/3, DOT5215.
51 J. A. S. Grenville, *The Major International Treaties, 1914–73* (London, 1974).
52 A. Willert to E. F. Crowe, 18 Dec. 1928. FO395/426, P1679/14/150.
53 Report of the British Economic Mission to South America led by Lord D'Abernon, 18 Jan. 1930. FO371/14178, A1908/77/51.
54 Introductory memorandum, FO431/1, no. 1.
55 Taylor, 'Cultural diplomacy', *loc. cit.*
56 Speech by the Earl of Derby at the Mansion House, 20 Dec. 1928. FO395/435, P215/178/150.
57 Ibid.
58 Enclosed memorandum in L. A. de L. Meredith to R. Kenney, 1 Aug. 1929. FO395/435, P1140/178/150.
59 Ibid.
60 Speech by Lord Derby, 20 Dec. 1929. Public Record Office, Board of Trade BT61/54/2, (Department of Overseas Trade) DOTE14888.
61 Enclosed memorandum in Meredith to Kenney, 1 Aug. 1929. FO395/435, P1140/178/150.
62 Ibid.
63 Memorandum by J. D. Gregory, 21 Feb. 1925. FO366/783, A ix (f).
64 Gaselee and Fletcher to Arthur Henderson, 15 July 1931. FO395/449, P1757/3/150.
65 *The Projection of England*, p. 11.
66 Ibid, p. 17.
67 Vansittart to R. MacDonald, 28 Apr. 1931. Ramsay MacDonald Papers, PRO30/69/1/287.
68 *The Times*, 20 Mar. 1935.
69 Hoare to Kennard, 8 Nov. 1935. FO395/529, P3900/267/150.
70 Tyrrell's statement to the Chancellor of the Exchequer, 27 Jan. 1936. British Council Records, BCR BW2/109, F8412, GB/9/9.
71 Minute by Vansittart, 24 Feb. 1937. FO395/554, P823/160/150.
72 Foreign Office memorandum, 'Foreign cultural propaganda and the threat to British interests abroad', 19 February 1937. FO395/534, P823/160/150.
73 Memorandum by R. A. Leeper, 27 Jan. 1935. FO395/541, P332/332/150.

74 R. A. Leeper to Treasury, 9 Apr. 1935; R. V. Nind Hopkins to Foreign Office, 8 May 1935. FO395/522, P529/9/150.
75 D. McLachlan, *In the Chair: Barrington Ward of The Times* (London, 1971) pp. 128-9.
76 CAB16/127, MIC1.
77 Report of the Broadcasting Committee, 1935. Cmd 5091 (1936) paras. 115–24.
78 A. Briggs, *The Golden Age of Wireless* (London, 1965) pp. 397–8.
79 *Parliamentary Debates* (Commons) 5th series, vol. 321, 2 Mar. 1937, cols 196–7; 3 Mar. 1937, cols 337–8; 25 Mar. 1937, cols 3170–8; vol. 327, 7 June 1937, cols 1408–9; vol. 325, 23 June 1937, cols 1177–8; 28 June 1937, cols 1618–9.
80 Memorandum by Eden, 13 July 1937. CAB24/270, CP185(37).
81 CAB23/89, 31(37)6. 31 July 1937.
82 Cabinet Committee on Arabic Broadcasting, 1st meeting, 15 Sept. 1937. CAB27/641, ABC (37).
83 Report of the Cabinet Committee on Arabic Broadcasting, 22 Oct. 1937. CAB24/271, CP274(37).
84 CAB23/90, 39(37)9. 27 Oct. 1937.
85 Reith, op. cit., pp. 290–3.
86 *Parliamentary Debates* (Commons) 5th series, vol. 330, 21 Dec. 1937, col. 1796.
87 Memorandum by R. A. Leeper, 13 July 1937. FO395/546, P3261/1/150.
88 Mr Lees Jones, MP for Blackley.
89 *Parliamentary Debates* (Commons) 5th series, vol. 331, 16 Feb. 1938, col. 1953.
90 Ibid, col. 1969.
91 V. Lawford, *Bound for Diplomacy* (London, 1963) p. 271.
92 Eden to Chamberlain, 18 Jan. 1938. FO395/596, P359/359/150.
93 Chamberlain to Eden, 19 Jan. 1938. FO395/596, P359/359/150.
94 *Parliamentary Debates* (Commons) 5th series, vol. 331, 7 Feb. 1938. cols 670–1.
95 *The Times*, 8 Feb. 1938.
96 N. Henderson to Foreign Office, 9 Feb. 1938. FO395/597, P786/359/150.
97 Report of the Co-ordinating Committee for British Publicity Abroad, 28 May 1938. FO395/602, P1948/359/150.
98 Note by E. Hale, 'Publicity abroad', 2 June 1938. T161/933, S42850/2.
99 E. Mullins to R. Williamson, 15 Apr. 1939. BT61/72/9, DOTE188773.
100 M. R. D. Foot, *S.O.E. in France* (London, 1966) pp. 1–3.
101 Minute by R. A. Leeper, 18 Feb. 1937. FO395/554, P823/160/150.
102 *Parliamentary Debates* (Commons) 5th series, vol. 343, 15 Feb. 1939, cols 1866–7. The speaker was Mr Emmot.

2 'Showing the world what it owed to Britain': foreign policy and 'cultural propaganda', 1935–45

D. W. ELLWOOD

In his latest volume of memoirs, called 'Wartime', the Yugoslav writer and former revolutionary leader Milovan Djilas, gives us a tantalising glimpse of a most unusual occasion, a meeting in 1951 between himself and his country's former ally and then adversary, Winston Churchill, now a useful friend again. Only a few lines of their conversation are recorded. They run as follows:

Djilas: Now you too regard Yugoslavia as useful?
Churchill: I have always done so.
Djilas: But you made the 50–50 agreement with Stalin.
Churchill: Yes, but that agreement had to do not with territory but with influence.[1]

We might do well to ponder what that word 'influence' and its near-relation, the grand-sounding phrase 'spheres of influence' really meant in the context of Britain's international position towards the end of the Second World War, when the famous percentages-of-influence deal with Stalin was arranged. The Americans, of course said they hated the whole concept of 'spheres of influence', (their own system in the western hemisphere being somehow different). To them it smacked of imperial rivalries, of *realpolitik*, of cynical nineteenth-century style power bargaining. In their 'one world' of free trade and collective security, there would be no place for such primitive

methods as such either. E. H. Carr recalled in 1947 that there
had been outrage in American circles when at the end of the war
the British had thought of capitalising on their presumed
influence in western Europe to create some sort of alliance system
or bloc. It was wasted anger said Carr for 'had the power been
there, a positive policy on the part of Great Britain would scarcely
have been needed to bring the western bloc into being. Since it
was not there, no positive policy could have availed'.[2]

To study the propaganda, information or 'cultural' policies of
nation-states in the twentieth century is one way, perhaps the
most concrete, of discovering how they see their role in the
international arena, how they perceive their own *influence*, how
they measure their own prestige. For propaganda and
information policies represent ways of managing these things, of
organising influence and mobilising prestige to reach certain
policy objectives, in alliance with the normal instruments of
power. In other words, in these policies we have a means of
looking at the confusing interplay between national power and
national influence in a given historical context.

In the case of Great Britain in the first half of the twentieth
century this is a theme of outstanding interest. It brings us to the
questions of how the British Empire and its machinery reacted to
their loss of weight and cohesion between 1918 and 1945, how
Britain herself sought to relate to the newly emerging world
powers of Russia and the United States and how the British
governing class strove to compensate for its deteriorating power
position in a world of permanent technological revolution, social
upheaval and fierce ideological competition.

Of all these new factors in the international situation of the
interwar years, the most exasperating according to many
contemporary observers was the last in this list, the unprecedented ideological challenge thrown down to most of western
civilisation by the so-called totalitarian powers, Soviet Russia and
Nazi Germany. T. S. Eliot, writing at the end of the Second
World War, saw political thought attempting to seize by force the
title of 'queen of the sciences', prepared to organise every
department of life, even culture itself, according to set schemes.
Eliot wrote

The conviction, which seems to be deeply implanted in the
Muscovite mind that it is the role of Mother Russia to

contribute not merely ideas and political forms, but a total way of life for the rest of the world, has gone far to make us all more politically culture-conscious.

The Nazis had gone even further, using 'culture-consciousness as a means of uniting a nation against other nations', but in every country the politicisation of culture was spreading, an assumption 'shared by the most opposed parties'. In Britain there was the British Council which although not overtly political reflected the ill-health of British culture, now needing state intervention to prop it up and look after it. Eliot concluded

> A body like the British Council by constantly sending representatives of the arts and sciences abroad, and inviting foreign representatives to this country, is in our time invaluable – but we must not come to accept as normal and healthy the conditions which make such direction necessary.[3]

Even in the 1930s when the new-born British Council was struggling obscurely for its existence on a few tens of thousands of pounds per annum, there were those who complained of the threatening 'nationalisation of thought'. But as E. H. Carr emphasised in October 1939, propaganda agencies in all their varied forms, from the BBC to the Third International, from the Dante Alighieri Societies to the British Council (the first pro-paganda agency set up in Britain in time of peace) had come to stay. The era of *laissez-faire* was over: just as economic controls were necessary to compete with totalitarian states, so were controls over *mass-opinion*, that product of an industrial society which had vastly increased the numbers whose judgement was politically significant.[4] Carr's analysis of the new role of propaganda in international politics was unique at the time, and it is worth noting that even now conventional histories of British foreign policy in the period make little reference to propaganda, and none at all to the birth of the British Council. Carr on the other hand covered most of the important issues surrounding foreign publicity. He noted the slowness and reluctance of the liberal democracies in taking it up. He recalled the role of the Bolsheviks and the Third International and noted in contrast the British tradition: first a discreet influence from official quarters, particularly in times of crisis, over broadcasting, films and the press, then the direct intervention of the state through the new foreign language broadcasts of the BBC and the British Council, with its rigorous if questionable declaration of faith in the separateness of cultural work from political propaganda. But one lesson Carr hammered home again and again:

> the success of (all forms of) propaganda in international politics cannot be separated from the successful use of other instruments of power . . . it is an illusion to suppose that if Great Britain (or Germany or Soviet Russia) were disarmed and militarily weak, British (or German or Soviet) propaganda might still be effective in virtue of the inherent excellence of its content.[5]

This was a crucial warning, not only for Carr's future colleagues at the new Ministry of Information, but also for the pioneers at the British Council. Would it be heeded?

Of the founders and early patrons of the British Council one thing cannot be said: that they wasted their time in long analytical discussions of their objectives, or in evolving theoretical definitions of culture, cultural relations or 'international understanding'. In the beginning it was fairly rapidly agreed that the Council should aim to:

> . . . make the life and thought of the British peoples more widely known abroad; and to promote a mutual interchange of knowledge and ideas with other peoples. To encourage the study and use of the English language . . . to bring other people into closer touch with British ideals and practice in education, industry and government . . . to afford them opportunities of appreciating contemporary British work in science and technology, literature, the fine arts, drama and music. To co-operate with the self-governing dominions in strengthening the common cultural tradition of the British Commonwealth.[6]

And this definition of aims was to endure unchallenged and uncriticised for many years. The question of methods tended to be interpreted in organisational terms. As in other national efforts of the kind, particularly that of the French, there were to be overseas schools and anglophile institutes, programmes for English teachers, documentary films, distribution programmes for books and periodicals, exchanges and scholarships for students, tours for lecturers and artists. When the war came the Secretary-General said simply:

> I think ... the most important role of the British Council in wartime is to let the world know that the people of this country are able to continue to live, think and act like civilised human beings with the barbarians at the gates.[7]

The fact was that Britain, the only true world power in the 1930s had been rather roughly forced to stoop to the level of the rest and improvise a defence on foreign shores of her predominant ideas, traditions and way of life, things the British were as unused to defending or spelling out as they were their Constitution. As the principal speaker Mr Lees-Jones said in a 1938 Commons debate on British news abroad:

> Up to 1914, we in this country were somewhat indifferent to the opinions of other nations and peoples, with the result that we took few steps to advertise ourselves. Pride of race was partly responsible. Also we thought that our position in the world was quite sufficient to make our actions and views speak for themselves ... I think we were justified in that ... we were a democratic country in the midst of democratic countries ... Today things are different. In some countries the democratic form of government has gone, and with it, that freedom of exchange of views which resulted in knowledge and ... understanding.[8]

Yet the British Council started off in 1935 with £5000 only and was obliged, against the inclinations of its Foreign Office sponsors, to seek help from industry. The Federation of British Industry adopted a positive attitude, but it was soon apparent as Philip Taylor has shown, that the industrialists expected to see quick commercial results, while the Foreign Office sought to construct lasting 'goodwill', with or without economic benefits.[9] Rex Leeper, head of the Foreign Office News Department and a key figure in the birth of the Council put the Foreign Office view as follows:

> ... if this country does not play its proper part in Europe, the

latter will drift into war . . . but I do definitely cherish the hope
that the influence of this country in Europe may avert war . . .
In my view the part of the world which matters most to us in
the next few years is Europe and the Near East. If we could
strengthen our influence very considerably in these countries
with adequate sums at our disposal we could use our cultural
work as a very definite political instrument. This work should
go hand in hand with our foreign policy.[10]

The founders were congratulated by *The Times* for avoiding
any mention of 'culture' in the title of the new body, saying it was
a word which came 'clumsily and shyly off the Englishman's
tongue'. And indeed Britain's first efforts 'to which the uncouth
name "cultural propaganda" was often applied' (as Neville
Chamberlain said), got under way clumsily and shyly.[11] Existing
British institutes and cultural societies in Paris, Florence and
Buenos Aires were helped and new ones were founded in Egypt,
China and Latin America. A Students Committee brought a
small number of foreign teachers of English to British universities
and placed student trainees with British firms.[12] Experts on
cultural themes were sent on lecture tours by the Lecturers
Committee, 40 per year by 1939. A typical example was Harold
Nicolson's Balkan tour of 1938, when he was asked unofficially by
the Foreign Office to 'do what he could to bolster Balkan morale
against Hitler's south-eastern drift'.[13] Committees on Fine Arts,
Music and Books and Periodicals enlisted experts such as John
Masefield, Sir Arthur Bliss and Stanley Unwin, the publisher, to
allocate the small sums available for concert tours, exhibitions
and the stocking of British libraries. To concentrate the effort in
areas where German and Italian propaganda was particularly
heavy, regional committees for Latin America and the Near East
were set up under Philip Guedalla of the Ibero-American
Committee and Lord Lloyd, lately British High Commissioner in
Egypt.[14] Guedalla also chaired the first Film Committee of the
Council, which examined documentary film from various sources
for possible use abroad and began to think how the Council itself
might get into the film-making business. This was in spite of great
scepticism from figures on high such as the Chancellor of the
Exchequer.[15]
From the beginning, as Leeper's comment indicates, the
Foreign Office was convinced that effort must be concentrated in

certain areas of first priority, political and economic, if it was to have any effect at all in diluting German and Italian influence. These areas were northern and western Europe, and the Latin American and Near Eastern zones mentioned above. But when His Majesty's representatives in Scandinavia and Poland were told early in 1935 that their areas would lead off, they made it very clear that although they were anxious to begin and convinced action had to be taken, there could be no half-measures. Kennard, the ambassador to Poland wrote:

> I feel that if we are going to follow the nauseating example of all others, of conducting propaganda, we should do it well. The French, German and Italians, who have plenty of money at their disposal, send their best representatives in every branch to lecture, their films are effective, and their exhibitions and representation at commercial fairs etc. is generally superior to ours. We only reduce our efforts to the level of minor powers if we furnish second-rate performances.[16]

Kennard cited a specific instance from his own past experience. In Berne the local theatres had asked for British films and two had been sent, 'one showing the promenade at Eastbourne and a new dancing hall of a rather inferior type, and the other similar scenes at Scarborough'. Naturally these were not even shown. Kennard warned:

> The German, French and Italian films of this kind are quite first-rate and it is worse than useless to send out inferior films which have no intrinsic interest, and I would suggest that those showing the distinctive side of English life should be given preference.

The programme should be a mass one, insisted Kennard, aiming directly at the intelligent middle class, 'those who are going to count for something in the political, administrative and above all economic life of the country'.[17]

There was no question of a campaign in northern Europe on this scale, let alone in areas such as the Near East and Latin America. Kennard himself had been told that there could be no big Anglo–Polish Institute in Warsaw. The Council's grant went up to £60,000 in 1937/8 under the chairmanship of Lord Eustace

Percy, the educational expert, and then to £200,000 in 1938/9 after Lord Lloyd took over.[18] Even so, said Lloyd in justifying this increase to Lord Halifax, the sum was far smaller than that of any other great power, one quarter of the Italian propaganda budget for example. The only hope could be to meet the most urgent needs on a purely defensive basis.[19]

Nevertheless the arrival of Lord Lloyd at the head of the Council gave a decisive boost to its fortunes. Forbes-Adam, his biographer, recalls:

> George threw all his immense energy and enthusiasm into the work. He had the advantage of knowing with some precision the goal at which he was aiming, and the methods by which he thought it could be achieved.[20]

The goal, in Lloyd's own words, was 'free access to our civilisation and free opportunity [to judge] our outlook and motives', the method, expansion of the British Council everywhere possible. As for the crucial question of power and influence, Lloyd said simply: 'What most interests the outside world, beyond the fact of our power, is the use to which that power will be put. The answer to that question lies deep in our national character....' This latter, Lloyd saw, in *The British Case* published in 1939, as a product of national independence, individual liberty and Christian civilisation. It was not apparently seen as incongruous at the time that, in this same context, Lloyd chose to laud Italy.[21]

But as Forbes-Adam wrote afterwards, the 'important and melancholy fact was that [the Council] started far too late in a race where the competitors, Germany and Italy, had several laps start and infinitely greater resources'.[22] The Council knew that it could not compete directly, so what could it do? The Foreign Office expected results in the future, while hoping as already mentioned to use British 'influence' to avoid another European war. Yet how could parties of Swedish gardening experts, 150 foreign scholarships, a scattering of anglophile institutes and a few dozen lecturers stem the tide?[23] Even the French with their vastly superior organisation, admitted in 1937 they were engaged in 'open battle' with Nazi and Fascist intellectual propaganda, and 'losing ground rapidly in Belgium, Rumania, Yugoslavia, Turkey and even Czechoslovakia...' Meanwhile the Council found it was being called on to do 'crash' programmes in countries as different as Turkey and Japan, with results of little or no value, as a Council official admitted in 1943 looking back on the pre-war efforts in Japan.[24]

In purely contingent terms, the Council was a desperate last hope, one more expedient in the British struggle to maintain the European balance of power without war. But other, truly long-term considerations *were* present, considerations which went beyond the emergency, and were in fact based on the premise that somehow the power balance in Europe would be maintained. Militant nationalism was not just a problem of the continent, but was emerging throughout the British Commonwealth and as George Lloyd well knew, in the Near East and Arab world too. Both Percy and Lloyd were convinced that Britain had somehow neglected her moral and intellectual responsibilities in the Empire – hence the growth of nationalism. They believed the menace had to be faced on a long-term basis by the Council, irrespective of Europe and in fact presuming implicitly that the danger there would sooner or later be liquidated.[25]

Yet once again the question of means came up. It was Lloyd's policy in 1939 to expand the Council's work over the maximum area as rapidly as possible, but with hindsight it was possible to see that because of the low standard of Council pay and conditions, only 'the mediocre, the déraciné and the failure' had cared to enlist. Such types had given the Council's work in southern Europe, for instance, 'a thoroughly bad reputation', said the Foreign Office afterwards. But it had been that area and the Middle East (not Europe) which had received most Council attention before the war broke out. As for the Empire, the Foreign Secretary had been told that it could not be touched at all under budgets such as that for 1939/40.[26]

But the greatest deterrent of all to effective action in the long and the short term was the repeated manifestation of Britain's weakness in conventional power terms before the dictators; even George Lloyd admitted that British prestige was 'flat' in Eastern Europe after Munich.[27] Pondering on 'the meaning of prestige' before a Cambridge audience in 1937, Harold Nicolson claimed that in the Abyssinia crisis the British had got away with it, they had exposed a flagrant decline in their power, 'yet our prestige (much to our surprise) remained almost undamaged'. But this could not continue, Nicolson insisted. Traditionally prestige reflected 'the general confidence inspired by reputation', based in turn on national character, and which made the direct exercise of power unnecessary. But British prestige could no longer be maintained by reputation alone: 'all reasonable people will agree that the proportion of power in our prestige must rapidly and largely be augmented'.[28] Meanwhile (though Nicolson did not mention it) a new body would manage directly and consciously the proportion of reputation. Would 'cultural propaganda' and rearmament suffice to maintain prestige and win the struggle? That was the crucial question facing the British Council just as much as the rest of the British defence machine as war broke out.

When war did finally break out, there was rapid agreement at the top that there could be no question of asking the nation to fight for the status quo ante. There had to be war aims which would support the military strategy and guarantee that a new start would somehow be made.[29] As a War Cabinet paper of October 1940 on propaganda policy stated, a formula had to be found that would 'sustain the spiritual motive force of our own people, appeal to our supporters abroad (especially America) and counter the German conception of a new order'.[30]

In spite of its obvious relevance to this task, the British Council was not immediately enlisted. Although Rex Leeper, still the Council's Foreign Office patron, had insisted as early as April 1939 that Britain too must have a model, a kind of ideology for the future to offer the world, nothing was immediately done in his circle or in the Council.[31] Instead the Council battened down the hatches and prepared to ride out the storm. Most of the staff went off to join the army or the Ministry of Information, leaving at one point only four full-time staff in London. Lord Lloyd became Secretary for the Colonies, while keeping his Council post.[32]

Yet the fact that the Council not only survived but began to expand rapidly after the summer of 1940, gaining its own Royal Charter at the end of the year, showed that in its way cultural propaganda too was passing from the defensive to the offensive and seeking to construct its own set of aims for the post-war world. In spite of having to withdraw in haste from western Europe and the Balkans (where there had been many teachers and 3000 students in the Bucharest Institute alone), in spite of having to give up in Italy, in spite of being barred from the United States in deference to the traditional American suspicion of European propaganda, the Council's budget more than doubled as the war began, reaching £550,000 in 1940/1. The Council had already planned before the war that work with students and lecturers should continue wherever possible, including hopefully in America, and that film and press activities would have to be tackled on a new scale. The foreign press in London would be cultivated and 'prestige' articles provided. There would also be a newsletter, 'Britain Today', Beyond that, the Council predicted that providing hospitality to foreigners would be important.[33] In fact this turned out to be one of the Council's outstanding wartime achievements, with national centres being set up for exile communities, hostels provided for foreign servicemen and close attention given to the needs claimed by the unruly exile governments. A vast effort was made in welfare, education and English teaching, 'with the short-term object of making foreigners in Britain more at home and so of more likely value to the war effort, and in the long-term hope that they would be better equipped to encourage a friendly understanding of this country on return to their own lands', as the Council's Secretary-General recalled.[34]

But this was only a part of the campaign to rally allies, neutrals and other friends by explaining British life and thought. In 1941 the Empire Division was set up to begin work in the Dominions and Colonies. Work in Europe, at the only available contact points, Sweden, Spain and Portugal, was expanded and the ambassador in Portugal, stated at one point that 'the Institute in Lisbon is by far the most efficient propaganda carried out by Britain'.[35] China, Switzerland, Iceland, French North Africa, Portuguese West Africa and the Belgian Congo all received Council attention for the first time, and late in the war a Council man based in the embassy in Moscow cautiously began to organise scientific exchanges and visits, and contacts between libraries. The regions receiving most attention, however, were once again Latin America and the Near East.[36] Latin America, wrote the Secretary-General, was important to Britain for certain commodities needed for the war effort, such as food from Argentina and oil from Venezuela, and also as a great potential market for British goods. This illustrates just how concrete the Council's aims could be when necessary. On the ground, the Council was able to rely on a substantial area of anglophile sympathy organised in local societies.[37]

But even in Latin America there was nothing to compare with

the scale of operations in the Middle East. The British commander-in-chief in the area reputedly stated that the Council's normal work, if extended, 'would be worth several divisions', and both the Middle East War Council and London 'pressed for urgent expansion' as the vital importance of the area to British strategy became clear.[38] By 1941, nineteen institutes were functioning in the area, with eight in Egypt and four in Palestine alone. British schools, particularly in Egypt, received strong support; in Cyprus there were three institutes and a local newspaper, the *Cyprus Post*, was in Council hands.[39]

The key country in the area was of course Turkey, as it had often been in the past. Turkish neutrality was not simply a thorn in the side, it was a major obstacle to British war strategy, blocking the encirclement of Germany, alienating the ever-sceptical Americans and revealing to all the limits of British power. No doubt one day the story will be told of the unceasing British efforts of every kind to win over the Turks; the British Council deserves a chapter of its own in that story. By the end of the war £300,000 was being spent and over 10,000 pupils taught English. The list of activities included: instruction in 150 Turkish social and educational centres, classes for Turkish army officers, eight British professors in Istanbul University and six at Ankara, two periodicals for students of English and bulletins in Turkish on medical, agricultural and engineering subjects. There were even six sports specialists for Turkish clubs and schools.[40] Turkey took the largest single slice of the Council's budget, and in fact it seems reasonable to suggest that nowhere outside the Empire itself was so much British influence concentrated in any one spot for such a sustained length of time.

And all to very little avail. Neither the threat of Hitler nor the blustering of Churchill nor the systematic blandishments of the British Council were enough to get the Turks' co-operation when it mattered. The Council in any case was sceptical about the short-term possibilities of its work, though gratified to be considered 'an indispensable ally of foreign policy' and the war effort, as Eden declared at one point. The Secretary-General in contrast emphasised long-term objectives. It was understood by all concerned that the government too had its eye on the post-war period when it gave out large sums to enable Latin Americans, Portuguese West Africans and Persians to learn how the British formally saw their own thought and work.[41]

   Inevitably then post-war planning became a major activity at
headquarters from very early on. One thing soon became clear:
while the Council's work should be the same everywhere, whether
under dictators or democrats, it had to be based on some form of
concrete, inspiring *idea*. The Atlantic Charter had shown there
was a need for this, not only for the future but to boost the morale
of resistance movements immediately. What could this idea be?
'Unity through diversity' symbolised by the British Empire was
one suggestion, from Lord Snell. Much more promising was that
of the Deputy Secretary-General, Seymour, who proposed 'the
free exchange of ideas throughout Europe', and a large-scale
offer by the Council to rebuild schools, universities and hospitals,
train doctors and teachers, provide lecturers and schoolbooks.
'The extension of British cultural propaganda would follow', said
Seymour. A recommendation was included that a conference
between representatives of the big powers and the exiled governments might meet to plan conventions on the exchange of ideas
and on rebuilding cultural resources.[42] Together with similar
ideas in the Board of Education this formed the starting point for
the successful conference of allied Ministers of Education, which
first met in November 1942, and which in turn laid the founda-
tion stone of UNESCO, a story which would repay further study.[43]
   By the summer of 1942 plans were under open discussion for
'the re-education of Germany' and especially for the development
of ties with Free France. Lord Bessborough, of the French
Welfare Section of the Foreign Office, hinted strongly that 'the
Entente in all its diverse forms [might] be recreated', and the
Council was asked to start thinking of the part it might play in
French reconstruction.[44] By the middle of 1943 the present was
rapidly catching up on the Council's post-war planning. The
Chairman said there was no question of rushing into places like
Italy with the first British or Anglo–American military adminis-
trations or with the first exile government which returned. But
the campaigns in North Africa and Sicily had indicated that the
Council might be needed quickly, especially in areas such as the
Balkans where the Council stood ready to execute the book
distribution schemes already planned by the Ministry of
Information and the Psychological Warfare Executive.[45]
   It was in fact these two bodies, not the Council, which jointly
produced the most significant document of this period entitled
'The Projection of Britain'.[46] This paper aimed to show what kind

of image the British people would present and what their impact
on the future world would be.

> In presenting this image it is essential that we should give full
> emphasis to the cultural aspect; and by 'cultural' in this context
> is meant much more than the contents of our art galleries,
> museums and old country houses.

Culture was much broader than this, a reflection of 'daily life and
thought whether in war or peace'. Then came the definition:

> Our culture is embodied in every phase of our national life and
> institutions, social and economic, industrial and scientific. It
> enters into the design of the goods we export, the interior
> decoration of our embassies abroad, the quality of the films,
> posters and pamphlets we produce for overseas consumption,
> and it is by these manifestations no less than by the output of
> our authors, painters and architects, past and present, that our
> cultural standards will be judged and our cultural influence
> will make itself felt.

This document, the background and immediate purpose of
which remain to be discovered, contained in addition a
remarkably frank assessment of the strategic situation (culturally
speaking) in which Britain would have to operate. First there was
the greatly increased importance of the English language;
secondly, America had now become Britain's chief competitor
though Britain had superior culture;[47] thirdly, France had
fallen, leaving a cultural and intellectual vacuum which Britain
should strive to fill. Inevitably, ran the conclusion, the main
burden would fall on the British Council, but its efforts should be
supplemented and co-ordinated with those of the BBC, the Board
of Trade and what remained of the Ministry of Information after
the war, as well as with the film and export industries.

Whether the Council ever saw this document and what became
of it is not clear. By the end of 1943 the Council was engaged in
its own plans for future development, independently of the rest,
and by the beginning of 1944 produced a paper for the Foreign
Office. To explain the background, Sir Malcolm Robertson, the
Chairman, wrote to Eden personally, saying that he was worried
about the scale of Council activities in relation to the under-

developed organisational side. Two million pounds were being spent in 1943/4 and four million were being sought, yet the Chairman could decide nothing, everything of any importance had to be referred to the Treasury or the Foreign Office, or to one of the special internal committees; staff shortages were chronic. Moreover, continued Robertson, 'there is no real plan, no order of priority as between parts of the world or countries'. Nor was there a clear vision of the relationship with the central government. Convinced that the Council was 'a British conception and had come to stay', and could help bring about 'a better understanding of the peoples of the world as distinct from governments', Robertson asked for an official enquiry. This was eventually set up under Sir Findlater Stewart, a former Permanent Under-Secretary of the India office.[48]

In fact by the beginning of 1945 a crisis point had been reached in the Council's development. A number of knots had reached the comb, to adapt an Italian phrase, of which the toughest was the relationship with the Foreign Office and the Treasury. The Foreign Office admitted at the beginning of the year that they were asking the Council to be prepared to start up in 14 new countries in Europe, to develop their work in China and to be ready to expand in Russia, as well as to continue expansion in Syria and Persia. Yet Council salaries and conditions were quite unattractive, and the Council's request for another budget increase, this time to £4.67 million, would be refused; all this work was to be done on the same £3.5 million as in 1944/5.[49] Although the Cultural Relations Department never said so directly to the Council, the fact was that they had lost confidence in the Council's system of management, both as individuals and as a system, and to some extent they had lost confidence in the Council's product too.

The Treasury complained of indiscriminate expansion and lack of control, and the Foreign Office agreed.[50] As to the image of Britain projected by the Council, there had been criticisms at intervals during the war from the Cultural Relations Department about the bucolic 'England's heritage' approach which seemed to predominate in Council films and the Government Cinematograph Adviser had complained that the Council 'cut the war out altogether'.[51] Now this charge was renewed: 'they often fail to produce effective propaganda by aiming at too wide a public, by attempting too wide a range of subjects, and often by giving too

rosy and self-satisfied a picture of life in Britain', wrote a Foreign
Office official. And this criticism was beginning to appear in the
press. J. B. Priestley boomed: 'Show them the real Britain in
shirtsleeves . . . the kind of castle-and-thatched-cottage-England
that appears in British Council films could not have kept this war
going for half a morning'.[52]

When Stewart's report was handed in, Treasury and Foreign
Office observers only found their fears confirmed, as its main recommendations centred on the replacement of the existing
management structure, and for some time a complete take-over
of the Council by the Foreign Office was under consideration,
again without the Council being informed.[53] However the
Council's work had always been praised in Parliament and in the
serious press, and on its tenth anniversary in July 1945, it was to
enjoy an almost unanimous round of applause. Opinion on the
Council's future among the ambassadors was divided. The
Middle Eastern representatives were almost all for unofficial
status and expansion, while such outstanding figures as Duff-
Cooper in Paris said the Council employees were neither civil
servants, business men 'or even impresarios', and should become
proper officials as soon as possible.[54] All in all the ministries knew
that they could not get away with a straightforward absorption
but were unable to produce an alternative scheme. At the end of
May 1945 Malcolm Robertson resigned his chairmanship in
protest against the indecision of his patrons and paymasters.[55]

In reality this crisis was the product of much more than a
bureaucratic power-struggle. The lack of planning and of any
clear conceptualisation of British cultural policy in general were
now producing their bitter fruits. The Council for its part had by
this time officially embraced the American concept of cultural
relations as pronounced by Archibald MacLeish in particular.
This referred to multilateral exchanges, 'popular relations
grounded upon community of interest', and the broadening of
channels of communication between peoples, and clearly derived
much of its force from the hopes surrounding the birth of the
United Nations.[56] Yet at the same time the Council was obliged to
carry a large unallocated reserve to finance 'crash' programmes in
particular countries at Foreign Office behest as political
circumstances changed. Sir Findlater Stewart saw the Council as
required to present 'a selection of the elements of our living and
thinking and achievements of which we are proud and which are

characteristic of our aims'. These might include 'the helpfulness
and equanimity of a London policeman or the behaviour of a
queue at a railway booking office', but should somehow stop short
at things like fried fish shops in the Barking Road. Sir Findlater
also thought that mutual understanding between peoples was the
overall aim, but he had almost nothing to say about Britain's role
in relation to the United Nations, nor about the Council's
effectiveness at that time, nor even about how it worked in the
field.[57]

What irked the Cultural Relations Department most however
was that the Stewart report said that Council work would never
benefit the Foreign Office or Board of Trade directly. 'The
Council is an instrument of long-term foreign policy, and long-
term as well as short-term foreign policy is the province of the
Foreign Office', Montagu-Pollock, the head of the Department
wrote bluntly.[58] In his own important statement on 'The Case for
Cultural Publicity', written in May 1945, Montagu-Pollock
attempted to spell out the Foreign Office conception, without
referring to the British Council and its difficulties, much less to
any Foreign Office responsibility in creating them. In this view
the conventional emphasis was placed on transmitting life,
thought and achievements, and on education, but this
information was to be directed to 'those sections of foreign
communities which are most capable of appreciating it and of
using it to the advantage of Great Britain'. There was no
reference at all to 'mutual understanding' in the MacLeish sense;
instead cultural publicity was expected to 'help maintain the
nation's present influence and prestige by establishing our foreign
relations on a broader basis than in the past', and this it would do
by aiming not at the mass but at those sections of the population
most influential over the future 'thoughts and actions of their
countrymen'.

What is most striking about Montagu-Pollock's paper however,
and what makes it one of the most important documents in our
story, is its analysis of the importance of cultural work in relation
to Britain's position at the end of the Second World War.
Montagu-Pollock wrote:

> Viewing the present international situation we see this country
> enjoying enormous prestige and popularity but possessing only
> limited means in the political and economic fields of living up
> to its newly acquired reputation.

In eastern Europe in particular, the Soviets would exploit their strategic position to reduce British presence and influence to a minimum:

> in these circumstances cultural policy becomes one of the principal means by which we hope to maintain the goodwill which we at present possess, and in fact in such countries as Yugoslavia and Finland it is the only form of penetration which we can undertake at present.

And to endorse this point of view Montagu-Pollock included a sheaf of quotations from His Majesty's representatives in Athens and Cairo, China and Czechoslovakia, all testifying to the likely importance of cultural work and the British Council in the post-war era. There was a letter from Cadogan to Malcolm Robertson of January 1945, which also showed that the long-term, indirect influence of the Council was expected to be important in eastern Europe.[59]

Here then was the Foreign Office apparently transgressing the first and foremost rule of organised influence by suggesting that reputation could in some degree substitute power. It was in fact a commonly held view at the time in British foreign-policy circles that 'British influence in the whole world', and especially in western and southern Europe, had been 'raised to new heights by the events of the last six years', to use Montagu-Pollock's own words, that is by the stand alone in 1940 and by the nation's conduct during the war.[60]

On this basis the British chose to make their stand in western and southern Europe between 1944 and 1946. The story of course is one of brutal disillusionment. The French immediately set out to reconstruct their own position as an independent great power and devoted 36 per cent of their first post-liberation foreign-policy budget to cultural propaganda.[61] In the Mediterranean, Churchill decided that Greece and Italy should be Britain's 'bastions', and the Foreign Office instructed the British Council in July 1945 to give 'the highest priority' to work in those two countries, a move which signalled the first use of the Council in the developing ideological struggle between the Western Allies and Soviet Russia.[62] In Greece of course, the British had been very heavily committed from the 1930s onwards, to the point in 1944 when a British army found itself fighting to prevent a local 'rebellion', stop a civil war and restore a king to his throne. Yet

even in the midst of all this the ambassador, Rex Leeper, and
Council representatives insisted there was substantial goodwill
only waiting to be cultivated.[63] In Italy from late 1944 onwards,
the British were up against increasing American resentment at
their attempts to run the country exclusively, while America
paid. The Foreign Office in fact had expected Italian political life
to evolve along British lines, and foresaw Italy as 'a member of the
European family under British direction'. Yet at the same time as
the British Council was instructed to mobilise there, Harold
Alexander, the military commander, was recommending that the
Americans 'take the lead' in Italy, while Harold Macmillan, the
resident political expert, told London that the only hope for
stability lay in materials and money for reconstruction, goods
which only the Americans could provide.[64]

The Americans for their part understood perfectly well that the
British system of authority as a whole in such places as the
Mediterranean was in crisis. They saw such changes as the shift
from a direct military presence to an indirect cultural effort in
Egypt as a diplomatic rear-guard action attempting to slow down
the tendency towards national independence.[65] The American
ambassador in Athens told Roosevelt that 'the new growth of
class-consciousness and proletarianism [had] altered the whole
aspect of the problem of retaining British control', and that every
day brought 'its evidence of [British] weakness and dispersion, of
consequent opportunism, and dependence on America's
nucleated strength'.[66] Yet the same American observers admitted
that if some sort of stability and progress was to be achieved (on
American terms) they could not do without 'the comprehensively
penetrating influence' of the historic British system. It was, they
said, an organic growth composed of 'diplomatic experience,
commercial exchanges, cultural contacts, long-standing and
nearly always honoured commitments and strong strategic
positions'. And without it American resources could never be
applied effectively; an equivalent American system would not be
put together overnight.[67]

The Americans of course had more than just resources to
apply; they had ideas and energy: the Four Freedoms, collective
security, free trade, raising living standards everywhere. That was
why their influence had the kind of impact it did in developed
and semi-developed parts of the world. Against it the British hope
that the Dunkirk spirit would somehow inspire seems a wan and

almost pathetic illusion. The British had no *future* to offer the rest of the world in 1935 nor in 1945, and they paid the price. Still something had to be done and something was done and as George Lloyd once said the British did not – usually – force their influence down other people's throats but gave other people the chance to learn what the British were thinking. The British Council represented, at least up to 1945, a ramshackle, almost self-effacing attempt by the British governing class to codify and propagate its form of nationalism, its set of values, serious only where it was indeed seen as a rear-guard action in the old areas of hegemony. Perhaps events simply moved too fast for the Council and its patrons, certainly it always seemed to have difficulty in portraying *change* and the way the British faced up to it. Mr Churchill said in 1945:

> It is beyond the power of this country to prevent all sorts of things crashing at the present time. The responsibility lies with the United States and my desire is to give them all the support in our power.[68]

The tragedy was that the British did not even have a cultural relations programme in America. It was one more proof that power and influence were seriously adrift in British foreign policy by the end of the Second World War.

NOTES

1 Milovan Djilas, *Wartime* (London, 1977) p. 422.
2 E. H. Carr, *The Moral Foundations for World Order, Foundations for World Order* (Denver, 1949) p. 65
3 T. S. Eliot, *Notes Towards the Definition of Culture* (London, 1948) pp. 89, 93–4.
4 E. H. Carr, 'Propaganda in International Politics', *Oxford Pamphlets in World Affairs*, No. 16 (Oct. 1939) p. 21.
5 Ibid., pp. 7, 26.
6 Cited in Philip M. Taylor, 'Cultural Diplomacy and the British Council: 1934–39', *British Journal of International Studies*, IV (1978) 256.
7 Correspondence between Charles Bridge, Secretary-General, British Council and Sir Trenchard Fowle, January 1940 in Public Record Office, British Council Records (henceforth BCR), BW2/88.
8 Cited in Ruth Emily McMurry and Muna Lee, *The Cultural Approach. Another Way in International Relations* (Chapel Hill, N.C., 1947) p. 145.

9 Taylor, op. cit., pp. 254–5.

10 Cited in ibid., p. 255.

11 *The Times*, 23 Mar. 1935; Chamberlain to Lord Derby, letter, 26 Mar. 1935, FO395/528, P1128/267/150.

12 McMurry and Lee, op. cit., p. 140; Taylor, op. cit., pp. 256–9.

13 Harold Nicolson, *Diaries and Letters, 1930–39* (London, 1969) p. 328.

14 On the work of the committees see, British Council pamphlets, 'The Work of the British Council' (1937) and 'Outline of Activities' (1939).

15 E.g., Sir J. Simon to Lord Halifax, letter, 3 May 1939, FO395/641, P1819/44/150.

16 Sir A. Kennard to Rex Leeper, letter, 3 June 1935, FO395/527, P2006/201/150.

17 Sir A. Kennard, 'A Suggested Programme for British Cultural Propaganda in Poland'. 3 June 1935, FO395/527, P2006/201/150.

18 Eustace Percy, *Some Memories* (London, 1958) pp. 160–1.

19 Lord Lloyd to Lord Halifax, letter, 29 Dec. 1938, FO395/641, P74/44/150.

20 Colin Forbes-Adam, *The Life of Lord Lloyd* (London, 1948) p. 283.

21 Forbes-Adam, op. cit., pp. 284–5; Lord Lloyd, *The British Case* (London, 1939) pp. 13, 17, 37–8.

22 Forbes-Adam, op. cit., p. 282.

23 McMurry and Lee, op. cit., p. 141.

24 On the French see ibid., p. 27; on the programme in Japan see memorandum, 1 June 1943, BCR, BW2/95.

25 Percy's comments in *The Times*, 16 Nov. 1936; Lloyd's view in Forbes-Adam, op. cit., p. 282.

26 On the situation in 1939 see memorandum by Director of Appointments Department, British Council, Appendix D, Foreign Office Cultural Relations Department Report on the Findlater Stewart Report, 26 Apr. 1945, FO924/113, LC 2017/19; on the Empire see note 19; Taylor, op. cit., p. 261.

27 Sir Walford Selby, *Diplomatic Twilight, 1930–40* (London, 1953) p. 103.

28 Harold Nicolson, *The Rede Lecture: 'The Meaning of Prestige'* (Cambridge, 1937) pp. 20, 25, 30–4.

29 Cf. Michael Howard, 'Strategy and Politics in World War II: The British Case', paper presented to the XIV International Congress of Historical Sciences, San Francisco, Aug. 1975.

30 War Cabinet Joint Planning Staff, 'Propaganda Policy', 23 Oct. 1940, FO371/25174, W3839/49.

31 Memorandum by Leeper, 16 Apr. 1939, FO395/641, P2262/44/150.

32 Memorandum by Director of Appointments Department, see note 26; on relations with the Ministry of Information cf. A. J. S. White, 'The British Council: The First Twenty Five Years, 1934–59: a Personal Account' (a British Council internal document 1965) pp. 30–1, 34. I am grateful to Philip Taylor for the opportunity to see this document.

33 On the general situation see White, op. cit., pp. 35–6 and The British Council, *Report for 1940–1*; on pre-war planning see Secretary-General to Sir E. Fass, Public Trustee's Office, letter, 30 Jan. 1939, FO395/641, P345/44/150.

34 McMurry and Lee, op. cit., pp. 160–1; *The Times*, 11 July 1945 (a

concentrated survey of the Council's wartime achievements); citation from White, op. cit., p. 41.
35 White, op. cit., p. 39.
36 Ibid.
37 Ibid., pp. 38–9.
38 Ibid., p. 36.
39 Ibid., pp. 37, 39.
40 Ibid., p. 38.
41 Ibid., p. 37.
42 Memorandum by Lord Snell, 10 Oct. 1941, BCR BW2/94.
43 Cf. files in BCR BW2/302–7 and FO370/719–21; also McMurry and Lee, op. cit., pp. 231–2.
44 Bessborough's message in circular memorandum to British Council and various Anglo–French societies, 23 June 1942, BCR BW2/94; correspondence, minutes and content of Foreign Office directive on France (July 1943), FO370/756.
45 Chairman to Sir M. Palairet, letter, 26 July 1943, BCR BW2/95; book scheme mentioned in Seymour to M. Grant, British Council representative at Ankara, letter, 18 Aug. 1943, in ibid.
46 Ministry of Information and Psychological Warfare Executive, Special Issues Committee, memorandum, 'The Projection of Britain', 23 June 1943, FO370/721, L6115/47.
47 The Council were naturally disturbed to learn that a quota system had been decided on for the distribution of films in liberated areas, a system by which American films would outnumber British ones by 40 to 12. But as the matter had been settled 'at a very high level indeed' they were powerless to intervene. Internal British Council minutes on the question, Oct. 1943, BCR BW4/52.
48 Robertson to Eden, letter, 23 Dec. 1943, FO370/782, L6529/4874; a file entitled 'Memo on Future Development of the Council' is to be found in British Council Records (BW2/101); this contains detailed comment on a memo of this title by the Deputy Secretary-General, Nov 1943, but does not contain the document itself. Foreign Office minutes on background to Stewart enquiry, FO924/1; copy of report and associated correspondence, FO924/112, LC624/19.
49 On tasks for 1945 see minute by Hedley, Admin. Dept., Foreign Office, 24 Jan. 1945, FO924/117, LC209/11; Council budget request, Robertson to Eden, letter, 13 Jan. 1945, ibid.; reply signed by R. Law, 8 Feb. 1945, ibid.
50 Treasury view in letter to Foreign Office, Feb 1945, ibid. (with Foreign Office comments).
51 For example of criticism during the war see Foreign Office to British Council Films Dept., 7 July 1941, BCR BW4/62; views of Government Cinematograph Adviser (J. G. Hughes-Roberts) in letter to Primrose, B. C. Films Dept., 2 Mar. 1942 and in a meeting of the B. C. Films Committee, 17 Feb. 1942, BCR BW 4/17.
52 Foreign Office criticism in comment on Robertson to G. Hall, Parliamentary Under-Secretary Foreign Office, letter, 11 Jan. 1945, asking for a parliamentary debate on the Council's future, FO924/112 LC160/19; Priestley's comments in 'Monthly Review of Mentions in the British Press of

Council Activities, Dec. 1944', BCR BW2/162.

53 Foreign Office report on the Findlater Stewart Report, 26 April 1945, see note 26; Treasury view, see note 50.

54 For appreciations in parliament see *The Times*, reports of debates on 18 Feb. 1941, 7 July 1942, 18 May 1945; tenth anniversary press comments collected in 'Monthly Review of Mentions ... July 1945', BCR BW2/162; ambassadorial opinion summarised in Foreign Office minute, 16 April 1945, FO924/113, LC1947/19; Duff Cooper to Foreign Office, tel., 30 Mar. 1945, ibid., LC1231.

55 Montagu-Pollock to Treasury, 24 May 1945, letter, FO924/113, LC2018/19; Robertson's letter of resignation (to Sir M. Palairet, Foreign Office), 28 May 1945, ibid., LC2096; also cf. White, op. cit., p. 56.

56 Report of the British Council, 1944/45, pp. 8–9; before Congressional Committees, however, MacLeish made it clear that he hoped to see a boost for American trade, through the opportunities cultural work gave for the export of American 'know-how'; citation from MacLeish statement on State Department budget for 1946 to the Appropriations Committee, House of Representatives, FO924/114, LC2134/19.

57 On the unallocated reserve see Davies, Finance Officer, British Council to Sir F. Stewart, letter, 24 Oct. 1944, BCR BW2/151; Stewart's comments in report cited in note 48; also cf. White, op. cit., p. 54.

58 Foreign Office report on the Findlater Stewart Report, see note 26.

59 'The Case for Cultural Publicity', 30 May 1945, FO924/114, LC2134/19.

60 Montagu-Pollock's view in ibid.; that of Sir M. Robertson in letter to Palairet, see note 55.

61 McMurry and Lee, op. cit., p. 34.

62 Churchill's declaration cited by Sir N. Charles at meeting in the Foreign Office to discuss British Council activities in Italy with Montagu-Pollock and Seymour, 17 July 1945, FO924/181, LC3027/82; Foreign Office directive formalising British Council commitment to Italy and Greece, Montagu-Pollock to Seymour, letter, ibid.; the possible role of the Council (and parallel US agencies) in a long-term effort to 'democratise' the Italians and combat the growth of the left was explicitly mentioned in a long report by Rear Admiral Ellery Stone, Chief Commissioner of the Allied Commission in Italy entitled 'The Future of Italy', 23 June 1945, excerpts in *Foreign Relations of the United States. The Conference at Potsdam*, vol. I, pp. 688–94. This report was cited, together with a Cabinet decision of 12 July 1945 to 'speed up our propaganda in Italy so as to convince the Italians of the advantage of a western democratic way of life', in Harvey, Foreign Office to Scott, Ministry of Information, letter, 20 July 1945, which stated that the ministry and the Council would be required to give high priority to Italy, ibid., LC3027/82. Research so far has not indicated any evidence that the Council thought in anti-communist terms in 1945.

63 Leeper's view attached to Montagu-Pollock paper, 'The Case for Cultural Publicity', see note 67; views of Council representative in notes on 'Visit to Greece and Italy', Oct. 1945, FO924/181, LC5810/82.

64 D. W. Ellwood, 'Allied Occupation Policy in Italy, 1943–46', unpublished PhD thesis, University of Reading, 1977, pp. 207–8.

65 William Reitzel, *The Mediterranean. Its Role in American Foreign Policy*

(New York, 1948) pp. 160–1.
66 J. O. Iatrides, *Revolt in Athens* (Princeton, 1972) pp. 124–5.
67 Reitzel, op. cit., p. 161.
68 Cited in Elisabeth Barker, *Churchill and Eden at War* (London, 1978) p. 294.

PART II
Film propaganda in Britain and France between the World Wars

3 The people and the pictures. The British working class and film in the 1930s

PETER STEAD

'Nothing but films, films, films' was J. B. Priestley's complaint about the entertainment available to him in Leicester one autumn evening in 1933.[1] A few years later the Welsh novelist Jack Jones recalled his mother's resigning herself to the fact that it was 'Nothing but pictures now'.[2] We are reminded then that what was increasingly referred to as 'going to the pictures' had become a popular form of recreation in the 1920s and then almost a way of life in the 1930s. There was no shortage of social observers to record the staggering statistics: London had 266 cinemas by 1921, Liverpool had 69 by 1932; by 1938 some 20 million tickets were being sold every week which meant that 40 per cent of the people went to the pictures once a week and 25 per cent, the first and perhaps only genuine 'movie buffs', went at least twice a week.[3]

The people, or the public if you like, had helped to clinch a revolution in popular entertainment and to consolidate a new component in the culture. As so often happens when the people firmly opt for something new, the self-appointed guardians of the culture panicked and rushed to identify 'going to the pictures' as yet another symptom of that general decay consequent upon the rise of the masses. D. H. Lawrence you will recall found much that was 'ugly, ugly, ugly' in the Tevershall of the late 1920s including 'the plaster-and-gilt horror of the cinema with its wet picture announcements, *A Woman's Love!*'[4] At much the same time J. B. Priestley's creation Inigo Jollifant found himself 'condemned' to an afternoon in one of Nottingham's 'huge sensuous caverns that called itself a picture palace' and to films 'with their bludgeoning sentimentality, their glycerine tears' and to listening to a cinema organ, an experience that could only be compared to 'being forcibly fed with treacle'.[5] Priestley was to return to this theme in the 1930s when he made it clear that, whatever his attitude to film as such, he had no hesitation in relating the new 'giant cinemas' to the decline of his beloved theatre and even more to the rise of a New England whose seedy monotony was American in origin, most blatantly obvious in Blackpool and symbolised by Woolworths.[6]

In some ways the intellectuals spoke for a wider group of socially-conscious Christians and politicians from all walks of life who saw the cinema as inherently second-rate as it was killing off not only live theatre but many other forms of recreational activity that had called for active and creative participation. Many of the more serious working-men would have said 'amen' to Inigo Jollifant's condemnation. Bert Coombes, a miner whose writings faithfully recorded the conditions of every-day life in the 1930s and early 1940s was quite happy to leave 'the pubs and pictures free for that night to those who want them' and to settle instead for 'Saturday Night Theatre; then the books until late'.[7] In earlier days he too had witnessed the demise of theatre in his village. To him films were but 'shadows' but for his colleagues Pearl White was irresistible. A touring company had offered that great classic *Bo-peep* but one member of the audience reacted strongly by crying out 'Bo-peep be b——I'll Bo-peep 'em! They can't see, let alone peep' and by demanding that the projectionist 'just shove on Pearl – I'll learn 'em what acting is'. 'That' concluded Coombes 'is about the history of the theatre in our village'.[8] But in general it was the sheer passivity of those who went to pictures that annoyed the advocates of participation. Cinemas were seen as helping to confirm that new apathy which was thought so typical of those years of mass unemployment. It was a subistitute which enticed precisely those groups which had no real grasp of the concept of citizenship. It was by its very nature a kind of opting out which appealed to the unemployed themselves, to women (several contemporaries stressed that women more than men were susceptible to the spell that was being cast) and of course to juveniles.[9] Film was attacking society at its weakest points.

The social historian is faced with the task of evaluating an experience. He can hardly fail to detect what the intellectuals and the agencies thought but it is perhaps more difficult to detect what the film-goers thought. Again it is the novelist who comes to our rescue for in *A Frost on my Frolic* Gwyn Thomas beautifully caught that mixture of apathy and anticipation that led so many millions to drift to the pictures in the late 30s and early 40s. The cinema 'is called "The Laugh and the Scratch" or simply "The Dog" from the way people have of itching after a few minutes inside it, kids hang around the cinema in the hope that adults will treat them.

> . . . The older people make this concession not because they have any love for these young elements whom they consider noisy and more in need of gaol than cinema but because, if driven to desperation through a long winter evening, these kids will create a whole seam of dark diversions like crawling into The Dog by the back way and setting the screen alight.

The commissionaire Talfan had been so shocked by finding work after years of unemployment that he has swung violently to the right and is delighted by patriotic films: 'What are the big pictures?', 'Very good for morale, both of them', 'Oh God, that sort again' and Merlin Pugh the projectionist was quite capable of showing the film backwards.

> . . . And we got used to the sight of a man right at the beginning of a film being buried, then shot, then drinking gaily with his friends, then working his way up gradually to being a baby, throwing in his mother's courtship as the final climax.

After a newsreel, a serial and two features Gwyn Thomas's protagonists find themselves 'out on the road in the pale mid-evening light', 'staring at the rounded hills, our minds tiny, hollow sepulchres'.[10]

Gwyn Thomas's superbly comic novel is a useful reminder that for every Oscar Deutsch 'Odeon' and for every 'Pleasure Dome' there were many more very ordinary cinemas of the 'Jeyes Fluid' variety, but it also serves to illustrate the sociological and psychological complexities involved in an evening at the pictures. There were multiple and powerful forces at work. Thomas's character had just drifted into The Dog, and Archie Lush reported that for young people picture-going had just become 'routine'. There is evidence that for others the cinema offered a very necessary escape from the drudgery of everyday life, a young wife told Fenner Brockway that the 11*d* it cost her to go to the pictures once a week with her two children was 'a big slice in the week's money, but for me it's pictures or going mad. It's the only time I forget my troubles'. It was precisely this forgetting of troubles that was to worry the left-wing politicians and there was soon a vociferous contingent who had no doubt that film was deliberately being used in this way. In 1933 the Communist writer Allen Hutt listed the cinema as one of the powerful cultural instruments which the bourgeoise had perverted so that it served its own class ends.[11] But it was perhaps only the more acute observers and those who themselves loved film who knew at what kind of level film was making its appeal. There was a strange kind of chemistry going on at the pictures and to appreciate it in full we must again resort to a writer. Dylan Thomas had been seduced by film at an early age and it was to be an interest that he never lost. In his very autobiographical story *Old Garbo* he describes the impact of an American film on a young reporter,

> Then I entered an American college and danced with the President's daughter. The hero, called Lincoln, tall and dark with good teeth, I displaced quickly, and the girl spoke my name as she held his shadow, the singing college chorus in sailors' hats and bathing dresses called me big boy and king, Jack Oakie and I sped up the field, and on the shoulders of the crowd the president's daughter and I brought across the shifting-coloured curtain with a kiss that left me giddy and bright-eyed as I walked out the cinema into the strong lamplight and the new rain.[12]

During the course of the 1930s then film had become big business and a very fundamental but as yet very confusing aspect of the social scene. In a way its commercial success and popular appeal had caught intellectuals, critics, politicians and social leaders napping. There was a distinct element of haste about their attempts to evaluate this social, technological and artistic revolution and their sociology and criticism were always to be well behind public taste. The people knew what they wanted and had

made their preferences clear long before writers began to refer to
the physical warmth of cinemas or the power of images, the
dangers of distraction and the realism of Cagney's acting. As had
so often been the case in the history of popular entertainment the
new and successful formula had been rather effortlessly determined by the collusion of nouveau-riches entrepreneurs and
audiences, leaving cultural and political establishments to hoist
themselves into a new age. In particular they were left to worry
about how this formula had been arrived at. Who was manipu-
lating whom? They could hardly believe that audiences were
actually choosing what they wanted. Archie Lush was convinced
that his young adults just went to the pictures out of habit and
that they were not in any way 'activated by intelligent interest'. It
took more sophisticated research to reveal what Leonard England
of Mass-observation had learnt by 1950 that

> ... box-office seems to point to the fact that the public is more
> intelligent than it is often given credit for, being faithful to its
> stars once having accepted them, not being unduly impressed
> by the allure of 'glamour' and liking in its films a story that
> exercises its mind.[13]

The popularity of film was certainly something that leaders
and students of society had to come to terms with but there was
another even more perplexing factor and that was the popularity
of American films. The 1930s saw the traditional leaders of
British culture realise that much of their power had been usurped
by an imported form of entertainment. They had lost their
constituency to another culture and who knew what harm that
would do to the traditionally organic nature of British society.
When even a Welsh writer could complain that 'Americanisms
have come to the Rhondda ... and the delightful local accent is
broken up by such words and phrases as "Attaboy!", "Oh Yeah!"
and "Sez You", we can well imagine the consternation caused in
more fashionable shires'. But in the South Wales fashion H. W. J.
Edwards could not leave this subject without giving his
community some kind of boost for he added that 'Rhondda
refuses to have anything but the best in films and anyone who
tries to foist some unworthy film on a Rhondda audience will hear
his patrons comment in very loud tones before they walk out
again'.[14] Here precisely was the rub for who could doubt that it

was the Americans who made the best films. This was thought to
be in part a question of finance and in part a matter of production standards but what really perplexed was the widespread
realisation that, as Raymond Durgnat was later to argue, 'that
American movies sometimes came nearer the actual attitudes of
British audiences than most British ones'.[15] The people had not
just been seduced by Hollywood rather they were quite decisively
opting not only for high standards but for entertainment that
meant something in personal terms. In 1937 Gilbert Seldes tried
to spell out for the British the secrets of the Hollywood formula,
secrets he thought that British producers in particular urgently
needed to learn, and for him 'good intentions and high purposes
and subtle aesthetics' were as nothing compared to 'that candid
pleasure in the work produced, that sincere belief that it is good,
added to the instructive feeling for the essence of the movie as
movement'.[16] For Seldes America 'moved' and its films 'moved',
but what needed to be explained more precisely was why this
'movement' in American films meant so much to the British, and
as we shall see these speculations by Seldes took their place
amongst many other contemporary attempts to diagnose why the
moguls of Hollywood had so totally captured the British millions.
    Since late Victorian, and certainly since Edwardian days, one
clearly identifiable British response to the challenge of mass
culture had been attempts to develop a pattern of adult
education, and it is not surprising that by the 1930s there were
many who wanted to incorporate film into this tradition. Behind
the backs of social leaders Film had become a mass medium and
now traditional British agencies responded to what had almost
been a silent revolution and they responded in a dead-pan,
didactic and pragmatic way that was typical of the culture and
ideally suited to missing the elusiveness and magic of the movies.
We are presented with the spectacle of men who were in so many
respects late Victorians attempting to handle a twentieth-century
miracle and of course they did not understand either the
language or the psychology, they were not up to 'carrying moon-
beams home in a jar'. There was a new power in the land and so
the people had to be instructed. This feeling and the general
mood of earnestness which accompanied it are best recalled in the
pages of *Sight and Sound*, a journal which first appeared in 1932
following the Second Exhibition of Mechanical Aids to Learning
and which was meant to 'provide a permanent channel of

communication between the producers of those instruments and all those who in the education world taken at its widest are interested in their possible application to cultural ends'.[17] The first number included an article 'Films You Ought to See' by C. A. Lejeune and the recommendations for *Kameradschaft, Tabu, A Nous La Liberté* and so on were prefaced by an introduction in which it was explained that 'in this page C. A. Lejeune gives, particularly for the benefit of our readers in the provinces a short list of outstanding films which have been shown in London during the last quarter. Ask the manager of your local cinema whether he is including any of them in his coming programme'.[18] The second issue brought a report from F. G. Thomas on how the WEA in South Devon had been using film as part of its education programme in twelve villages whilst readers of the eighth issue were told by D. F. Taylor that 'today cinema is shaping towards its ultimate realisation as a social service'.[19] In the spring number of 1934 R. S. Lambert thought it worth pointing out that 'to get better films you must be first a filmgoer and secondly be an intelligent filmgoer – train yourself' and he advised members of film societies to 'make friends with those who are engaged in the business of running the local picture houses'.[20]

Sight and Sound was only a minority-interest journal aimed at adult educationalists and intellectuals but it reflected what was a more general response to film amongst traditional, social and political agencies and for the historian its pages help to explain the context in which so much film criticism and film politics developed in the 1930s. It is in this context of established cultural elites confronting a new mass phenomenon that we should examine many of the strands that made up the story of film in Britain in the 1930s, and it is precisely the general sense of earnest concern which justifies the historian's treating these strands as a unity. We can see concern in heavy-handed government involvement and censorship, in what Rotha rightly calls the 'shady' role of the BFI under its first chairman the ex-Tory Minister the Duke of Sutherland, in the endeavours of the adult education and social-service agencies, in the more sophisticated theories of Grierson and much of the documentary movement, in the whole ambience of that so very English Film Society Movement, and in all the efforts of those intellectuals on the Left who wanted to show *10 Days That Shook the World* and *Potemkin* in every welfare hall in the country. Whenever the British talked about film, attempted to evaluate it or explain it, or whenever they attempted to make films in some purely indigenous way the earnestness, didactism and self-consciousness were all too obvious. The response to film was an integral part of a very distinct chapter in that story of how British elites have reacted to popular developments in society in the era since the industrial revolution. This episode in which film became a part of a wider debate on British society is now best evoked by a reading of those *Daily Worker* advertisements which announced screenings of *Isatoff* and *Ivan the Terrible* at clubs in Woolwich and Hammersmith or of the pages of *Sight and Sound* in which D. F. Taylor enthused over the prospect of '50,000 projectors in the hands of private individuals, hospitals and schools'. The period will always be represented in the history books by Grierson who was to this phenomenon what J. S. Mill was to nineteenth-century liberalism. You will recall that he called for his disciples to

> Go out and ask men to mobilise themselves for the destruction of greed and selfishness. And mean it. Ask them to forget their personal dreams and pleasures ... And I haven't a doubt whatever that they will march with you till the skies open and the future is born.[21]

Grierson's sermons represent Thirties Concern at its most sophisticated, but my favourite image of the period is that of the sixteen '23 horsepower Thorneycroft [sic] vans with specially designed bodies operated by a one-man driver and showman' and whose engines drove the projector which went on to the road for the Conservative Party in the 1931 General Election. 'If you can't beat them join them' was a lesson that was soon learnt in some quarters. After the election the vans were taken over by British Films Ltd., which used them to promote milk and other agricultural products.[22]

Film and the phenomenon of picture-going occasioned then a complex and many-sided debate in the 1930s – a debate which takes the historian right to the heart of social and political relationships in the Britain of the day. As we have seen, that debate was characterised by many anxieties over the effects on a mass audience of a cinema which was dominated by certain modes of production and by films of a fairly limited range. As the decade progressed so those debating the nature and impact of film came to worry more and more about one quite overwhelming aspect of popular cinema in Britain and that was the simple fact that the millions who went to the pictures in this country were almost never seeing films that dealt with the every-day realities of the world in which they lived. In a decade in which intellectuals had become politicised and in which many political activists were more aware than ever before of danger and disaster in international affairs, they were being presented with statistics which clearly revealed that the people were more than content to allow what was perhaps the most powerful technique of instruction yet devised to merely entertain them. The plain facts and statistics of picture-going led directly to a debate on what kind of films were being taken up by those who controlled the cinemas but it went beyond that to the more fundamental point that films dealing with the vital social, political and international matters that affected the British people were just not being made. The belief that film was a major art form was now widely accepted as was the notion that one of the functions of all art was to illustrate, develop and complicate the question of human relationships. But in what sense was film in Britain complicating anything? In 1936 Aburo Vessolo attempted to resolve that troublesome question of how art and propaganda could be reconciled in film and in so doing he outlined what was becoming a very general view in late thirties Britain. His view was that 'the prime duty of art is to reveal reality with truth and insight'.[23] Who then could possibly be satisfied with British films? Concern was most fully expressed on the Left but in this Popular Front era left-wing critics were talking for a significant segment of informed opinion. Many non-Communists would have agreed with Maurice Orbach's view expressed in 1936 that 'It is time for the making of workers' films in this country with the punch and power of Eisenstein' and with Jane Morgan's fervent hope printed in the *Daily Worker* of 1938 that Grierson's projected film on the history of Manchester could in changed circumstances be the *'La Marseillaise* of Britain'.[24] There was a general desire for better and different British films and this need was nicely illustrated by *The Times* New York correspondent in 1939 who, when discussing what British films should be shown at the New York Fair, quoted a Middle Westerner who had 'solemnly declared that in his part of the world, none thought of an Englishman without also thinking of a monocle' and then was quoted as adding, 'Show us your factory workers at a football match . . . Let there be stories of work-a-day England, but do not forget or ignore the aristocracy'.[25] All of which tempted *The Times*'s man to ask 'But what is the average Englishman?', a question which clearly British film-makers of the 1930s had in no way definitively tackled.

There were two great questions and, given the aesthetics of the later thirties, these tended to become one; why were there so few good British films and why were British films so disinclined to deal with what was generally accepted as reality? 'No artist in movie can afford to ignore social realities', argues Paul Rotha in perhaps the best known and most influential statement of the time, but this was a challenge that seems to fully substantiate Francois Truffaut's later comment that, 'Well, to put it bluntly, isn't there a certain incompatibility between the terms "cinema" and "Britain" '.[26] Why then was there no British Eisenstein and no British Renoir?

To answer this question in full would involve an examination of many different factors and here it might be appropriate to concentrate on those factors which related most closely to the lives and experiences of the British picture-going public, the 'people' of my title. Perhaps we should first note the general background against which social and political factors operated. Britain was, of course, swamped by Hollywood and so the native industry was from the outset swimming against a strong tide. The ensuing 'quota' saga, a story so dear and meaningful to many in the film establishment, was never of much interest to the man in the Clapham cinema, for as P. L. Mannock pointed out in the *Daily Herald*, 'all this discrimination between Hollywood and British films is a great mistake. Audiences don't care twopence where a film comes from so long as it entertains them.'[27] Moreover, Hollywood not only offered a plenitude of glorious films it also enticed the British film industry into imitation. About this time *The Times* film critic pointed out that 'perhaps the greatest advantage enjoyed by French films is that they are not, as a matter of course, expected to have luxurious settings. It may be that the natural frugality of the French would disapprove of indiscriminate opulence.'[28] The British, of course, emulated Hollywood and went for opulence. But the emulation went much further than this and amounted to nothing short of an attempt to develop in a number of London suburbs replicas of what had become concentrated in one suburb of Los Angeles. The outcome really was the disappearance of anything that could be termed 'British cinema' and the rise of a cosmopolitan cinema dominated by what Rotha called 'a scintillating galaxy of talent from Europe and Hollywood'.[29] This 'Korda era' was best summed up, as Gilbert Seldes noted, in the decision to name the studio which was to show that the English could outdo Hollywood in an English manner 'Pinewood', something which reminded Seldes of the producer who wanted to make a great African picture that was going to have nothing to do with *Trader Horn* and then asked 'What shall we call it, *Trader what?*'[30] And then there were the simple but all important facts about distribution in Britain and the way in which the few chose for the many. Going to the pictures soon came to mean for most people going to see that small percentage of films which were guaranteed to be popular. P. L. Mannock was of the view that if films were good people would go 'to the oldest, pokiest hall' but the combines were rapidly imposing their policy of popular films shown in palatial surroundings. The price to be paid was that 'millions of people in this country never see many magnificent films' and Mannock instanced a town not fifty miles from London with 9,000 seats in seven cinemas, all of which were owned by the same firm thereby denying citizens 'half the good films of 1937'. He knew also of a town in Kent whose cinemas were controlled in such a way that 'Greta Garbo is almost unknown there'.[31]

All these commercial and entrepreneural facts constituted a formidable obstacle to the development of an indigenous cinema and one able to respond to Rotha's challenge. It is in the context of this colonial or Banana Republic infrastructure that we should examine the story of the Documentary Movement with its dependence on its sponsors and its inability to do very much about the distribution of its films. '*Shipyard* is a serious and important contribution to documentary cinema' claimed J. R. Fawcett-Thompson in a *Sight and Sound* of 1935, then adding 'What will Barrow-in-Furness think of it?', a question that reverberates within thirties film-writing like a stone bouncing its way down a deep well.[32] But the very anomalous mention of Barrow in the pages of *Sight and Sound* jerks the historian into a realization that restricting as the commercial conditions of the British film industry were, they still did not in themselves sufficiently explain the nature and quality of home-produced films. Quite apart from the fact that there have been at least a few examples in history of

artistic masterpieces being produced against the grain of entre-
preneurial norms, there is a case for arguing that the kind of films
shown to the people of Barrow were determined as much by
cultural and political factors as by straightforward economics. Is
it not perhaps as true to say that cultures produce the films they
deserve as it is to say that we get the films our businessmen want
us to see? Film in thirties Britain was very nicely illustrating
aspects of the culture.

The mushrooming suburban film studios were in so many ways
operating in a cultural vacuum. This after all was a country
whose literature had, as yet, hardly come to terms with the urban
and industrial experience. There were few creative writers able to
measure up to the artistic demands of Rotha's and Vessolo's
definitions of art, and surely it was quite reasonable to have
expected this more established artistic form to have pointed the
way towards a treatment of social reality? In 1936 Graham
Greene argued that 'The novel has long ceased to make any effort
at being a really popular art: the novels of Mr. Priestley or Mr.
Brett Young represent the people about as much as do the pros-
perous suburbs of Balham or Streatham' and he went on to doubt
whether 'we have had any popular art in England since the
Shakespeare theatre'. He welcomed the cinema as a new
possibility but greatly regretted that 'the fictional film is more-or-
less stabilised at the level of middle-class taste'. For Greene
cinema had become horribly middlebrow and mediocre and for
this he wanted to blame critics and reviewers 'for they are doing
as much as any Korda or Sam Goldwyn to maintain the popular
middle-class Book Society status quo'. Greene was surely right in
pointing to the suburban values which dominated the British
cinema world but the really vital and interesting question is how
individual film-makers reacted to this milieu. The sad truth
would seem to be that commercial cinema in Britain never
recruited individuals with the artistic confidence and social
awareness needed to stand up to the entrepreneurs and that the
metropolitan and cosmopolitan film world with its emphasis on
technical excellence and commercial success was allowed to
smother genuine artistic freedom. Apprentices of the technical
and literary sort were sucked in to the glossy and opulent studio
atmosphere which was so very far removed from the drab Britain
outside the studio gates. When rebellion came it came not in
terms of fictional film but in documentary and in films which had

far more in common with the way in which middle-class poets were discovering and then using an urban world than with the popular romance with the movies. The Documentary Movement created images of the thirties just as surely as did Arden, Spender and Isherwood and they were and remain images which tell us more about the artistic tasks of intellectual elites in England than they do about British society. Documentary was an aesthetic mode and it could never have been a popular art form. There was no British Renoir because no British film-maker knew enough about his medium or knew enough about his country and its people.[33]

We must, however, be fair to the potential British 'auteurs' for there were obstacles other than economics and middlebrow taste to overcome. We should never underestimate the extent to which the domestic taste for films was determined by government policy. The story of how the newsreels and even *The March of Time* were neutered is now well known but not enough attention has been given to the way in which even the feature film was controlled. In a way the British film industry was carefully guided away from the streets and in through the studio gates. The Cabinet Papers, Home Office and Metropolitan Police files all indicate the concern of various governments that political dissent should not be filmed but an earlier file does much to explain why so little of Britain was filmed before the nineteen thirties. In 1929 Norman Lee, a film director, wrote to the Prime Minister to complain that 'British Picture Companies are not receiving sufficient facilities for filming London', that directors faced 'innumerable setbacks' and that during his shooting of a film on London life he 'was hunted by detectives in Hyde Park and eventually turned out'. Later uniformed officers came to his home and yet he argued 'soon we are to see the German film *Berlin*. Everywhere we can see pictures of New York'.[34] 'Auteurs' then were kept off the streets and away from the people. This nervousness about film-makers on the loose must be recalled together with all those difficulties that surrounded the showing of foreign films in the 1920s and the tense relationship that existed between the censor and the young Film Society. Throughout the period British film-makers were fairly clearly told to avoid 'controversy' and as Grierson said of the censor, 'it is not surprising that his slogan of "No Controversy" – which to philosophy and all the world is "No Reality" – is abjectly obeyed'.[35] British film was stunted in its adolescence and the historian in his search for cultural generalisations must not lose sight of those policemen and bureaucrats who lurk through the pages of our film history. Herman Weinberg talked of the way in which 'anger' had always 'made American film directors great' and 'pumped the life-blood into their best work': British directors did not come from the right class or ethnic background to be angry but they also knew that anger would take them straight into the courts or into unemployment.[36] The story that unfolded was one in which a film industry and its own Board of Censors for the most part collaborated with an anxious and nervous body of civil servants and politicians. The nation seemed little concerned with the asides in which Graham Greene, Forsyth Hardy and Rotha protested.

Protest was what was needed and it would have taken a body of film-makers closely connected to a deeply concerned political movement to change the ethics of the British film world. Britain, though, was to have no very meaningful Popular Front; there was never any meaningful fusion of artists and the workers and, in any case, the country's powerful Labour Movement had never shown any great interest in artistic or cultural matters. The entre-preneurs and the censors wielded their influence alongside a supine and philistine Labour leadership and it was this, as much as anything else, which forced the potential auteur into a terrible isolation and a cultural vacuum. The Labour Movement as a whole only showed a spluttering interest in film and the social his-torian of film has to look hard for his tit-bits. In Llanelly in the 1920s the Constituency Labour Party developed its own news-paper which in 1924 printed a story welcoming the *Union of Post Office Workers Film* which had just been premiered at the Kilburn Picture Palace and praising the Union to which belonged 'the distinction of being the first organisation to adopt the possibility of the cinema screen to Trade Union propaganda.' The film had made 'a forceful plea for industrial solidarity' and its success was taken to indicate 'a new era which has remarkable potentialities'. The 'animated diagrams' were thought to be particularly effective and the correspondent did not think it was 'belittling the power of the spoken word in any respect to say that no platform orator, no matter how eloquent, could have conveyed the point with equal forcefulness'.[37] The following year this same *Labour News* embarked on a detailed examination of

'capitalism and the Cinema – The Money Behind the Movies'.
The writer traced the rise of cinema in the constituency – there
were now 'a score of cinemas', many of them 'sumptuous Palaces'
and he concluded that 'a curiosity has evolved into an entertainment'. His concern was that 'the Pictures are being cleverly used
to dope the workers' and he went on to relate the general nature
of the industry to the detailed statistics of local cinema
proprietorship. He saw the need for the British Labour
Movement to face up to this situation and he reminded his
readers that 'at a good many Halls controlled by miners in our
area there is a cinema', so 'why not run the cinema yourselves?
There is money in it and by controlling it yourselves you will in a
measure determine what kind of Pictures you show.'[38] This brave
challenge was never really taken up. Bert Hogenkamp has
recently given us the detailed story of how in the 1930s Workers
and Labour films were made but neither those films nor the films
of the Documentary Movement ever reached a mass audience.[39]
For the most part they joined the Soviet films in the programmes
of selected London clubs, or in the case of the provinces they were
used in what we may term flickering experiments. Occasionally
constituency parties would show films and miners halls would
react to the *Daily Worker* advertisements, but it was never a
sustained or glorious story. In 1934 the film *Russia: Past and
Present* was shown in 18 South Wales locations and was very
much appreciated by some 2000 people, but this venture bank-
rupted the Rhondda Labour College and brought its other
activities to a temporary halt.[40] Such episodes reveal how divided
the Labour Movement was in the thirties, of how sensitive the
wider Movement was to Communist influences and of how
difficult it was in such a tense and fragmented society to get any
co-operation for cultural initiatives, whether in the sphere of
cinema, adult education or any recreational activity. The lead of
the Post-Office workers was not followed, the challenge of the
Llanelly *Labour News* not taken up and even those resources that
Unions and Labour branches did have (such as the cinemas in
miners halls) were not fully developed as instruments of
education. The unions had other priorities, the Labour Party as
such was always a little suspicious, and it was always easiest to give
the public what they wanted. Nevertheless, it was still staggering
that the Labour Movement produced nobody with a genuine
interest in film or with the imagination to see the wider
possibilities.

The explanation of why the reality that was Britain did not get onto the screen has taken us to many parts of the nation's life but for one final point we should return to those middlebrow values to which Graham Greene had drawn our attention. In the films of the 1930s language was becoming more and more important and quite remarkably the film-going public showed, as were later generations of young television viewers, that they had no difficulty in following the very different American language. It was soon widely appreciated that part of the genius of American film-makers was that they could write realistic dialogue and use actors who spoke lines not only as if they meant them but also as if they were their own. American cinema was classless and even in Britain the atmosphere of the cinema had always been déclassé – it was perhaps the first genuinely classless social activity in British history. In such a world most British films could only be an embarrassment for they had to employ actors and even more actresses who had been trained for the West End stage. In 1938 Jane Morgan spoke of a need for 'actors who have not had every spark of humanity ironed out of them by the strange conventions of the West End stage' and 'who are not either deadly anaemic or absurd caricatures of the characters they are supposed to represent'. P. L. Mannock quoted a correspondent who thought that 'three-quarters of the country will not have the overdone "Oxford" accent' and another who told of how Scottish patrons 'wander up to the house, look at the displays and say "Och, it's ane o' they English. Let's go somwhen else" '.[41] British films were unpopular (with the very notable exceptions of those made by the ex-music halls comedians) because they sounded so awful, a stilted language was spoken in 'posh' accents and that high-pitched twang, which reproduced so badly, was interrupted only by the interventions of provincial caricatures in the form of servants or policemen. No other country has had so many problems with language in public life and whereas the BBC could arrive at a formal language for public pronouncement, it could be argued that British cinema took at least another twenty years to catch the rhythms of the people. Roger Manvell authoritatively summed this up when he spoke of British films which 'prattle when they should be swift and precise' and of how, by contrast, 'American idiom is clipped and pert, insolent and free, quickened with imagery, and spoken with speed'.[42]

In this respect, as in so many others, Hollywood was good and was getting even better for suddenly in the later thirties British intellectuals began to realise that Hollywood was not only making well-made films but films which matched up to the current notions of what constituted art. Hollywood was manifestly tackling reality. Suddenly even the *Daily Worker* found itself praising American films and there were recommendations for *Oil* ('The film touches the fringe of reality'), for *King of the Damned* ('takes the side of the underdog') and *Fury* ('one is conscious of the tremendous force for progress that the cinema can be without in the least sacrificing entertainment value'). How could one account for 'Hollywood's sudden outburst of social honesty'? 'Were these good films strange flukes?' asked Victor Shannon or, as Trevor Blewitt suggested, a case of Hollywood being 'ready to cash in on the class struggle'. Certainly they seemed 'to be going funny that way in Hollywood'.[43] The truth was that American films, just like American literature, were quite prepared to deal with almost any individual experience and perception of America that confirmed the general principles of the American credo, even to the extent (as in the case of the widely praised Capra films) of criticising the dominant economic values. In America the culture was, in part, a product of the sum total of individual experiences and it invited people to convert their own histories into statement. In Britain we are talking of a received cinema in which individual experiences were as nothing compared to the industry's conventions and broad social generalisations.

The people then did not see themselves in the cinema and perhaps they were not too unhappy with that state of affairs, for the actors employed in Hollywood were not at all bad proxies. British cinema audiences felt far more comfortable when love, ambition, bravery and adventure were depicted by American professionals than when they were entrusted to West End actors or even to their own kind. In American films they saw their own reality, albeit related in strange accents, set in exotic surroundings and somewhat speeded up, but the sentimentality, the humour, the feel for family and community, the sexuality and above all the celebration of the individual constituted a new but thoroughly intelligible, immediately recognisable and infinitely appealing version or interpretation of life. The conventions of an industry had made the most of the medium's magic and had created a universal language. Above all American films did not patronise in the same way as so many British films. In British

feature films directors had relegated the people to the status of
'yokels' and to documentary film-makers they had often been no
more than picturesque figures in a landscape. The American
cinema had created individual heroes and heroines whose point
of view audiences were asked to share or at least to understand.
This individualised perspective allowed audiences to perceive
social relationships and history with something that approxi-
mated to their own sense of reality. In the British cinema
people were far too neatly packaged. Listen for the voice of an
authentic individual in British film and you will find it difficult to
find. Actors created types rather than expressing their own
quiddity and documentary and newsreels were only interested in
clichés. Only very occasionally did the strident and earnest
sermonising of the commentators give way to a 'vox populus'. In
Eastern Valley an unemployed miner was allowed to say that a
relief scheme had been characterised by 'lots of mistakes', in
Today We Live another miner, John Adlam, helped to explain
the background of another relief scheme, and in *Housing
Problems* a Mrs Hill told the world and history that 'Vermin is
wicked'. In odd moments then we can glimpse real people
nervously addressing the camera but there is not much of this
material and its novelty is symbolised in the way in which those
two names *Bill Blewett* ('a fine character') and *Dai Jones* (who
now 'digs for souls not coals') leap out of the title-catalogues.
George Orwell was horrified by the thought that Spartacus was
one of the very few slaves that history remembered and we,
perhaps, should have the same feelings about how few British
people of the 1930s have been introduced to us by film. British
films of the thirties did not come to terms with reality and largely
responsible for that failure was the inability of film-makers to
realise that social reality can only be meaningfully interpreted
through individual experiences. The country in general and the
film industry in particular seemed happy with a few general social
assumptions. There is no sense in this cinema of history as process
and experience, or of society offering and being determined by
options. Directors then did not become 'auteurs' and apart from
Mr Baldwin, Oswald Mosley and an eccentric choice of assorted
politicians, no real person was allowed to speak for him or
herself.[44]

Of course things improved. Whether it was because Hollywood
had shown that realism could be good box office, or whether a

Popular Front mood was catching on as war approached, but the last years of the decade did see a sense of individuality within society begin to creep into British films. The mediocrity was diluted by films like *South Riding* in which John Clements played a young Socialist councillor, and *Pygmalion* which in a way satirised many of the film world's own conventions. Most impressive were two adaptations of A. J. Cronin novels; first *The Citadel* which got its working-class politics horribly wrong but managed a very radical critique of the medical profession, and then *The Stars Look Down* in which Michael Redgrave told his fellow students about the coal owners shortcomings as images of working miners flashed on the screen, and in which Margaret Lockwood's brilliant portrayal of feminine opportunism is as frightening an illustration of what the Depression really meant as any shot of an unemployed miner. Neither Cronin film was interested in political ideas or organisation but, at last, British films were realising the drama inherent in the social issues of the day and creating characters who determined their own values and realised that there were options.[45]

In the war years the people were the heroes and the cinema was allowed and encouraged to publicise their efforts. In this sense we can talk of British cinema as of Britain as a whole 'coming of age' but of course it was to be many years after the war before films as good as *The Stars Look Down* were made again. The story of the people and the pictures in the 1930s is not just one chapter in a synoptic tale but rather a wider illustration of the relationship between political and artistic elites in Modern Britain. We are reminded that art fails where, in Michael Wood's term, it does not complicate, that if we do not create images of ourselves then others will use us in their images, and that in tackling reality there is no substitute for the creation and projection of individuality. Only artistic genius coupled with a strong sense of the worth of every individual can save film, literature or politics from being propaganda.

NOTES

1 J. B. Priestley, *English Journey* (1934) p. 121 of 1937 cheap edition.
2 Jack Jones, *Unfinished Journey* (1938) p. 185.
3 Taken from various references in C. L. Mowat *Britain Between the Wars* (1955) which is still unrivalled as an account of the era.
4 D. H. Lawrence, *Lady Chatterley's Lover* (1928) p. 158 of Penguin edition.
5 J. B. Priestley, *The Good Companions* (1929) p. 227 of Penguin edition.
6 Idem, *English Journey* p. 401 *et seq.*
7 B. L. Coombes, *Miners Day* (1945), p. 28.
8 Idem., *These Poor Hands* (1939) pp. 140-1.
9 For the unemployed see Hilda Jennings, *Brynmawr* (1934), for women J. B. Priestley, *English Journey*, p. 201, and Fenner Brockway, *Hungry England* (1932) p. 33 *et seq.*, and for juveniles A. J. Lush, *The Young Adult* (1941).
10 Gwyn Thomas, *A Frost on My Frolic* (1953 – reprinted 1968), chap. VII.
11 Allen Hutt, *The Condition of the Working Class in Britain* (1933) p. 177.
12 Dylan Thomas, *Portrait of the Artist As A Young Dog* (1940).
13 'Popular Taste in the Cinema', in *The Cinema 1950* (ed. Roger Manvell).
14 H. J. Edwards, *The Good Patch* (1937) p. 162.
15 Raymond Durgnat, *A Mirror for England* (1970) p. 6.
16 Gilbert Seldes, *Movies for the Millions* (1937) p. 4.
17 *Sight and Sound*, vol. 1, no. 1, Spring 1932.
18 Ibid., p. 25.
19 *Sight and Sound*, vol. 1, no. 2, p. 38 and vol. 2, no. 8, p. 128.
20 Ibid., vol. 3, no. 9, p. 6.
21 'Education and the New Order' in *Grierson on Documentary* (1946) p. 202.
22 *Sight and Sound*, vol. 1, no. 2, p. 49.
23 Ibid., vol. 5, no. 18, p. 30.
24 *Daily Worker*, 13 April 1936 and 16 May 1938.
25 *The Times*, 2 January 1939.
26 Paul Rotha, 'The Movies and Reality', *Sight and Sound*, vol. 6, no. 22, p. 90. Truffaut is quoted at the outset in Roy Armes, *A Critical History of British Cinema* (1978).
27 *Daily Herald*, 7 Jan. 1938.
28 *The Times*, 17 Jan. 1938.
29 Paul Rotha, *Rotha on the Film*, (1958) p. 255.
30 Ibid., p. 2.
31 Mannock almost more than any other critic attempted to come to terms with the sociology of provincial cinema-ownership and film going. See the *Daily Herald*, 14 and 28 Jan. 1938.
32 *Sight and Sound*, vol. 4, no. 14, p. 76.
33 The outstanding book on Documentary is William Stott, *Documentary Expression and Thirties America* (1973) and the world in which British documentary film-makers worked is best explained in Samuel Hynes, *The Auden Generation* (1976).
34 File on 'Police and Filming', Public Record Office, HO45–17415.
35 Quoted by Rotha in his comments on censorship in 'The Movies and Reality', op. cit.

36 'American Film Directors and Social Reality', in *Sight and Sound*, vol. 7, no. 28.

37 *Labour News* (Llanelli), 14 Oct. 1924.

38 Ibid., 29 Aug. 1925.

39 Bert Hogenkamp, *Workers' Newsreels in the 1920's and 1930's (Our History* No. 68) and 'Film and the Workers' Movement in Britain 1929–1939', *Sight and Sound*, vol. 45, no. 2.

40 A story to be told in a forthcoming University of Wales PhD thesis by Richard Lewis of Teesside Polytechnic, to whom I am grateful for the reference.

41 *Daily Worker*, 2 May 1938, and *Daily Herald*, 14 Jan. 1938.

42 Roger Manvell, *Film* (1944) pp. 67–9 of the Pelican edition.

43 See reviews in the *Daily Worker*, 28 and 29 Sept. 1936, and 26 Oct. 1936.

44 My comments here arise out of my extensive viewing of thirties footage when preparing my compilation film *The Great Depression*, InterUniversity History Film Consortium, Historical Studies in Film, No. 5 (1976). I discuss these questions in an accompanying booklet.

45 *The Citadel* (1938), directed by King Vidor, and *The Stars Look Down* (1939), directed by Carol Reed.

4 The political censorship of films in Britain between the wars

NICHOLAS PRONAY

The question of the aims, machinery and impact of the censorship of films can scarcely be described as a subject which has excited much discussion amongst historians of Britain in the twentieth century. The impact of the cinema itself has indeed been long noted in our 'standard books', such as *Britain Between the Wars* by C. L. Mowat[1] and *English History 1914–45* by A. J. P. Taylor[2] or social history such as *Britain in the Age of Total War* by Arthur Marwick,[3] but there is no mention of the subject or even the existence of censorship at all. The specialist literature of 'film-history' of recent years has also relatively little to say about the subject. Professor Thorold Dickinson's *An Appreciation of the Cinema*[4] deals with the existence of censorship and its impact by implication only. Mr Basil Wright, who has been personally associated with the socially and politically committed film ideas of John Grierson, does not mention the subject at all in his massive study of the cinema *The Long View*.[5] The most significant, and indeed pioneering, historical study concerned with the impact of political ideas projected by the cinema in the inter-war years, Jeffrey Richards' *The Visions of Yesterday*[6] makes no reference at all to censorship as far as Britain's 'Imperial Cinema' was concerned. Censorship was certainly not like some other aspects of the history of the inter-war years which, having been shrouded in official secrecy, could only now become a subject of historical interest. On the contrary, it was so far from secret that its existence was announced in some 4000 places every night. No historian who has ever been a cinema goer himself could have been unaware of the fact that, like every one else in the cinema, the films which he was going to see had been examined and passed by a body plainly described as the British Board of Film Censors, located at 'Soho Square, London' with the name and signature of the President of Censorship reproduced on the screen itself.

Censorship not only appeared however so disarmingly, indeed boringly, open, its activities were also regularly discussed in the media particularly during the 1960s and 1970s. It staggered through the pages of the press, ever more fatuously, from row to row over such questions as the permissible angle from which certain parts of the human anatomy may or may not be filmed. Worse, it was also evidently futile, for local authorities cheerfully licensed or banned such films as *Emmanuelle*, irrespective of its judgements or the statements issued on behalf of the Board by its chief officials – being themselves people no-one has heard of and manifestly of no political standing, connections or significance. One tended to derive from all this an image of the British Board of Film Censors as that of a body which fusses over bosoms, bottoms and violence and which tries to bowdlerise common English usage. One tends to picture the film censors as people wielding a pair of scissors, snipping out frames or sequences and who occasionally stir up big storms in teacups, either because of some particularly silly cutting of an artistically meritorious film, or as often, because they let through some cleverly disguised piece of pornography which upset the self-appointed guardians of our moral welfare. Altogether our image of the British Board of Film Censors is that of a comical, if not pathetic, minor aspect of the panorama of a liberal nation subject to occasional fits of morality. The image of film censorship in Britain today, and for at least the last two decades was thus hardly conducive to attracting historical examination, particularly since in contemporary accounts of the cinema, such as Paul Rothas' or Roger Manvell's, the salient features appeared to be similar: a self-appointed body of the cinema trade itself, of no legal or political consequence or standing, run by men of no position in the political world and exercising a censorship dedicated to the maintenance of a Victorian ideal of morality and religion. A subject which therefore can safely be excluded from the general study of the period.

The *political* censorship of films, if it existed, would be a different matter. Political conditioning by negative propaganda, preventing the promotion of alternative ideas to those projected as

the basis of the authority, legitimacy and policies of the government – that is, political censorship – is of historical significance
and interest. Particularly so if exercised over a medium which
reached some 18 million of the population each week, including
the great majority of young people during their most impression-
able age and those whose lack of education made them least able
to turn to other media. And, if that medium happened to be the
sound film with its peculiarly persuasive combination of being
both able to create totally photographic illusions of actuality/
reality, unlike the theatre, yet also convey ideas in spoken
language, like the theatre, in the verbalised form of politics.

But was political censorship of films, in this sense of deliberate
negative propaganda on behalf and with the backing of the
powers of government, actually practised in Britain during the
years of peace which lay between abolishing the first and
establishing the second ministries of 'Information'? Published
views differ markedly on this basic question. Miss Rachel Low in
the fourth volume of what surely deserves to be called the 'official'
History of the British Film, covering the period 1918–29, after
discussing the moral and religious censorship exercised by the
British Board of Film Censors (BBFC) noted that: 'Probably the
most stultifying group of objections was that designed to protect
existing authority and the social establishment.'[7] She takes the
view that the Board was essentially a private organisation run by
elderly personages, certainly agreeable to the Home Secretary but
not involved in the progaganda work of the government. She
believes that 'political censorship', a phrase which she avoids
otherwise, was confined to occasional ham-fisted attempts by
certain ministers, usually the Foreign Secretary, the worst of
which concerned the attempts to ban a British film, *Dawn* by
Herbert Wilcox, which upset the German Ambassador, and the
importation of the revolutionary epics of the Soviet cinema, such
as *Battleship Potemkin*.[8] Dr Roger Manvell, who co-authored the
first volume of *The History of the British Film*, and may be
regarded as high an authority on British films while at the same
time being a distinguished author in the field of the history of
propaganda, listed 'Religious', 'Political' and 'Social' as the triple
concerns of censorship before the war. He defined the aims of the
'political' section as the suppression of 'Anything calculated to
wound foreign susceptibility' and 'Anything calculated to foment
social unrest and discontent'.[9] He also emphasised, however, that

'The British Board of Film Censors was set up *by the trade itself* and was financed by it in order that the trade should gain respectability in the eyes of the community'. (italics in the original)[10]

On the other hand, Guy Phelps' *Film Censorship* does contain a chapter plainly titled 'Political Censorship'.[11] It is an excellently researched and lucid book which draws upon Home Office material, the papers of the BBFC, as well as the papers and recollections of some of its officials, although its concern is with the present position and future of censorship rather than its history. The author has no hesitation in endorsing, from his own research, the conclusions of Paul O'Higgins' legal study, *Censorship in Britain*:

> Open censorship on political or social grounds appears no longer to be practised by the BBFC, as it certainly was in the 1920s and 1930s, although social and political attitudes still appear to colour some decisions.[12]

This view, that political censorship, most regrettably, had in fact been practised in the bad old days but nothing could be fairer from the present position, has been frequently expressed by BBFC officials during the 1960s and 1970s, such as John Trevelyan and John Murphy, although not much weight on its own can be attached to such public statements for current consumption as regards the historical position.

The fullest legal examination of the history of film censorship to date has been provided in Neville March Hunning's *Film Censors and the Law*.[13] 'Political censorship' is regarded as a part of the system of several foreign countries, but the term is only used three times in the context of British film-censorship and always as part of quotations from contemporary statements either referring to the 'dangers of political censorship' should the BBFC be replaced by a government department of censorship, or opposing attempts at its extension to 16mm films or newsreels, or statements by the government to the effect that it would be most reluctant to so extend it – without comment.

> Almost for the first time reference is made to the dangers of political censorship: 'The British Board concerns itself – or is supposed to – with morals only. A Government Department would almost certainly concern itself with many other things'.[14]

> The County Councils Association ... referred especially to the dangers of 'uncensored films (non-flammable, sub-standard stock used for 16 mm and other non-cinema type filmshows) being used for subversive purposes.'[15]

The Merseyside Film Institute Society expressed 'uneasiness at recent attempts to impose a political censorship upon films, especially ... sub-standard films'.[16] Perhaps, because the author's interests are primarily legal and philosophical, or perhaps because this pioneering study was undertaken in the early 1960s when most of the political records were still under a 50-year rule, the fact is that while it provides a vast amount of material of political significance, it avoids discussion of the issue of political censorship altogether as far as Britain is concerned.

There is little difficulty, however, in establishing the rules applied by the BBFC, and what is even more useful, the practical form in which they were applied for, until 1932, they were printed annually for the benefit of film producers and films importers in Britain as an appendix to the Annual Report of the BBFC.[17] It was also sent to foreign producers wishing to market films in Britain, so that they also should be aware what the Board would not pass. The point of a new list each year was that either new rules came to be added, which was rare, or that the application of the existing rules to new scenes or story-lines during the preceding year should help to clarify their meaning in practice. The first set of 'rules' was presented in the course of the hearings of the Cinema Commission set up by the National Council of Public Morals in 1917, five years after the establishment of the BBFC. The Board then operated 43 rules already, listing the 'subjects' about which films should not be made at all, if they were to receive a certificate from the Board and indicating the form of treatment, 'scenes', of acceptable subjects which were to be avoided in the first instance, or were to be ordered to be 'cut' by the Board. Of these rules 34 dealt with either religious matters (such as no. 3 'Irreverent treatment of sacred subjects') or matters of sexual morality (no. 36 'Prostitution and procuration') or indecency and indecorum (no. 10 'Nude figures'; no. 11, 'Offensive vulgarity and impropriety in conduct or dress') or cruelty, mental or physical, to humans, or of course, animals. Rules 15–22, however, covered the following:

15 References to controversial politics
16 Relations of capital and labour
17 Scenes tending to disparage public characters and institutions
18 Realistic horrors of warfare
19 Scenes and incidents calculated to afford information to the enemy
20 Incidents tending to disparage our Allies
21 Scenes holding up the King's uniform to contempt or ridicule
22 Subjects dealing with India, in which British officers are seen in an odious light, and otherwise to suggest the disloyalty of the Native States or bringing into disrepute British prestige in the Empire.[18]

These rules, grouped together as they actually were, reflect accurately and intelligently wartime political needs: to avoid raising party-political controversy in a period of Coalition Government; endangering industrial relations; casting doubts upon the actions or motives of organs of government or justice; jeopardising recruitment; the care needed about information which film cameras may give to enemy intelligence; the protection of good relations with allies who may not so readily take traditional jokes about unmilitary and undersized Frenchmen; the authority and competence of the officer corps and the confidence upon which depended, in the final resort, British rule over the peoples of the Empire. In wartime, political censorship aimed at fostering confidence in the government and unity at home is essential and the BBFC was the natural body for exercising it over films. These manifestly neither 'moral' nor 'security' rules call for no comment, except that these rules went no further than the minimum necessary and a lot less far than in most other belligerent countries. What is surprising, however, is to find that once peace came and the Ministry of Information was wound up and the press, postal and telegraphic censorship discontinued for purposes other than counter-intelligence and crime detection, film censorship continued to apply all but one of these rules. The only rule which disappeared – though it was resuscitated in 1936 – was the rule about 'affording information to the enemy'; even the rule about disparaging our Allies came to be retained in the form of 'wounding the just susceptibilities of Friendly Nations' – it being left to the Foreign Office to decide from time to time, who they were.

In fact the British Board of Film Censors not only continued in peacetime to apply these rules, it went on to add to them and to elaborate them almost year by year. In 1919, the year of 'Bolshevik Agitation' and the 'Red Clyde' for example, there came the rule banning 'Subjects calculated or possibly intended to foment social unrest or discontent'.

By 1930 there were no less that 98 rules instead of 'O'Connor's Forty-three', as they were called within the BBFC for whose officials they appear to have fulfilled the same role as the Ten Commandments do for canon lawyers. Of the original eight political rules the rule concerning holding up the King's uniform to contempt or ridicule came to cover: 'British Officers' and 'Forces' shown in 'disgraceful', 'reprehensible' or 'equivocal light' and also 'situations including reflections on the wives of responsible British officials'. The rule about bringing British prestige in the Empire into disrepute was extended to cover: 'inaccurate or objectionably misleading "themes" (the new term for "subjects" after 1922) purporting to illustrate parts of the British Empire' or 'representing British possessions' as 'lawless' or 'iniquitous'. A new dimension to this rule was added with the extending of the ban against British officials, etc. to their being shown in 'equivocal situations' overseas involving coloured women. This began in 1923, and was developed with the introduction of a clutch of new rules between 1926–30 which banned: 'The showing of white men in a state of degradation amidst Eastern or Native surroundings'; 'Liaisons between coloured men and white women', 'Equivocal situations between white men and coloured *people*' (my italics) and finally, 'Equivocal situations between white girls and men of other races' not necessarily 'coloured'.

The rules about scenes tending to 'disparage public characters or institutions' came to cover: 'Royal Personages' both 'British' and 'Foreign', at home or abroad; 'Lampoons on the institution of Monarchy'; prohibition of any 'incident' which 'Conveys a false impression of the police forces in Britain' or upon 'The administration of British justice' or its officials.

The rule prohibiting films whose subject dealt with 'Relations of Capital and Labour' was joined first by the rule concerning

'Subjects calculated or possibly intended to foment social unrest or discontent'. These were followed by a series of rules banning the showing of 'scenes' or 'incidents' in films whose subject as such could not be seen even by the BBFC as coming within these definitions, such as: 'Inciting workers to armed conflicts' – extended after 1926 to the 'incident' occurring in any part of the world not only in a British or Imperial setting; 'themes or incidents' dealing with 'Industrial unrest or violence'; 'Mobs attacking unarmed police'; 'scenes or incidents' showing 'Soldiers and police firing on defenceless population' and showing in any way 'Conflicts between the armed forces of the state and the populace'. This rule was first only applied to British or Imperial settings but was extended to cover any state by 1928. One should perhaps note in the context of these provisions that, as O'Connor explained to the Cinema Commission as early as 1917, the Board was particularly conscious of the power which the cinema screen had over young people in respect of evoking a desire to emulate in real life what they vicariously lived through on the screen.[19]

The general rule about 'controversial politics' came to be extended, in 1931, to 'offensive political propaganda'. 'Controversial politics' was a rule taken over verbatim from the rules of the Lord Chamberlain's Office where it had always been applied to mean 'current' political issues.[20] It was, however, extended by the Board to cover issues which were not in the least 'current' nor involving the 'representation of living persons' as was the case with the Lord Chamberlain's rules. Thus, when it suited the Board, any of the rules could be extended to cover any objectionable 'theme' which films tried to treat in an historical setting. The rule which prohibited the depiction of British forces as oppressive in Imperial or colonial settings, was thus extended to ban D. W. Griffith's epic *America* in 1925 and in 1936 a production company seeking the Board's advice about a script concerning the life of Judge Jeffreys was told that 'no reflection on the administration of British justice at any period could be permitted'.[21]

It might be thought that while this set of rules would strike the historian today as being manifestly political in intention, they might have been regarded by the Board itself in a different and less politically conscious or sophisticated light. Indeed, Miss Rachel Low, for example, quoted the rules about 'white men' and 'white girls' with particular emphasis in arguing that the rules of the BBFC were vaguely designed merely to 'protect existing authority and the social establishment'.[22] The evidence however does not support this view. From 1920 the Board classified its annual list under headings: 'Religious'; 'Political'; 'Military'; 'Administration of Justice'; 'Social'; or 'Cruelty' and so forth. The 1928 list of additions and re-applications under the heading 'Political' ran as follows:

POLITICAL

1) References to H.R.H. the Prince of Wales
2) Libellous reflections on Royal Dynasties
3) British possessions represented as lawless sinks of iniquity
4) Themes likely to wound the just susceptibilities of Friendly Nations
5) White Men in a state of degradation amidst Far Eastern and Native surroundings
6) Equivocal situations between white girls and men of other races[23]

Distinctions between some of the categories were not absolute – indeed they could hardly be so – and this is especially true of the 'Political' and 'Military' categories. In the same year 'Military' included not only 'Officers in British uniforms shown in disgraceful light' but also 'Conflicts between the armed forces of the state and the populace'. In 1930, the 'White men . . .' and the 'White girls . . .' rules appeared under 'Political' and so did 'Inciting workers to armed conflict'. – But 'Conflicts between the armed forces of a State and the populace' appeared under 'Military' while 'Soldiers and police firing on defenceless populace' headed the list under 'Administration of Justice'.[24] Whether any particular significance attached to the occasional movement of certain rules, in and out of the 'Political' and into the 'Military', 'Justice' and 'Social' categories – beyond perhaps the overall impression of the drift of particular films – is doubtful. This is particularly so if we bear in mind that the classifications were applied by very busy officials when they filled in the 'red' forms, informing the producer or distributor that the Board 'objected' to his film and giving the particular rule and category under which the censor thought his objection rested. What is unquestionable however is that the Board exercised *political* censorship as well as sexual, moral and religious censorship and openly described it in its own printed list as 'Political'. It shows a remarkable degree of political sophistication that, for example, the white men and white women rules invariably were listed under 'Political' and not under 'Sexual'. This was also how the Home Secretary, Sir William Joynson-Hicks, during whose tenure of office these rules came to be added to the Board's list, saw the issue. In 1929, in a pamphlet *Do We Need a Censor* – his answer was in the affirmative and especially in the case of films. – He wrote:

> . . . of terrible and far-reaching importance is the effect of films . . . showing the white woman in a state of degradation . . . it is undoubtedly essential that all nations which rule Eastern countries should see to it that the pride and character of their womanhood is maintained unimpaired.[25]

By 1931 the political rules of the Board were fully developed. During the next decade certain rules came to be re-emphasised or given a more specific or severe interpretation according to the needs of the moment. The Board showed itself to be wise to the possibilities of historical parallelism as a propaganda technique and extended the force of its rules to forbidden themes appearing in a historical guise, as they did in 1936 for example in the case of the script for a film about Judge Jeffreys which we have already noted. The Board added for good measure that not only would they not tolerate 'reflection on the administration of British justice in any period' but that 'no phrase as lurid as "Bloody Assizes" could be used'.[26] From 1929 and with increasing vigilance as long-term unemployment and real hardship came to settle on the land, the Board laid special emphasis on the principle, already laid down by T. P. O'Connor in one of the circular letters to all producers and distributors which the Board issued relating to matters of general policy – that it will not permit:

> Stories in which sympathy is enlisted for the criminals; and in which they are made out to be either victims of unavoidable circumstances or of early environment, and as such held more or less irresponsible for their social delinquencies. There is also an almost invariable tendency in such films to hold up the

recognised authority of the law either to odium or ridicule, a procedure the constant repetition of which cannot be considered in the best interests of society.[27]

The rule relating to 'Wounding the just susceptibilities of friendly nations' was not extended or altered during the 1930s. It merits mention again because it caused the greatest amount of public fuss over 'political censorship'. The Board was obliged to fly in the face of powerful public feeling in following the policy of the government in striving for good relations with Germany from the Treaty of Locarno onwards. Banishing the Hun abruptly from the screens was a clumsy policy, the wisdom of which O'Connor, in his last year as President in 1928, doubted so much that he took the strongest step available to him. He made it clear that a film dealing with Nurse Cavell was not banned under the normal political rules of the Board, but that it had been refused a certificate merely because its exhibition had been deemed 'inexpedient in present circumstances' – leaving for once the Foreign Secretary exposed to the very limelight against which it was the job of the British Board of Film Censors to provide a shield.[28] Thereafter the Board loyally banned all manner of films about Germany reaping odium for its pains, such as *Professor Mamlock* dealing with Nazi anti-semitism, as late as 1938.

There was in fact only one substantive expansion or addition after 1930, to the scope of the political censorship of the Board. In 1933 the Board decided that the rules concerning 'Objection-able political propaganda' would in future extend to films made up entirely of 'photographs of current events', already exhibited or not, provided that the compilation used actuality footage more than a fortnight old and had captions or, in particular, a commentary added. Films, the Board explained, 'made up of a series of topical events, for instance, before and since the War, strung together with a running commentary of a definitely pro-pagandist nature' would be liable to be examined by the Board and the test of 'Objectionable political propaganda' as well as other rules applied.[29] This was a major step indeed for it removed any lingering doubts, or wishfully perceived veil, over the question of whether the Board was concerned with the impact of indecent or otherwise objectionable *pictures* being exhibited to the general public – or with the censorship of the ideas or viewpoints communicated through the screen. The Board was itself aware of the significance of the step. It sought Counsel's opinion, of not one but two leading constitutional lawyers, Stuart Bevan KC, and F. D. Morton KC, concerning the legality and enforcability of this extension and sent copies of their opinions supporting the Board to all producers and importers.[30] A 'series of topical events strung together with a running commentary of a definitely propagandist nature' is, of course, an inelegant but succinct definition of the genre of the 'documentary compilation film'. And, of course, since the arrival of the soundtrack, it was, and still is, one of the most compelling forms of political argument in the medium of film or television.

The evidence, provided by the statements of general policy principles issued by the Board from time to time, by the rules themselves, by their frank classification system, by the elucidation of the application of those rules in practice by the Board itself, year by year, is quite clear. It leaves little room for doubting that the British Board of Film Censors did actually exercise censorship over the political ideas which might be communicated through the medium of film in Britain. There can be no doubt also that, whatever definition one might apply or whatever qualifications one might seek to find, these rules do provide conclusive evidence that the cinema screen – the most widely accessible medium of communications to the largest number of the population – was subject to a coherently thought-out and consistently applied, politically conscious censorship. If the function of censorship is to act as negative propaganda, preventing firstly, the presentation of arguments which question the premises of policy and their application in practice; preventing secondly, the presentation of alternative interpretations of the causes of the problems to which the government is devising remedies and thirdly, preventing the projecting of alternative solutions, alternative methods and alternative aims to those projected by the government – then the rules operated by the Board manifestly fulfil these criteria too.

It *was* permitted to present arguments and even to make state-ments through the cinema screens: in fact the 1930s came to be the golden age of long, rolling captions spelling out what the film was about and also of the tedious technique of speeches directly to the camera breaking up dramatic action. But only if they were not those which the Board banned. It was, for example, perfectly permissible to argue that Africa was 'Vast, *empty*, magnificent and fertile' (my italics); that England suffered economic and social problems because she was overpopulated, must expand or perish and that Rhodesia was the answer to where 'our teeming millions at home' should emigrate (*Rhodes of Africa*, 1936). This could not be described as a viewpoint which was wholly uncontested in Britain at the time and thus not 'controversial'. It was not permitted to put, however, say, the Marxist or 'Left' interpretation of the problem or of their view of the solution offered or project their alternative solutions – in film, though perfectly permissible in print. It was equally impermissible to argue either the Fascist or the Marxist alternative interpretations of the causation of crime and delinquency, or suggest alternative penal or social policies for dealing with them – in film. It *was* permitted to portray a British Member of Parliament as a scoundrel who spread Red ideas amongst the simple folk in order to reap personal gain and power (*The Return of Bulldog Drummond*, 1934). It was permitted even to show this MP dunked in a creek in full shot – so much for simply trying to protect 'all figures of authority and establishment' – and, by 1939, it was even permitted to plan the assassination of a British MP who was a Pacifist, as a laudable act (*The Four Just Men*, 1939).

It *was* even permitted to take 'a series of topical events before and since (and during) the war' and to 'string it together with a running commentary of definitely propagandist nature' yet obtain the Board's certificate. Such a film, for example, was *The Soul of a Nation* (1934) – financed by the Conservative and Unionist Film Association, though the credits made no allusion to that. *The Soul of a Nation* argued that the best way of bringing about desirable political and social changes and of securing solutions to serious problems facing the country was by avoiding the accentuation of political differences of opinion which had led to strife and even revolutions elsewhere; that this had been the secret of the success of the British people through the ages, and that the Crown was there to facilitate such national unity in time of trouble. The film did not actually use the phrase 'National Government', it should be said, and the BBFC was doubtless not informed that an Election might be contemplated. As important as content control was the control of exemplars and stereotypes: as a dramatic form the cinema operates through heroes and villains. It was not permitted to present as heroes Union leaders, strikers, guerillas or mutineers, nor any political activist other than those who employed constitutional methods.

But, if the BBFC did indeed exercise censorship in the full sense of negative propaganda over which political ideas could be put before the public through the powerful medium of the cinema, did it do so actually on behalf of the government? Were its Presidents men in the confidence of government, for without that 'negative propaganda' is a meaningless phrase? Was the Board not just a private organisation of the cinema trade itself which assumed a high-sounding name, like Mrs Mary Whitehouse's 'National Viewers Association' with absolutely no official standing? Were they not a set of self-appointed nobodies who took it upon themselves to prevent the British people from being treated as adults, politically as well as morally, assuming that Londoners would storm Buckingham Palace if they were allowed to sit through Comrade Eisenstein's *October*? In this case they may have thought that they were exercising 'political censorship' in this matter but the term in its natural meaning would be inappropriate.

John Grierson *seemed* to think so. As the self-proclaimed 'propagandist' he was, however, his writings represent not what he actually thought but what he judged would best achieve the purpose in hand. – But he memorably and lastingly encapsulated this view when he wrote in 1935:

> ... poor dear censor Wilkinson, with his Blake's poetry and his beloved pre-Raphaelites, has, in the jungle of Wardour Street, the strength of ten. Great figure he is, for on his charming old shoulders he carries the burden of our servility and shame. Created by the Trade as an image of gratuitous fright it is not surprising that his slogan of 'No Controversy' – which to philosophy and all the world is 'No Reality' – is abjectly obeyed.[31]

Poor dear Joseph *Brooke*-Wilkinson was the Secretary of the Board from 1913 to 1949. Unknown to Grierson, and indeed to all except those in very high position, he was also a member of the (secret) CID Subcommittee on Censorship, alongside the representatives of Press Proprietors Association, the Security Services and so forth under a Ministerial head. He might have known about Blake's poetry, but for his background experience it might be more relevant to recall that he had been in charge of British film-propaganda to neutral nations during the First World War.[32] This was also of course an official secret still in

1936, and it is not quite irrelevant to note that he started as a Northcliffe journalist in 1906 when the Chief was teaching Fleet Street how to influence the new 'office boys' readership.

Brooke-Wilkinson was only the Secretary, however, not the President of the Board. The President was Edward Shortt. Shortt entered the Commons as MP for Newcastle in 1910. As chairman of the Select Committee set up to review the administration of the Military Service Acts, he made a name for himself as a person capable of handling matters of great potential for public outcry, and was appointed in 1918 Chief Secretary of Ireland to deal with the new outbreak of Sinn Fein troubles. Through his handling of the situation he acquired a reputation as an expert on counter-subversion techniques, as well as a tough man who did not hesitate to resort to wholesale arrests. In 1919 he was therefore brought back by Lloyd-George to take over the Home Office to deal with the extremely dangerous situation presented by 'Red Clyde' agitation, the threatened General Strike and the disaffection in the police which led to actual police strikes in March in London and in August in the provinces – all in the wake of the disaffection and mutinies in the army which so shook the Cabinet. As Home Secretary, Shortt's work in dealing with novel problems of subversion was thought to have been brilliantly successful in the immediate run – gaining a tremendous loyalty and respect from the higher officers of the police – and he put into train regular counter-subversive preparations, including the planning of measures against the General Strike. He remained Home Secretary until the fall of Lloyd-George. Thereafter he continued to serve on several of the secret anti-subversion committees, as well as acting regularly as Chairman of a string of Committees concerned with Home Office matters throughout the 1920s, under both Conservative and Labour administrations. He also acted once in that role under the National Government after he had already become President of the BBFC, in November 1929, at the request of the Home Secretary, J. Clynes. He was also, of course, and remained, a member of the Privy Council.[33]

Edward Shortt thus was a front-rank politician and Parliamentarian intimately connected with one particular area of the activity of government: internal security, counter-subversion and counter-insurgency. Counter-propaganda is of course, an integral conceptual component of this area and had come to be recognised as such after the experiences of the First World War.

Moreover, he continued to be involved in the Parliamentary and Committee side of the work of government all through the period including the National Government. The mere fact that such a person regarded the job of the President of the BBFC as a job which was worth his while to undertake should give us some pause for thought before accepting the BBFC as something 'created by the Trade as a symbol of gratuitous fright'. Nor did Shortt regard the job as a sinecure. On the contrary the surviving papers of the BBFC, the Home Office files and his lectures and addresses to 'the Trade' all show it to have been an arduous job indeed which he carried out with considerable industry. He was a front-rank politician and knew not only about counter-propaganda and subversion, but also about films and the way they actually work as instruments of attitude formation. In 1935 in a paper read to the Summer Conference of the Cinema Exhibitors Association he said 'I can not believe that any single film can have any lasting effect on the public – but the same theme repeated over and over again might be most undesirable'.[34] It was this recognition of the same themes, of stereotypes, as the distinguishing feature of film, which helped the BBFC to be effective.[35]

Edward Shortt died in harness in 1936 and was succeeded by Sir William, by then Lord Tyrrell – commonly described in the film-history literature as 'a retired career diplomat who had a spell as Ambassador in Paris',[36] not the sort of person who could be expected to be able to exercise political censorship of a serious kind. In view of Dr Philip Taylor's contribution to this volume, little needs to be said about Tyrrell's actual qualifications: Permanent Head of the Foreign Office; pioneer in Britain of the concept of cultural propaganda and of news as a new addition to the conduct of diplomacy; one of the founding fathers of the News Department, Head of the Political Intelligence Department, and finally chairman of the British Council, the institutional embodiment of the cultural propaganda approach. Altogether Tyrrell was the highest ranking Foreign Office expert on propaganda and was made a Peer in recognition of his life's work there. He was indeed retired from the Foreign Office when he accepted the job of the President of the British Board of Film Censors in 1936, but he held it together with the Chairmanship of the British Council. Thus the conduct of positive cultural propaganda directed abroad and censorship of the mass-culture medium at home were united in the same hands. Like Shortt himself, but to a splendidly flamboyant degree, Tyrrell was anything but a 'moralist' likely to be concerned with sexual propriety or virtuous living on the screen. He was so fond of 'wine, women and song', even by the highly convivial standards of the upper echelons of the Foreign Office, that it gave cause for considerable concern and contributed to a somewhat curtailed tenure as Permanent Head. Lord Tyrrell of course was part of that very top of the Civil Service which is wholly privy to government itself, and there can be little doubt that the BBFC, in his particularly well-informed eyes, must have had a place in the scheme of things more significant than protecting the morals of cinemagoers. For that, there were many better qualified and less busy than Tyrrell! Tyrrell was also no career diplomat to whom the cinema itself was a strange new world. On the contrary, not only had Tyrrell been closely interested in the cinema as part of his interest in cultural propaganda, but he himself wrote the script of the highly successful major British film *Sixty Glorious Years: The Life and Reign of Queen Victoria* – a much-quoted example of value propaganda.

The significance of the backgrounds, particular fields of expertise and the positions held by Edward Shortt and Lord Tyrrell, for the question of 'political' or non-political censorship, needs little elaboration. They prove the existence of high-level contacts, of wide experience of politics and government at the highest level, and of knowledge about other operations being conducted in the field of propaganda and counter-propaganda which are the essential prerequisites for conducting political censorship. They also reveal the top-quality minds, political finesse and personal authority without which an operation requiring as great intelligence and sophistication as the conduct of political censorship in a country such as Britain, could not survive for a moment. It was these personal qualities which brought men like Shortt and Tyrrell to the top in the first place.

The formal position of the BBFC is of relatively little importance in itself, if it was run by men such as T. P. O'Connor, Edward Shortt and Lord Tyrrell. If Edward Shortt or Lord Tyrrell was willing to accept the utterly unprestigious, indeed odium-gathering job of President of the British Board of Film Censors when asked by the Home Secretary to do so, it was of no significance whether their salary was paid from the revenues of the Duchy of Cornwall, Cable and Wireless Ltd (as was for example the salary of Sir Campbell Stuart who moved from Deputy Director of Crewe House after 1918 to Chairman of the Imperial Communications Committee) or some other source – provided it was not paid by any one particular cinema producer or a particular cinema trade association with direct interest in the fate of particular films. We should only note that, although it is commonly stated by historians of film, it is not the case that the British Board of Film Censors was a private organisation financially 'maintained' by the Cinematograph Manufacturers, or Reuters, or Distributors. The censorship was financially maintained from the examination fees payable by those who wished to receive a certificate from the Board – a sensible arrangement mirroring that of the Holy Office of Censorship of the Roman Church which was also self-financing. The niceties of the position of the 'private' British Board of Film Censors with its President 'elected' by a Trade Association upon 'suggestion' from the Home Secretary need not concern us here. It was a convenient arrangement, which led to such exquisitely British occasions as the dinner at which Baron Tyrrell of Avon, PC, GCMG, KCB, KCVO, Grand Cordon Légion d'Honneur, thanked the assembled chieftains, of what Grierson did accurately describe as the 'Jungle of Wardour Street', for the honour of electing him their President.[37]

The *modus operandi* of the relationship between the Home Office, the Chief Constables, Local Authorities and the BBFC is a subject in its own right which I shall discuss elsewhere. It would be impossible here to do justice either to a 30-year-long story or to the volume of documentation in the series of Home Office files relating to it.[38] The details of the arrangements, interesting as they are, in fact make little difference to the question of the official standing of the Board. In the British style of government it is the man who makes the office and not the office which makes the man – especially in new or 'secret' areas of government. What mattered was that the person installed in Soho Square should be someone like Edward Shortt or Lord Tyrrell, whose experience and background ensured that he could be relied upon to know what was needed, who was 'fully in the picture' knowing not only what was known to members of the public and whom it was 'safe' to 'contact' or consult. It made no difference to his 'official' standing either where the money for his salary came from or what position, if any, the organisation formally possessed.

We need only to note three aspects concerning the relationship of the film censorship with the Home Office. From before the First World War the Home Office never wavered in its belief that censorship of the cinema was necessary; that it should be concerned with other matters as well as morality and that it should be ultimately under Home Office control. But there was an on-going debate about the best way of realising these objectives in Britain. Britain was a country where politicians and public alike were genuinely committed to liberal ideals of government though they also shared a realistic and pragmatic approach to the realisation of any ideal, including freedom of expression. It was thus common ground that children and those of insufficient upbringing and education were not fit to be exposed to the full range of ideas about moral and political alternatives. There were also well-established and tried precedents. There had been since 1737 a compulsory, preemptive censorship for the stage, exercised by a single, centralised state organisation, the Lord Chamberlain's Office[39] and enforced, via the local authorities, by the Chief Constables. Punitive post-censorship existed for books and was exercised by the courts, with the decision whether or not to proceed in the hands, of the Home Secretary who also had the power to prevent the importation of written matter. Also there was the brand new concept of 'voluntary censorship' which was formulated in the course of one of those wide-ranging formalised debates, or enquiries, which are such a fundamentally important part of the British system, in this case by the *Joint Select Committee of the House of Lords and the House of Commons on the Censorship of Stage Plays*, in 1909. The idea of 'voluntary censorship' was explained in 1916 by Sir Herbert Samuel the Home Secretary and the Chairman of the Select Committee to a conference of local authorities discussing film censorship:

> To have a central tribunal under Government authority to which any author could, if he wished, submit his play. If the Censor opposed his play . . . he would be free from the risk of proceedings against him. . . . If he did not wish to present it to censorship or if it was presented to the censorship and the censorship did not approve it . . . on general grounds of liberty he might still be allowed to produce his play but he would run the risk of having proceedings taken against him.[40]

The advantages and disadvantages of the two long-established systems for the stage and books were well known, the new idea arose from considering that experience, but was an unknown quantity in practice. No wonder therefore that the Home Office and successive Home Secretaries veered back and forth between the idea of establishing a State Film Censorship Board, on the model of the Lord Chamberlain's compulsory pre-emptive censorship, which Sir William Joynson-Hicks preferred believing that it was inevitable in the long run; a State Film Censorship Board operating on the 'voluntary censorship' principle which Sir Herbert Samuel preferred; compulsory pre-emptive censorship exercised by local authority committees under guidance from the Home Office and supervision by Chief Constables, which Sir Edward Cave preferred – and the British Board of Film Censors approach preferred by McKenna, Sir John Simon, Edward Shortt and Clynes, and which was an amalgam of some elements from all the others and some of its own.

The nub of the problem was, as far as the Home Secretaries were concerned, which approach would allow them to exercise the most effective, the most unfettered and discretionary control over determining what films should or should not be able to obtain access to the mass-audience. They were much less concerned with totally preventing almost any kind of film from reaching *some* people – as long as they were freely able to control *general* release. Herein lay the difference from the Lord Chamberlain's operations though a measure of it was there too in the 'Theatre-club' provisions. The trouble with the State Censorship Board approach was that it could only be established by legislation. It would thus have to have a legislative definition, and indeed limitation of its powers. However skilfully the Act might be drawn up it could not give the Home Secretary *carte blanche* – least of all in matters other than the protection of morality. And, being established by legislation each exercise of its powers would be subject to Parliamentary scrutiny. Once it became clear that it could not be done even in wartime (1916), although the scheme got as far as the actual circulation of its regulations drafted by the Home Office, it was dropped. Sir Herbert Samuel's advocacy of the 'voluntary' version of the State Censorship Board approach was founded on his belief that it should be possible to establish it without *specific* legislation.[41]

The prospect of Parliamentary limitation of his discretion, and

especially Parliamentary scrutiny, was the reason why Home
Secretaries strenuously resisted the frequent demands in the
1920s, chiefly by 'liberal' MPs but also from the occasional
simple-minded right-winger, that the BBFC should be replaced
by a State Censorship Board under the Home Office.[42] At the
height of the most serious attempt, after three MPs put down a
formal request for the Prime Minister to establish a State
Censorship Board and in the course of a debate running for over
3 weeks with tempers rising very high, the Home Secretary burst
out in a moment of exasperation: 'Just imagine the Home
Secretary's position if every single film, as might be the case, were
to be the subject of a question in this House. It would be an
impossible position.'[43]

The issue was also understood outside the House. Two years
later when there was a nationwide campaign for making moral
censorship much more severe than the liberal morality of the
BBFC, led jointly by the London Public Morality Council
(LPMC) under the Bishop of London and Sir Charles Grant
Robertson, Vice-Chancellor of Birmingham University, the
argument which tilted the issue in the LPMC against petitioning
Parliament for a State Censorship Board was:

> The real danger is this: that owing to our national instinct the
> Home Secretary is the whipping-boy of the country . . . if you
> had a government censor working through a Board, his
> decisions will inevitably be attacked in the House of Commons,
> in the press and multifarious ways in which the present Board
> of Film Censors cannot be attacked.[44]

A 'British Board of Film Censors' was an original, and from the
point of the Secretary of State for the Home Department, a very
good idea: a 'private' body which did not depend on legislative
authority or the taxpayers' money, thus free from Parliamentary,
public scrutiny. Its constitution laid down no rules, no criteria, no
appeal procedure, no duty to explain: it simply stated *'as far as
Censorship is concerned, that matter is entirely under the direct
control of the President (named) whose decisions in all cases will
be final'*. The President was 'elected' by the Manufacturers' and
Exhibitors' Association, the only candidate emerging after
consultation with, and prior approval by, the Home Secretary.
The President was therefore a personal choice of the Home

Secretary unbound by any civil service or other problems. His constitutional connection with films was not with film-makers but with the exhibitors of films: not with the sort of people who might have temperaments and interests difficult to deal with but with associations of businessmen, naturally dominated by the biggest, most successful businessmen, with whom harmony of outlook and interests could be readily maintained. They sought only to give the public what it was willing to pay for and reap profit. The Home Secretary had no objection to that and was equally mindful of the cinema as a source of revenue. Like pubs, sports and entertainment, the cinema too needed to be kept in balance with the feelings of a fairly moral country but the exhibitors, the Home Secretary and his officials were also alike in being men of the world, not moral crusaders. In fact the Board was far more widely attacked for being too liberal in matters of morality and especially vulgarity, than for being too prudish.[45] Political censorship was in fact the *essential* function of the partnership of the Home Office and the British Board of Film Censors.

Neither of them 'looked on the cinema as a pulpit', while they were aware of the influence it had over the kind of people who gave its mass audience. They were also at one in not wanting the cinema to be available to be used 'as a propagandist' by people of Grierson's persuasion or much worse. The Home Secretary thus could also expect from this arrangement to derive vitally important support from those who commercially controlled the distribution of film, which helped to diffuse the issue of censorship. Films which were not going to be taken by major distributors could safely be let through to end up in the *Cosmo* in Glasgow or the *Everyman* in Hampstead, to delight the leftish *literati* and show the liberality of the Board.

> We have [Lord Tyrrell told the Exhibitors' Association] a duty to perform, which is at times a very difficult task, and that is to prevent films being shown which are likely to give offence to the public and imperil the Industry itself. In the carrying out of these duties I know, that I shall have not only your sympathy, but when necessary, your co-operation.[46]

A constant source of strength to the Board was Sir Albert Clavering who combined, throughout the 1930s, the Chairmanship of the Exhibitors' Association with being Organising Director of the Conservative and Unionist Film Association.

It is little wonder that when representatives of the distributing side of the cinema industry first put the gist of the idea of a 'British Board of Film Censors', to be formally established by themselves and headed by a person approved by the Home Secretary, to McKenna in 1912 he felt that 'it is a project which smiles at me'.[47] It remained to be seen whether it could be made to work of course, and for the next eight years the Home Office explored alternative possibilities and kept its options open. T. P. O'Connor, President from 1917, showed that it could be made to work and from the Home Secretaryship of Edward Shortt, the Home Office worked in harness with him to overcome the only difficulty which such an unorthodox arrangement without legal sanctions entailed. This was the need to cajole and bully a particularly independent-minded minority of local authorities, with help of the Courts, to insert into their conditions of cinema licence a suitable formula requiring the films to possess a certificate from the Board. The Home Office succeeded in that task by 1931. The problem of official status for the President in sole personal charge of 'matters of censorship' was also solved *where it mattered* – with access to confidential information and bound by the Official Secrets Act – by making O'Connor a Privy Councillor, in 1924. So were of course Shortt and Tyrrell.

What most of all ultimately mattered, however, were the convictions of the governments of the 1920s and 1930s. The conviction that in the special circumstances of the times, it was both right and their duty to prevent the spread of certain types of political ideas to the mass of the people of Britain – by whatever practical arrangement would do it most effectively and quietly. Stanley Baldwin dominated, and represented, the governments of the inter-war period more than any other person. His views sum up the views of the governments of the inter-war period concerning the place of political ideas in that first 'age of the masses' and of the mass-communications media. In his stunning speech in America in August 1939, a speech which was in so many ways the political testament of the Baldwin Age, he said through the medium of film to the largest audience imaginable yet:

Science has brought the nations of the world jostling together and ideas laugh at frontiers. And there are ideas so loaded with dynamite that they may blow systems which appear founded on rock into fragments. I need not tell you that such ideas are those of Bolshevism and those propagated by the Nazis and the fascists. No-one can foresee what effect they may have on the future of the world, how far they may spread, what their ultimate form may be. But of one thing be clear, they can not exist within the same boundaries of what you and I understand as democracy.[48]

Within this perception, the censorship of political ideas was fully acceptable and indeed necessary for British Governments, particularly so in the medium which 'science' has perfected for reaching the great mass of 'people with immature minds and unstable judgement' as *The Times* often described the cinema audience, precisely for the protection of what Baldwin defined as 'the great traditions of our Nation: constitutional method, freedom and liberty: ordered freedom and ordered liberty'.[49]

Under Presidents who all had the high quality of mind, the high-level political contact and trust and particular expertise in matters of counter-propaganda and propaganda and who were supported by a Secretary who also had that expertise and was himself a member of the Censorship Sub-Committee of the CID, the Board evolved an intelligent, coherent and wide-ranging political censorship of the first, and until television, only true medium of mass communications. Based on nothing more than the characteristically pragmatic willingness of British courts to remedy situations where legislation might be difficult, in this case by extending an act solely designed to allow the control of inflammable celluloid to inflammatory messages which it could carry, it succeeded in developing an ingenious and flexible system of censorship. As Mrs Neville Rolf of the British Social Hygiene Council could report by 1931:

I have the privilege of sitting on international bodies on which sit censors of many countries. They all state with one accord, that we have a higher standard of censorship in this country than any National Board governmentally appointed has been able to bring about in any other country.[50]

And in 1932, the League of Nations recommended the world-wide adoption of the British system, which at that time moved a

stage further: from 1933 the BBFC succeeded in persuading all
the major studios in Britain to submit their 'scenarios' *before*
commencing filming. They would thus be able to exercise a much
fuller control and also provided a similar service, in co-operation
with the newly established Hays Office, to US production
companies wishing to export films to Britain. With justifiable
pride Lord Tyrrell could say to the Exhibitors' Association in
1937: 'We may take pride in observing that there is not a single
film showing in London today which deals with any of the
burning questions of the day.'

NOTES

1 C. L. Mowat, *Britain Between the Wars* (London, 1955).
2 A. J. P. Taylor, *English History, 1914–1945* (Oxford, 1965).
3 A. J. B. Marwick, *Britain in the Century of Total War* (London, 1968).
4 Thorold Dickinson, *A Discovery of the Cinema* (London, 1971).
5 Basil Wright, *The Long View* (London, 1974).
6 Jeffrey Richards, *Visions of Yesterday* (London, 1973).
7 Rachel Low, *The History of the British Film, 1918–1929* (London, 1971) p. 64.
8 Ibid., p. 66.
9 Roger Manvell, *Film*, revised edition (London, 1946) p. 170. Chapter 7 dealing with censorship is titled 'Censorship. No Controversy, Please: No Fires'.
10 Ibid., p. 169.
11 Guy Phelps, *Film Censorship* (London, 1975) pp. 144–60.
12 Paul O'Higgins, *Censorship in Britain* (London, 1972) p. 90, cited Phelps, op. cit., p. 160.
13 Neville March Hunning, *Film Censors and the Law* (London, 1967).
14 Ibid., p. 73.
15 Ibid., p. 106.
16 Ibid., p. 107.
17 In 1933 the BBFC announced that because 'ill-informed criticism has been made of the list of exceptions' on account of the publication of its rules by 'ill-disposed persons', in future the rules would not be published in detail. In 1929 Ivor Montagu, member of the Communist Party of Great Britain, one of the founders of the Cinema Society Movement, Kino and other left-wing film groups and distributor of Soviet films, incorporated virtually the whole of the 1928 BBFC Report, despite it being privately printed, in a pamphlet *The Political Censorship of Film* (London, 1929). After 1932 therefore the rules were not published and it became 'the practice nowadays to forward copies of the Board's exceptions both to British studios and studios abroad'. *BBFC Annual Report*, 1933, p. 6.

18 *The Cinema: its Present Position and Future Possibilities* Report of the Cinema Commission of Inquiry (London, 1917) p. 254, cited Hunning, op. cit., pp. 408–9.

19 Ibid., p. 251.

20 Thus the Lord Chamberlain banned *In the Red Shadow*, dealing with Ireland in 1924; *Red Sunday* – in 1929, deeming that the Soviet Revolution was a subject 'too recent' and that Tsar Nicholas II appeared in it which might still break the 'representation of living persons' rule. *Who Made the Iron Grow?* dealing with persecution of Jews in Germany was also banned in 1933 on account of it being a current issue. On the other hand a play plainly critical of Queen Victoria *The Queen's Progress* by Housman, was, after a good deal of argument, passed in 1931 on the ground that it was no longer 'current'. Dorothy Knowles, *The Censor, The Drama and the Film*, London 1934, pp. 120–3. This book based on a Leeds University Dissertation, is a mine of reliable information.

21 Forsyth Hardy, 'Censorship and Film Societies' in C. Davy (ed.) *Footnotes to the Film* (London, 1937) p. 264.

22 Low, op. cit., p. 64.

23 *BBFC Annual Report*, 1928, p. 5.

24 *BBFC Annual Report*, 1930, p. 6.

25 Viscount Brentford, *Do We Need a Censor?* (London, 1930) p. 16.

26 Forsyth Hardy, op. cit., p. 264.

27 *BBFC Annual Report* 1928, pp. 9–10. The matter was re-stressed in 1931 and 1933, when Hollywood studios were especially asked to note it for films to be released in Britain. Jack Vizzard *See No Evil: Life Inside Hollywood Censorship* (New York, 1970) pp. 17–21. Vizzard was the head of the Hollywood office of the Hay's Organisation; like the other American censors, he was a Jesuit seminary priest and shrewdly claimed that while the American censorship was a moral censorship, the British was political. The 12 rules and 36 sub-rules of the Hay's Office do not contain either 'Political' or 'Social' or 'Military' or 'Administration of Justice' categories. The only category which comes at all near to the BBFC is that of 'National Feelings' (cf. 'Wounding Just Susceptibilities of Friendly Nations'). It contains two sub-rules.
   1. The use of the Flag shall be consistently respectful.
   2. The history, institutions, prominent people and citizenry of all nations shall be represented fairly.
   Under 'Seduction or Rape', it did include a rule, II/6 'Miscegenation, sex-relationship between the white and the black races, is forbidden'. The contrast between the BBFC's various wordings and the American version is perhaps the clearest illustration of the difference between the ideas motivating the two systems. On the other hand, France which openly operated political censorship, as well as having Ministries of both 'Information' and of 'Public Instruction and Culture', produced rules which came much closer to those of the BBFC. They were summed up by the Director of the Sureté Générale as 'All films which are concerned with revolutionary questions, which show violent conflicts between capital and labour, clashes between the army and the people, revolts in prison, victims of police charges . . .'. Hunning, op. cit., p. 339. The French,

after 1932 included Newsreels, with a special commission, not only excising but also ordering the inclusion of items, in operation, and with an export licence system, after 1936, permitting the export of only such films as gave a suitably laudatory picture of French life and culture. See Remy Pithon, 'La censure des films en France et la crise politique, 1934', *Revue Historique*, 258 (1977) pp. 105–30.

28 See House of Commons Debates, vol. 214, cols 14–17, 27 Feb. 1928, for the fullest statement of this affair, also *The Times*, leader 22 February 1928, *An Inexpedient Film* 'a Government is bound to accept its share of responsibility for the vast influence which films exert on immature and unstable minds . . . nevertheless . . . Inexpedient is a dangerous word on a censor's lips. What is the nature of this inexpedience?'

29 *BBFC Annual Report*, 1933, p. 18.

30 Ibid., pp. 19–24.

31 John Grierson, 'The Course of Realism' in C. Davy (ed.) op. cit., p. 141. Grierson liked to boast that he had a thorough understanding of the political world and that he could lead the Treasury into things they would never sanction, had they not been led by the nose by himself and Sir Stephen Tallents. This view is part of the mythology of the Documentary Movement. A thorough study of the Treasury and other government records, including the GPO reveals a very different picture: that of a man well and truly seen through and manipulated by the Civil Servants and their masters. A man wholly kept in the dark too – and easily so because of his assumption that his opponents were rather less clever than himself. See Paul Swann, *The British Documentary Movement, 1926–1946*, unpublished PhD Thesis, University of Leeds, 1980.

32 For Brooke-Wilkinson's First World War activities, which also extended to newsreels, see his own account in Public Record Office HO45/10811/312397/121.

33 *Dictionary of National Biography, 1931–1940*, p. 810 for an outline of Shortt's background and career.

34 *BBFC Annual Report*, 1935, p. 4.

35 'Movies are entertainment, but they are also symbols, and behind every shadow on the big screen is the struggle to impose definitions upon what is and what should be. The power of any single movie to influence a viewer permanently is limited, although repetition obviously has its effect. Constant repetition that emphasises certain stereotypes . . . is overpowering.' Daniel J. Leab, *From Sambo to Superspade, The Black Experience in Motion Pictures* (London, 1975).

36 E.g. 'On his (Shortt's) death, he was succeeded by Lord Tyrrell of Avon, a career diplomat and ex-ambassador to Paris.' Hunning, op. cit., p. 128.

37 *BBFC Annual Report*, 1936, p. 12.

38 The main body of documentation for before 1920 is in Public Record Office HO45/10551; for the 1920s HO45/10811, for the 1930s HO45/21109. See also HO44/10533.

39 For an account of the Lord Chamberlain's Office and its policies before 1914 with particular reference to political censorship see Knowles, op. cit., and J. Palmer, *The Censor and the Theatres* (London 1912); for books see F. Fowell and F. Palmer *Censorship in England* (London, 1913).

40 HO45/10811/312397, cited in Hunning, op. cit., p. 62.
41 See account of the floating and death of the idea of a State Censorship Board in 1915–16 in Hunning, op. cit., pp. 55–68.
42 In 1925, for example, Capt. A. Evans asked the Home Secretary, 'If in view of the fact that the present BBFC has no responsibility to any authority other than the members of the industry, and in view of the number of foreign films shown in this country since the war the subject matter of which is detrimental to the best interests of public morals, safety and good order, will he consider setting up a Censorship Board responsible to his department?' The Home Secretary refused upon which Harry Brittain asked, 'Is not this a matter for the right hon. Member for the Scotland Division of Liverpool?' (T. P. O'Connor). The Speaker ruled that out. Captain Garro-Jones then demanded to know whether the question of foreign propaganda came within the purview of the Home Secretary's Department. *H.C. Debates*, vol. 183, 313–14, 30 April 1925.
43 *H.C. Debates*, vol. 214, 579. 1 Mar. 1928.
44 *BBFC Verbatim Reports, 1930–1931*. Private Cinema Conference of the London Public Morality Council, 12.1. 1931, p. 51. The BBFC operated a system of employing shorthand writers to take down verbatim not only its own meetings with outsiders, but also those of all sorts of organisations and pressure groups, including meetings of the LCC and other Local Authorities and even courts dealing with matters of interest to the BBFC: a curious system for a 'private' organisation. In the case of Courts it was doubtfully legal even, but of course standard Home Office procedure – and a boon to the historian. Surviving volumes of the transcripts are deposited in British Film Institute Library. The decision to 'use all our powers in fighting the present desire expressed in many quarters for a state censorship' was partly based on the assurance given by Brooke-Wilkinson that the BBFC is successfully seeking to establish pre-censorship of film scripts in order to have a wider impact on the 'themes' dealt with by films. 'As a matter of fact, at the present moment there are five film-plots lying on my table to be dealt with this week.' Ibid., p. 36.
45 Between 1930 and 1933 alone, the Board's standards of moral censorship were attacked by the following bodies. The Wesleyan Church; the Jewish Association; the Headmistresses Association; the Cinema Enquiry Commission representing 27 local groups of churchmen, educationists, psychologists and others; The International Council of Women; The National Union of Women Teachers, the Mothers' Union, and the Bishop of London.
46 *BBFC Report*, 1936, p. 12.
47 Public Record Office HO45/10551/163175. Shorthand note, cited in Hunning, op. cit., p. 52.
48 InterUniversity History Film Consortium, Archive Series No. 3, *Stanley Baldwin*, by John Ramsden, 1980, reproduces the fullest version.
49 Baldwin's newsreel address through all the reels, 23. Nov. 1936 reproduced in *Illusions of Reality* no. 5, 'Wonderful Britain', by N. Pronay, BBC Further Education, 1980.'
50 *BBFC Verbatim Reports*, 1930–31. LPMC. (12 Jan. 1931) p. 49.

5 Baldwin and film

J. A. RAMSDEN

Historians no longer underestimate the importance of Stanley Baldwin in their assessments of Britain between the world wars, and yet the exact nature of his dominance has proved difficult to define. There is no single piece of legislation that can be associated with his personal interest and direct intervention – with the exception perhaps of the Government of India Act of 1935, a reform that interested only very few of his contemporaries anyway. He developed no new line of political philosophy and he originated no novel political strategy. In the area of policy-making, he could be a constant trial to his colleagues and the stories of his ignorance, his apparent lethargy, and his detachment are legion. On closer investigation, he appears to have been less uninformed and uninterested than was sometimes thought, but the fact remains that his importance is not to be found in the areas for which politicians usually compete, the promotion of policies and ideas. His was indeed the rarer talent, that of a man who could influence the public not only on actual policy matters but on more fundamental attitudes. If the inter-war years were a 'Baldwin Age' as John Raymond suggested, or if he was the Hegelian 'man of the hour' who expressed the *zeitgeist* of Britain in the twenties and thirties as Keith Middlemas has put it,[1] then it was for two reasons. He certainly possessed an intuitive gift for interpreting 'public opinion', which is to say that he could usually gauge accurately what the articulate public on the Conservative side would and would not stand for. Neville Chamberlain said in 1937 that Baldwin had 'a singular and instinctive knowledge of how the plain man's mind works'. But the second reason for the coincidence of Baldwin's views and those of 'the public' was that he had quite extraordinary skills as a political communicator.

Not only could he interpret opinion, but he could also do a great deal to shape its course. One of the difficulties in assessing Baldwin's role lies in exactly this point; political communication is a talent that is essentially ephemeral and Baldwin's abilities were only partly grasped even by contemporaries. Neville Chamberlain conceded in 1934 that Baldwin 'provides something crucial in retaining the floating vote', but he does not seem to have understood how Baldwin did it; how much more difficult is the task after half a century.[2] This essay seeks to investigate Baldwin's approach to communication in the medium of film, an appropriate avenue not only because Baldwin himself gave it a high priority, but also because the timing of his career corresponded exactly with the zenith of film as a source of information and an influence on attitudes in Britain. He appeared in newsreels within days of becoming Prime Minister in 1923 and he continued to appear in them at regular intervals over the next fourteen years. During his later terms as Prime Minister the newsreels reached a mass audience of something like twenty million people a week; the Conservative Party gave great weight to the political newsreels in the 1935 election, and *The Times* reprinted Baldwin's newsreel address to the nation verbatim, for those who had not managed to see it – though every one of the newsreel companies showed it.[3] In this sense Baldwin may well have been the first British Prime Minister with whom the electors actually became familiar, the first premier whose voice, appearance and characteristic gestures would have been seen and heard by a majority of his countrymen. In the short time between the introduction of sound newsreels in 1930 and his retirement in 1937, Baldwin was seen and heard by vastly more British electors than ever heard Gladstone in his entire political career.

Film is thus an important political record for the historian seeking to understand how Baldwin communicated, a record that supplements and sometimes modifies the more conventional written material. The surviving film material does not of course constitute any sort of impartial or authentic record, but it does give the historian a chance to see exactly what contemporaries saw, and in similar circumstances. The material that survives is mainly in newsreel archives, but party propaganda film can also be viewed, and this presents a fascinating contrast between the statesmanlike, 'national' tone that Baldwin adopted for the newsreels and the more combative style he used for party films.

The surviving material can be used not only as a record of news and propaganda film as such but also as an incidental record of other forms of communication. So for example, the newsreels regularly included occasional speeches made by Baldwin in situations that were at most only semi-political. In 1930 he was filmed unveiling a statue of Mrs Pankhurst and in 1931 it was a statue of Lord Curzon.[4] He was particularly adept at turning out an appropriate speech for such an occasion and he was constantly in demand for them; in 1935 he was invited to deliver the BBC's tribute to George V, which he did so successfully that a gramophone record of it subsequently raised £300 for charity; in 1939, George VI turned to Baldwin in retirement to write his Christmas Day message to the Commonwealth. It was such non-partisan speeches that were published in the four volumes of Baldwin's speeches, and it was these occasions that made him a national figure with a following that went beyond politics. Thus he was also a regular contributor to the BBC, for example addressing the nation on 'The English Character' for 20 minutes in 1933. Such speeches read well enough in print, but in that form they convey only a part of the message, for it requires Baldwin's voice and appearance to bring them to life. The film archives also record a form of political communication now extinct, the mass political rally in the grounds of a country house; so Pathé went to Norwich in 1926 to film Baldwin addressing a huge meeting of supporters shortly after the General Strike. A year later the same company filmed a rally at Welbeck Abbey and their title clip claimed that 'over 72,000 listen to Mr Baldwin': the film itself gives irrefutable evidence of the Prime Minister's drawing power, at a time when the fortunes of his government were at a low ebb. Similar meetings can be seen in 1935 at Halstead and at Himley Hall, again meetings where the size of the crowds is as impressive as anything said by Baldwin himself.[5] Indoors, Baldwin's speaking style at meetings can be seen from an Albert Hall rally in 1931, in Birmingham Town Hall at the general election of that year, and most impressively of all at a meeting in Carnegie Hall in 1939.[6] There is of course no film material of Baldwin in the House of Commons, though his speech in the Canadian Parliament during the Ottawa Conference of 1932 probably comes close to capturing his despatch-box style. Extant film material therefore goes far beyond the recording of occasions on which Baldwin set out to address the nation on film.

Meetings of all kinds, partisan and non-partisan, formal and informal, can be seen, and from these a rounded picture of Baldwin's public face can be established. The InterUniversity History Film Consortium has recently brought together a lengthy compilation from these various sources as the third in its Archive Series.[7] Quite a large amount of film is extant in the archives but is not easily available, and it is hoped that the compilation will help to make the real Baldwin available again. Perhaps the clearest lesson that has emerged from a study of all the extant film, and from the IUHFC compilation, is Baldwin's sheer communicative skill. Even to a generation of viewers saturated by their exposure to politicians through television, Baldwin comes across as an impressive performer, as a likeable and easily identifiable character whose message is always clear and concise. And such reactions would need to be greatly magnified if we are to consider the impact of Baldwin on a generation that had never seen Prime Ministers playing their party games before.

Baldwin's technique was above all that of keeping his message simple, speaking for the most part in short sentences and always in easy vocabulary. He could therefore establish a rapport with his audience even when it was invisible; there was little danger that the message would go over the viewers' heads, or that his main thrust would be left unclear. This was especially important in the newsreels, since almost every item that was finally shown was short, often very short, and most of the more extended items were stitched together with separate sentences from three or four different places in a longer speech. In such circumstances, there was little opportunity to develop an argument that had much sophistication or that needed any great length for its exposition. There was thus a dispute between Conservative Central Office and British Movietone in 1931, when Movietone wanted to use only short extracts from a Baldwin film, thus considerably reducing its impact. This danger could be reduced when prime ministerial authority was available to impress the companies, but it could also be avoided in part by preparing only short speeches in the first place, which is what Baldwin's staff were doing by 1935. This effectively reduced the danger of their being cut before distribution. In any case, short and simple political messages came naturally to Baldwin, who was far from being a profound political thinker. He tended to think in sentences rather than in paragraphs, and it was perhaps this above all that made

him a suitable subject for the news media. Simplicity and
directness certainly came naturally to him as a film performer, so
that a very early film of him as Prime Minister in 1923 shows him
sitting pensively on a garden seat at Chequers, puffing at his pipe
and gazing into the distance, apparently contemplating the great
issues of state with calm and determination.[8] In much the same
way, he made a great impact with his first broadcast, during the
general election of 1924, during which he already sounded like an
experienced radio speaker. He spoke directly to the microphone
as if addressing an individual, rather than addressing a political
meeting – which was a trap that other politicians fell for when
speaking on early sound radio. Press comment on the broadcast
also centred on the fact that he had paused in mid-sentence to
light his pipe, striking a match in front of the microphone and so
conveying the impression of a man absolutely at his ease.[9] The
film-going public therefore had a clear visual impression through
the twenties of a Prime Minister who was calm, straightforward
and homely, exactly the impression that was made by his voice on
BBC radio. The impact was therefore greatly increased when
these two influences came together in sound films after 1930.
Baldwin had a very good speaking voice, deep and resonant, but
he also had a voice that matched his message and his established
image from the silent films. By the beginning of his final term as
Prime Minister in 1935, he had added to his natural talents a
considerable experience from the making of so many films and a
number of the tricks of the trade which emphasised rather than
weakened his professionalism. Thus by 1935 he was using a roller
mechanism to prompt his important speeches, and he was also
gaining other advantages from an industry that had made great
advances since 1930.[10] This can be seen clearly by comparing
most of the film of his final premiership with one that was made
in unusually difficult circumstances in 1936. It was decided to
record this latter item in November 1936, in order to prepare the
public for the abdication crisis, shortly to break, but it was
impossible to fit a day in a studio into Baldwin's schedules, so that
the film had to be made in Downing Street itself. The result was a
location that looked far less like the Prime Minister's room than
the film sets that he usually used; the lighting was uneven, the
sound was patchy (the noise of the camera always present), and
the prompter was placed at the wrong angle for the speaker to
read without looking away from the camera. Baldwin's tiredness

in the midst of a major crisis, and the fact that the film had to be shot at breakfast time, contributed to the film's poorness, but this item also showed how far his normal appearance was bolstered by the packaging that the film companies could offer.[11] With a prompter, he was a very fluent speaker, but without it easily to hand, he was less effective. All such judgments depend to some extent on the standard of the opposition, and in this sense the effectiveness of Baldwin was greatly increased by the lack of success of his main opponents on films. The disparity was clear from the radio broadcast of 1924, when the leaders of all the parties were given equal time. Baldwin broadcast a short speech written especially for the radio, but both Asquith and MacDonald had the microphone taken into public meetings; Asquith harangued the microphone as a part of the audience, creating a poor impression on an individual listener at home, while MacDonald followed his usual practice of walking about the platform as he spoke, so that only a part of his speech was even picked up on the microphone.[12] The same lack of any real feel for the medium can be seen in the film appearances of both MacDonald and Lloyd George in the thirties. In 1935, Baldwin's election speech contrasted greatly with that of Attlee for the Labour Party, the two speeches going out together which can only have heightened the contrast between them. Baldwin's fluency and experience were the more impressive when put alongside Attlee's hesitation and uncertainty, his obvious nervousness in front of the camera. Baldwin's fluency was certainly increased by the prompter in front of him, which Attlee did not use, but it is unlikely that Attlee would have been able to use one at that stage of his career anyway.

There is no doubt that Baldwin followed his own inclinations and his real personality in the impression that he gave on news films, but the success of his appearances also derived to some extent from the good advice available to him and from the advantages to the Conservative leader that accrued from the sympathies of the newsreel industry as such. So for example, that first success on the BBC in 1924 can be traced to the good advice of John Reith whom Baldwin consulted at the BBC office. Reith noted Baldwin's visit in his diary, and added 'many intelligent questions'. It was on Reith's advice that Baldwin made his broadcast from the studio and broadcast a special script, but it was Baldwin's decision after talking to Reith to take Mrs Baldwin with him to the studio to provide him with an audience.

> He placed her on a chair in front of him in the studio, and she
> sat there placidly knitting, with appraising ears open and alert
> while he talked to the microphone. He wanted to get the right
> atmosphere; he realised that most women ... would probably
> be doing much the same sort of thing as his wife in the studio –
> knitting calmly.[13]

The advice of Reith was important, but the reaction to advice was
perhaps equally important, and the same can be seen throughout
his career. So, Sir Patrick Gower of Conservative Central Office,
who was Baldwin's closest adviser on film and radio broadcasts
throughout the thirties, wrote in October 1931 to urge that he
should pitch his next film speech rather lower, since the previous
one had gone over people's heads; it was vital to say what the
National Government was, why it had been formed, and what
was the alternative – anything else was superfluous. The resulting
film was very effective on exactly those lines, and Gower wrote
again to say that the view of the Party was that it had been
successful.[14] A few months earlier, after Baldwin had recorded a
major film speech on the formation of the National Government,
Gower had to write to reassure Baldwin's secretary that the speech
had been well received in the country. In 1935, Gower's advice
was that Baldwin should make his appeal on a less partisan basis
than the other speakers at the election:

> In addition, it seems to me that many of the talks have been too
> formal. They sound like speeches delivered in a hall rather
> than talks to people sitting in their armchairs at home, and I
> have always held the view that the more personal, intimate and
> friendly these talks can be, the greater the influence they will
> exercise, and there is nobody who can deliver a talk of this kind
> better than yourself ... The more personal and homely the
> talk can be the better.[15]

Baldwin's Parliamentary Private Secretary, Geoffrey Lloyd,
made the same point, telling him that 'if you can put those simple
issues across to the working man and his family as they sit by their
firesides tonight all over provincial England, I believe we shall
have a great victory'.[16] The chief professional source of advice on

the actual making of films was Sir Albert Clavering, who was chairman of the Conservative and Unionist Films Association, making propaganda films for the Party as well as having direct personal interests in the newsfilm industry. Similarly, the Party could draw on advice from sympathetic film-makers like Alexander Korda; Campbell, Craig and Sanger of Movietone were all Conservative supporters, and both Craig and Sanger were on the committee of the CUFA. Through such people, Gower could get all the professional advice that was needed and pass it on to Baldwin, as he did. Baldwin's dependence on Gower may be gauged from the fact that his major speech for the 1935 election was actually written by Gower; because of shortage of time, Gower had sent it off through Clavering to the studio, for transmission on to the prompt-roller, before Baldwin had even seen it. In the event Baldwin made only two verbal changes to the speech: a promise 'to build up our defences' became a promise 'to make good the gaps in our defences' (much more cautious, in tune with Baldwin's view of the attitudes of the electorate in 1935); and an appeal for trust was strengthened by the addition of the quintessentially Baldwinian phrase, 'and I think you can trust me by now'. Gower was by no means the only one of Baldwin's staff to be called on to write a speech for him; by 1935, the style that he adopted for film speeches was settled enough for any one of them to have produced a text. But only Baldwin could have delivered it.[17]

Through the Conservative and Unionist Films Association, the Party had a source of funds and expertise for its own propaganda activities. These were conducted in the main through daylight cinema vans, showing cartoons with a political message as well as the Party's leaders, and Baldwin recorded a number of films for these 'talkie-vans'. Party reactions suggested that this novel form of propaganda could be a great draw; having gathered together an audience in the open air for a free film show, the meeting would be handed over to local speakers while the van moved on to another location. Large numbers of viewers were reported, and the effect must have been considerable when a number of vans were used together for a by-election or for a summer campaign in a seaside resort. But the number of vans available to the Party was never enough to have much impact on the electorate as a whole, and for this purpose the commercial newsreels were the vital medium. The Party film-makers almost seemed to recognise this truth in the way in which most of their films were made in conscious imitation of the newsreels and other commercial shorts. So most of Baldwin's film speeches for the Party vans were made in newsreel studios, as if the format and look of the film would encourage audiences to think of it as news rather than Party material. On at least one occasion, Baldwin made a newsreel film for general release and a Party propaganda film at the same studio session, using the same set; on that occasion, in August 1931, the measured bi-partisan tones that were used to describe the formation of the National Government for the commercial cinema circuits did not match the more partisan content of the film made for the Party. The Party film made on that day generated enthusiastic replies from Party agents, but it can have been seen by only a fraction of the number who saw film of Baldwin put out by all of the newsreels. The attitude of the newsreel companies was thus crucial.[18]

In general, the newsreel companies gave the National Government a very easy ride in the thirties, and treated Baldwin himself generously. The explanation for this is to be found not only in the personal opinions of the owners, commentators and editors of the individual companies, but in the natural sympathies of the companies themselves. It was after all hardly surprising that the capitalists who controlled the industry should show a clear preference for the Party of antisocialism. This was no more than was to be found among the proprietors of the national press, in many cases the same people, for the connection between Movietone and the Rothermere papers was not the only such overlap between press and film media. (What is less easily explained is why Labour was unable to gain a compensating advantage from the Labour sympathies of so many of the directors and the technical staffs who actually made the films. Presumably, as in the case of Baldwin, the control of distribution was more important than control of production.) The bias of the film companies in favour of the Conservative Party was probably made easier by the formation of a National Government in 1931; this enabled the newsreels to show men of 'all three political parties' attacking Labour, and it no doubt enabled the film-makers to convince themselves that they were still supporting a national, non-party cause. For such an approach, Baldwin was ideal, because his film speeches were low-key, non-partisan and

contained no attacks on Labour to upset Labour sympathisers in
the cinema audiences. He could thus be put on the screen as a
national leader, and because he was such a good screen
performer when compared to MacDonald, he became the
National Government's chief communicator on film. In that role
he was constantly in the public eye, for as a minister he could be
shown doing things on the nation's behalf without any need to
give an alternative point of view. So for example, the delegation
to the Ottawa Economic Conference which Baldwin led,
generated six separate news stories in July and August 1932. The
delegates were shown leaving from Southampton, arriving in
Canada, at the opening ceremony, signing the final document,
leaving Canada and arriving back home. On each of these
occasions, Baldwin spoke, usually for the sole benefit of the
camera; few of the words that were recorded had any real
political impact, but the fact of such routine interviews at regular
intervals was precisely what kept Baldwin always in the public
eye. By comparison, nobody from the Labour or Liberal Parties
was invited to say what they thought about Ottawa at any stage;
to the newsreels, the Opposition could make only party points
which were not 'news', whereas the Government was news in all
that it did. Nonetheless, the newsreel companies were by no
means wholly subservient to the wishes of the Conservative Party,
even in times of crisis. When Baldwin's speech 'Mr. Baldwin on
the Crisis' was made in September 1931, the party had difficulty
with Movietone, usually thought of as the most Tory of all the
companies. Gower reported to Baldwin:

I saw your film yesterday evening and I think that it is a great
success. Three of the agencies are so thrilled by it that they are
proposing to send it out with practically no cuts at all, and a
copy of it is already on its way to America. I am afraid that I
had a goodly scrap with the British Movietone people. I found
that they intended to push it out as part of a tripartite film
containing Ramsay MacDonald and Herbert Samuel. This
would have meant giving Ramsay about three minutes, and
yourself and Herbert Samuel less than a minute each. As it
seemed to me wholly contrary to the opinion which you had
expressed to me I put a veto on it and told them that in no circumstances could I agree to the film being used in this way.

They got a bit noisy about it, but after prolonged argument I told them that I could not give way one iota, so we left it at that.[19]

The full four-minute speech was put out by British Gaumont, Paramount and Pathé, even though MacDonald was Prime Minister, and Baldwin was only his deputy. It appeared that Movietone's reluctance to put out the full speech was based in part on the failure of their equipment during the joint recording, which meant that they had no soundtrack for the peroration. Gower eventually agreed to their using a cut version of Baldwin's speech, and he suggested that 'in order not to disappoint the British Movietone', they should be given a special film later. This finally took place when 'Mr. Baldwin's last word to the electors' appeared shortly before polling day, only on Movietone, in November 1931.[20] This whole dispute illustrates the symbiotic relationship between the political leaders and the film-makers; unless Baldwin made himself available, no company could show pictures of him, but the Party needed the film companies at least as much, and for the most part the two sides got along in mutual agreement.

The 1935 election gives the clearest example of bias in Baldwin's favour, and it came at a time when the appearance of political balance was made for the first time. It was agreed that Baldwin and Attlee should each be invited to speak for the same time, and that their speeches should be put out together by all of the companies, something very close to the modern television party political broadcasts on all channels. In this case though, there was consistent bias against Labour in everything except the allocation of time. The set that was built for Baldwin in the studio was an imposingly prime ministerial location, with a massive desk and chair set between two Greek pillars and backed by rows of leather-bound books. For Attlee, no desk at all was provided; instead he had to perch uncomfortably on the arm of a low chair, with a setting that looked like a Hampstead sitting-room. The visual impression of Baldwin as the man of experience and of Attlee as the rank outsider was inescapable. Added to this came Baldwin's fluent reading of the script from his rollèr, compared to Attlee's fumbling with notes on his knee. The camera level for Attlee was set too low, so that he was constantly looking down at the camera, and so that each time he bent to read his notes, the film lights shone on the top of his bald head.[21] All of this might be regarded as dirty tricks that loaded the dice against Attlee, but another less visible influence made it absolutely impossible that Attlee's speech would succeed. Gower reported this to Baldwin when he sent Baldwin the draft for his own speech:

As you will see, it is very much abbreviated, but I have endeavoured to include a good many points in it and answer in positive form some of the favourite allegations of our opponents. In this connection you will be interested to see the enclosed copy of Attlee's speech which will precede yours. I am not supposed to have seen it but I managed to secure a copy. I am told that his film speech is a very poor affair from every point of view, but I have endeavoured to counter his arguments in the draft I am sending you.[22]

As a result of this, Attlee's case was considered by the Conservatives before they composed Baldwin's speech, and the two were then distributed together. Any doubt about the actual sympathies of the film-makers would have been removed by the way in which they treated the election results a few weeks later. Gaumont British reported the National Government 'sweeping on to victory in all areas' with obvious satisfaction, and their results sequence finished by cutting back to extracts from Baldwin's speech; the item ended with Baldwin saying 'and I think you can trust me by now', after which the newsreel flashed up the words 'AND YOU DO!' to the sound of massive cheering.[23]

It should be added that the bias of the newsreels in Baldwin's favour was rather less apparent in and after 1936. When Baldwin made his emergency broadcast to reassure the nation before the abdication in November 1936, he made his film speech shortly before the crisis broke and he therefore made no mention of the king. He compared the unity of Britain under the National Government with disaster, dictatorship and civil war over the rest of Europe, and he also pointed to the country's economic recovery, stressing how far all of Britain's achievements rested on confidence and agreement. But Gaumont British immediately undercut Baldwin's picture of a happy people with returning economic prosperity. The very next item in the newsreel that showed Baldwin's speech was a report of a visit by King Edward to South Wales, a report which emphasised the depth of misery through prolonged unemployment and which treated the king very favourably – 'the King saw all of this and was appalled'.[24] It was perhaps fortunate for the government that the actual abdication crisis moved so quickly when it finally broke, for it seems likely that the newsreels would have taken the king's side if they had had time to do so. Over the years of his retirements, Baldwin was hardly ever in the news; an important speech that he made in New York in August 1939 was recorded by the American companies and sent over to their British associates, but its use by Gaumont British and by Movietone probably owed more to their need for something reassuring to put out in Britain in the wake of the Nazi–Soviet pact than to the fact that Baldwin was making the speech.[25] In his very last appearance on film, when British Movietone produced an obituary compilation in December 1947, Baldwin was subjected to a sustained piece of character assassination. The film was made up of the same clips which had been shown with an uncritical and often fawning commentary over the past 20 years, but now that Baldwin's reputation had crashed during the war, Movietone added a commentary made up equally of innuendo and abuse. There was reference to Baldwin's 'familiar gestures' (and nobody had made them more familiar than Movietone), but with the sly remark that the gestures were 'presumably unconscious'; it was pointed out that because Baldwin had been three times Prime Minister he must have commanded some fairly wide following, an expression that hinted clearly that Movietone had never been among that following; and the obituary ended by quoting from Baldwin's New York speech of 1939, when he had pledged that in the coming war Britain 'will play her part, and to the end'. The obituary commentator added 'He was right about *that*'.[26] In this sense, the newsreels present in an exaggerated form a mirror of the change in informed opinion about Baldwin, much as the popular press reflected the same changes and the same exaggeration, from the hero-worship of 1931 and 1935, through the doubts of 1936 to the abuse with which Baldwin was generally treated after 1939. While that change of heart certainly upset Baldwin greatly, it came too late to do him any real political harm; for almost the whole of his active career, he could count on getting most of what he wanted through the medium of news-film.

With this advantage, Baldwin concentrated on the propagation of a few simple themes, which he pursued with remarkable consistency. The impression given of a calm pipe-smoking and ordinary Englishman, so clear in the first silent films, remained the chief message of all his later appearances. He was able to turn this low-key approach to a particular advantage in 1931, when he could ask for support for 'the leaders of the *three* parties who have joined together in order to carry through a great policy of national reconstruction and international reconciliation'.[27] No matter that Baldwin had resisted the formation of the National Government almost to the last, he rapidly found it to be an excellent vehicle for the promotion of his political aims, and he found that it was particularly suitable for him to recommend the return of 'a National Government, consisting of men of all parties, resolutely determined to put the national interests first'. The 1931 crisis also gave him an opportunity to bring home to the viewer the real nature of the crisis, first by a simple explanation about what the financial crisis meant and second by a reminder of what had happened in Germany in 1923. People were reminded that

> Friendly societies, banks, insurance companies, trades unions and building societies, ultimately depend on credit, and if people lose confidence in the management of any of these institutions, they want to get their money out. And as with these institutions, so it is with the country . . . But the world is nervous, and people rich and poor alike are nervous where their savings are concerned . . . Cash is being withdrawn from London and put into foreign currencies, and if that process is not stopped – and stopped immediately – we have the lesson from Germany what may result. And you will all remember but a few years ago, when notes of thousands and thousands of marks were sold in the streets for a copper as a curiosity. It is no time for party considerations – there is no bankers' ramp.[28]

For Baldwin, 1931 represented the 'acid test of democracy', and his later speeches made regular references back to the great crisis; so he reminded an audience in 1935, 'I want you never to forget the way in which the British electorate rallied in a time of crisis. The political instincts of our people never showed to greater advantage'.[29] This last quotation indicates another constant theme, the Englishness of his political ideas. So, when unveiling the statue of Curzon in Carlton House Terrace, Baldwin commented on Curzon's knowledge, his sense of duty and his capacity for work, but he reserved his highest praise for

> that one quality which must appeal to an Englishman, and that is the possession of a passionate love for his own country, and what often goes with that, a passionate love for that corner of England with which he and his family had been connected for countless generations.[30]

The constant harping on England and the English character in his speeches was gradually assimilated into the more general argument in favour of the national government. He told a meeting at Halstead that 'you have been watching the bitter struggle that we have engaged in, to build a better Britain in the past four years. We, with our traditions and our love of law and order, we should all unite in this great object'.[31] Only a few weeks earlier, at Himley Hall in June 1935, he had concluded a review of progress since 1931 with a prolonged tribute to the British political instinct: 'I hope that's not insular pride, but I feel more than any country in the world today we are the guardians and the trustees for democracy – for liberty – for freedom, for ordered liberty and for ordered freedom'.[32] His November 1936 film speech made the same contrast even more clearly when he compared fears and suspicions, violence and disturbance throughout Europe with the position in Britain. Among the many reasons for this was the sensible policies of the government of course,

> but it is also due to the fact that we as a nation, true to our old traditions, have avoided all extremes. We have steered clear of fascism, communism, dictatorship, and we have shown the world that democratic government, constitutional methods and ordered liberty are not inconsistent with progress and prosperity.[33]

And he drew on the same sense of national history to impress his American audience with Britain's real determination to fight, in August 1939. 'Our little island has been in the danger zone for two thousand years. If war comes, it will find us as a people united as we have never been before, powerful in material resource and believing in our hearts that on the issue depends ultimately the freedom of mankind.'[34]

By the mid-thirties Baldwin was so experienced a politician that he could use his experience as a positive asset on the newsreels, not only in a technical sense, but because it could be referred to regularly to bolster his current point of view. Back in 1923, his very first film appearance within days of becoming Prime Minister, had recorded a visit to Downing Street of a group of employees from the family firm, calling to congratulate Master Stanley on his promotion; the impression given was of a man with direct industrial experience, and of a family firm where labour relations were harmonious and settled.[35] Ten years later, the experience he claimed was more directly political, as in the suggestion to the electorate that 'I think you can trust me, by now'. A Party propaganda film for the 1935 election made the same claim quite explicit:

I have spent many years in public life. I have studied the programme of the Opposition Labour Party, and I am honestly and sincerely convinced that if that party attempted to carry it out, not only would there be an end to the present trade revival, but this country of ours would be faced with industrial depression and unemployment on a scale that we have never experienced before.[36]

A large claim, and one that was underpinned solely by his claim to be a good judge of policy through his experience. At Himley Hall in July 1935 he had claimed that

I have served in many governments, and I assert without hesitation, and without fear of contradiction, that what has been accomplished in the last four years could not have been done by any party government, whatever it was and however strong it was in the House of Commons.[37]

The final theme that emerges clearly is that of confidence and trust – Baldwin had campaigned as early as 1929 as 'the man you can trust'. In 1931, he attributed a large part of the blame for the financial crisis on a lack of international confidence in Britain because of the Labour Government's policies:

... confidence in British credit, confidence in the pound sterling, has made the pound sterling the basic currency of the international trade of the world ... Our changing balance of trade, from a balance enormously in our favour to a very different state of things, and the fact that we have been borrowing in order to balance our budget instead of paying as we go along, has increased nervousness.[38]

In 1935 he told the electors that 'we have been faithful to the trust that you imposed in us'. In 1936, he attributed Britain's recovery to the confidence that people felt in their government.

It can be summed up in one word – confidence. Confidence in industry, confidence in finance, and confidence in one another. This confidence is largely due to the fact that when our country was faced with crisis there were men of all parties who put party politics on one side and united together to pull the country through.[39]

This verbal picture of a sensible and moderate people united behind their government, true to their historic traditions, was one that Baldwin put across at every opportunity. In the gloomy Britain of the thirties it was no doubt a reassuring message, and one that many of the electorate accepted, but it was also greatly reinforced by the sight and the sound of Baldwin himself, almost the incarnation of this simple, no-nonsense message. And in that lay the real secret of his success, for the idea that he was propagating was a matter of deep concern to him, and the film image of Stanley Baldwin was very close to the real man. If electors felt that they knew Baldwin through film better than they had known any previous premier, then they were right in their belief.

NOTES

1 J. Raymond (ed.), *The Baldwin Age* (London, 1960); Keith Middlemas, 'Stanley Baldwin' in H. van Thal (ed.), *The Prime Ministers*, II (London, 1975).
2 J. A. Ramsden, *The Age of Balfour and Baldwin* (London, 1978) pp. 295, 331.

3 *The Times*, 31 Oct. 1935.

4 Movietone 1/40, 10 Mar. 1930; Movietone 2/94, 22 Mar. 1931.

5 Pathé Gazette 1311, 13 July 1926; Pathé Gazette 1507, 31 May 1927; Gaumont British 163, 22 July 1935; Paramount 448, 13 June 1935.

6 Movietone 2/110, 13 July 1931; Movietone 2/124a, 22 Oct. 1931; Gaumont British 590, 24 Aug. 1939.

7 John Ramsden, *Stanley Baldwin*, InterUniversity History Film Consortium, Archive Series no. 3 (1980).

8 Pathé Gazette 985, 4 June 1923.

9 A. H. Booth, *British Hustings 1924–1950* (London, 1956) p. 46.

10 Gower to Baldwin, 27 Oct. 1935, Baldwin MSS., vol. 202.

11 Gaumont British 303, 23 Nov. 1936.

12 Booth, op. cit., p. 46.

13 Ibid., pp. 45–7.

14 Gower to Baldwin, 21 and 24 Oct. 1931, Baldwin MSS., vol. 45.

15 Gower to Fry, 10 Sept. 1931 and Gower to Baldwin 2 Nov. 1935, Baldwin MSS., vols 166 and 203.

16 Lloyd to Baldwin, 8 Nov. 1935, Baldwin MSS., vol. 203.

17 Gower to Baldwin, 27 Oct. 1935, Baldwin MSS., vol. 202.

18 Paramount 494, unissued; Pathé 31/72, 7 Sept. 1931.

19 Gower to Baldwin, 10 Sept. 1931, Baldwin MSS., vol. 166.

20 Movietone 2/124a, 22 Oct. 1931.

21 Gaumont British, 31 Oct. 1935.

22 Gower to Baldwin, 27 Oct. 1935, Baldwin MSS., vol. 202.

23 Gaumont British 197, 18 Nov. 1935.

24 Gaumont British 303, 23 Nov. 1936.

25 Gaumont British 590, 24 Aug. 1939.

26 Movietone, 19/967a, 18 Dec. 1947.

27 Pathé 31/72, 7 Sept. 1931.

28 Ibid.

29 Paramount 448, 13 June 1935.

30 Movietone, 2/94, 22 Mar. 1931.

31 Gaumont British 163, 22 July 1935.

32 Paramount 448, 13 June 1935.

33 Paramount 599, 22 Nov. 1936.

34 Gaumont British 590, 24 Aug. 1939.

35 Pathé Gazette, 983, 28 May 1923.

36 Election Speech for CUFA, November 1935, in the National Film Archive.

37 Paramount 448, 13 June 1935.

38 Paramount 55, 7 Sept. 1931.

39 Gaumont British 303, 23 Nov. 1936.

6 The workers' film movement in Britain, 1929–39*

BERT HOGENKAMP

During the pre-war decade the workers' film movement in Britain thrived as an important and colourful aspect of left-wing political, cultural and social activity. As with other media, film's political possibilities were explored partly under the influence of Soviet 'revolutionary' experimentation, but mainly under that of the fashionable aesthetic of social realism. The use of film by the workers' movement was paralleled by experimentation in 'proletarian literature', 'workers' theatre' and on the continent, 'workers' radio'. The international background, particularly the European, and the movement towards the politicisation of culture within left sections of the international workers' movement were of central importance to the development of the workers' film movement in Britain. The purpose of this short article however is to outline the activities of the main workers' film organisations in Britain and provide descriptions of a few of their most important films.[1]

It was only with the First World War and the use of the medium for government propaganda purposes that organised working-class movements in Europe began to realise the propaganda potential of the cinema. Yet, preoccupied with the

---

* For his invaluable criticism and extensive help with this chapter, the editors and author would like to thank Trevor Ryan of the University of Leeds, whose PhD thesis is entitled 'Labour and the Media: the attitudes of the Labour Movement in Britain, 1929–39, towards the new media of Radio and Film and its attempts to use them for political purposes'.

traditional, nineteenth century means of propaganda, newspapers, pamphlets, broadsheets, books and the public meeting, it was only after the Russian Revolution, and the development of the Soviet cinema that they began to see how film could be used in their own agitation and propaganda work. It was several years, however, before definite moves were made to produce workers' films. This was partly because there was a tendency amongst labour leaders to condemn the cinema, both morally, as having a corrupting influence, and politically, as attracting workers away from party meetings, evening classes, etc.

Where sections of the working-class movement had acquired cinemas, as in the case of a number of Belgian co-operative societies, these were run strictly along commercial lines, providing programmes which were no different from those of the ordinary commercial cinemas.[2] This delay was also partly because it took several years before Soviet films were shown in Europe in any substantial numbers.

A key role in the dissemination of these Soviet films was played by Willi Muenzenberg, Secretary of the Workers' International Relief (WIR), an organisation which he had established on instructions from the Executive Committee of the Communist International. Muenzenberg distributed in Europe and north America Soviet actuality films recording the devastating effects of the famine in the Volga area in 1921, as part of the WIR's campaign for relief assistance for the region. After the famine crisis had subsided the WIR maintained its propaganda role of generating international solidarity with the Russian people in opposition to anti-Bolshevik opinion in the West, and began organising sections in many countries to provide relief for workers in distress or involved in industrial struggle. In the mid-1920s Muenzenberg set up Prometheus-Film in Berlin as the principal distributor of Soviet films to foreign countries, and Weltfilm, to produce and distribute workers' films for showing in labour halls and working-class clubs. By 1928-9 workers' film clubs for production and exhibition were appearing in many towns and cities in Germany, France, the Netherlands, Denmark, Britain, Japan and the USA. Virtually all these groups originated within the Comintern national section – Communist Parties and their auxiliary organisations such as the Friends of Soviet Russia and the WIR.[3]

With the assistance of the WIR and the central organisations in

Berlin, Prometheus-Film and Weltfilm, these workers' film societies showed Soviet films and their own productions, and arranged exchanges between emerging national workers' film movements. They were also assisted by the strong avant-garde film movement in Europe which, keen to study the aesthetic innovations of the Soviet cinema, was involved in a prolonged struggle against censorship restrictions imposed on the exhibition of Soviet films.

In Britain the British Board of Film Censors (BBFC) banned most Soviet films from public exhibition, and commercial distributors were consequently unable to find outlets for them. Under the Cinematograph Act of 1909 local authorities (County Councils, etc.) were empowered to grant licences to exhibitors whose cinemas conformed to Home Office safety regulations; and no inflammable film (that is, nitrate film stock, the standard commercial film stock in Britain) could be exhibited to the public except in premises so licensed. Local authorities generally made it a condition of their licences that no film which had not been passed by the BBFC, could be exhibited without their express consent, in premises licensed by them. There was therefore a means of sidestepping BBFC prohibition; and led by Ivor Montagu, the Film Society, pioneer exhibitor of avant-garde and continental cinema in Britain, persuaded the London County Council after a lengthy debate on censorship to grant permission for the exhibition of Soviet films to its members under club conditions.[4] Apart from the Film Society other groups had been campaigning against the ban on Soviet films in Britain, ranging from art-film groups connected with the international film magazine *Close Up*, to prominent intellectuals and cultural personalities, and various workers' organisations and leading left-wing critics such as Henry Dobb of the *Sunday Worker*. The strategy of forming workers' film societies as the most effective means of avoiding censorship difficulties was commonplace in western Europe. As soon as the LCC accepted the principle of the exhibition of Soviet films before a private audience, Ralph Bond and Emile Burns, both prominent Communist Party organisers, and other members of the Minority Movement, the party's trade-union wing, established the Federation of Workers' Film Societies in late 1929. The Federation's aims were to encourage the formation of local workers' film societies, to supply film and apparatus to them as required, to provide legal advice for member societies, to encourage the production of 'films of value to the working-class', and to co-operate with other groups having similar aims.[5]

In November 1929 the London Workers' Film Society gave its first exhibition in a co-operative hall, and by March the following year was able to give performances at the Scala Cinema in central London. A distribution company, Atlas Films, was formed and Bond negotiated with Weltfilm in Berlin for the supply of Soviet and German films. The interest generated by the society quickly led to the formation of similar workers' film societies in large cities in Britain, including Manchester, Glasgow, Birmingham, Edinburgh, Cardiff and Liverpool. Encouraged by this support Atlas quickly commenced production. As with similar groups on the continent it concentrated on the most accessible cinematic form, the newsreel. Of the three which it made two have survived. Both are silent, made on standard 35mm film stock, and were shown within days of the events portrayed. *Workers' Topical News No. 1* was shown for the first time on 9 March 1930, in a programme arranged by the London Workers' Film Society which featured Viktor Turin's documentary *Turksib* on the construction of the Turkestan – Siberian Railway. The newsreel is concerned entirely with a demonstration organised by the National Unemployed Workers' Movement (NUWM) in London at Tower Hill on Unemployment Day 6 March 1930. In this five-minute film we see images of the mass demonstration, of the WIR food kitchen, and of various speakers, including Tom Mann. Brief titles provide the barest of information; and it is significant that Mann, seen in characteristic pose, was sufficiently well-known to the intended audience that his image is not identified.

Workers' Topical News No. 2 shows many of the same characteristics, although it is composed of images shot in different places, suggesting a larger and more organised film production unit. The reel covers two events: the NUWM Hunger March of 1930 and May Day in London. The hunger marchers are seen marching and during their rest-periods, and are portrayed in human terms: we see them eating, having their haircut, having their shoes repaired and playing football. Wal Hannington, the leader of the March, who is seen visiting one of the contingents en route, looks self-consciously into the camera. The newsreel continues with shots of the May Day Demonstration; and the numerous banners carried by participants, some with anti-

MacDonald slogans, clearly establish the political views of the section of workers which we see. Finally, we see scenes of the gathering in Hyde Park, including shots of the veteran Irish socialist Charlotte Despard, and the former Communist MP Shapurji Saklatvala, who also needs no identifying title.

Apart from a third newsreel, two other films were produced by Atlas, a compilation of Soviet footage on aspects of Soviet life, *Glimpses of Modern Russia*, and a propaganda film for the Minority Movement's campaign for a 'workers' charter', *1931*. The *Workers' Topical News* series was one of several attempts by workers' movements in various industrialised countries to gain access to the cinema screen. Newsreels and newsfilms were produced by workers' film societies in Germany, the Netherlands, Belgium, France, the USA and Japan. In all these cases workers' newsreels were seen in terms of providing working-class audiences with news of events of importance to the working-class movement, and countering the commercial newsreels, which were considered purveyors of politically dangerous ideas. They therefore had a cultural and political value, and the production of workers' newsreels must be seen in the wider context of the numerous workers' cultural organisations which flourished in the late 1920s and 1930s, such as the Volksverband für Filmkunst based in Berlin, the ILP Arts Guild based in London, and the International Workers' Theatre Movement, based in Moscow. These organisations related to a long tradition of working-class culture in its broadest sense, yet they also performed a particular function of which Ralph Bond of the Federation of Workers' Film Societies was well aware: 'We must learn to master in a practical way' he explained, 'the elements of film production so that when we have the resources after the revolution we shall know how to make use of them'.[6] The activities of workers' cultural organisations were seen as the continuation of a tradition and as a preparation for the work which would have to be done after a workers' revolution. The two issues of *Workers' Topical News* clearly express this double purpose: they were made for workers' audiences to see their own class, their own organisations, their own leaders on the screen; and they were part of an attempt to cultivate an interest within the workers' movement in film as a political and cultural medium as well as a vehicle for entertainment. These reels also performed a propagandist role, publicising what were considered by the Communist Party film-makers the most important revolutionary campaigns of the day.

The Federation of Workers' Film Societies and Atlas Films survived until early 1932, when the company went bankrupt. Due to the decrease in Soviet films available in Europe, as a result of the slow conversion to sound-film production of Soviet studios and the restriction of Weltfilm's activities amid the deteriorating situation in Germany, Atlas Films was unable to increase its stock, and with no new films to attract either audiences in London or the numerous provincial workers' film societies, custom slumped. Such problems were augmented by the effects of the censorship difficulties experienced by these societies: their programmes became so irregular that they almost all closed down, leaving Atlas with considerable losses and little income.

Censorship problems had punctuated the Federation' activities from the beginning. Similar experiences on the continent and in Japan had led to the use of 16mm film for exhibition in labour halls and clubs. Being made of non-inflammable stock this gauge had a particular attraction in Britain as the Cinematograph Act of 1909, which effectively conferred censorship powers on local authorities, referred only to inflammable film exhibited in licensed premises. There were no legal means relating to the films themselves for preventing the exhibition of film of this gauge in unlicensed premises. With 16mm films workers could therefore avoid being dependent on the bureaucratic whim or political prejudice of local authorities. The only disadvantage of 16mm exhibition was that it involved leaving the cinema for the labour hall.

The interest amongst the workers' movement which the Federation had generated did not wane, despite the collapse of Atlas, and as soon as a reliable 16mm film stock became available on the market a new workers' film group, Kino, was formed. The group evolved from London-based members of the Workers' Theatre Movement (WTM), whose work was largely agitational, performing short pieces on the streets, at political meetings and events. Kino was the outcome of a conference held in Moscow in 1933 by the International Workers' Theatre Movement, which decided that national workers' theatre associations should revitalise the ailing international workers' film movement. Within four months of the British representatives to the conference returning home a WTM Film Section was showing a 16mm film, *Soviet Russia: Past and Present*, to audiences on the streets.[7] In December 1933 the Film Section formed Kino, primarily as a distributor of Soviet films, but it soon began to produce its own material. While censorship problems did not abate, police harassment and LCC bans could not prevent Kino showing *Battleship Potemkin* and several other Soviet productions throughout London in unlicensed halls; and moves by the Home Office in 1934 to amend the 1909 Act to cover non-inflammable film were eventually abandoned on grounds of impracticality.

The scope of Kino's distribution and exhibition work quickly expanded and by 1937, when the group acquired sound film and equipment, it was providing a national film-hire service, offering a large library of Soviet films, and giving regular shows for workers' organisations and campaign groups. A number of its own productions were also available, mainly newsreels and reportage films, which concentrated on marches, demonstrations and other working-class events of political or cultural importance.

In late 1934 Kino's production unit established itself as the Workers' Film and Photo League, to allow Kino to concentrate on distribution. The League survived until 1939 and produced roughly thirty workers' films, which were distributed either by itself or Kino.[8] In its early days at least the League remained faithful to the decisions taken at the Moscow Cinema Conference and encouraged the formation of local film production units, provided classes and instruction in both production and criticism, and generally tried to popularise the workers' film movement. Members of the League believed that film was of particular value in political work because, through the careful construction of images, it could provide powerful and evocative insights regarding the nature of capitalist society. By exposing the contradictions of capitalism, it was argued, film could be used as an important agitational weapon in the class struggle. A number of the League's films possess this agitational quality, relying on the technique of intercutting to juxtapose images as a means of conveying appropriate messages.

The silent film *Jubilee*, co-produced by the North London Film Society Cine Unit and members of the League, is one of the best examples of workers' films of this type. *Jubilee*, 'An anti-war picture [which] hits the bull's eye right in the centre every time', according to the *Daily Worker* critic,[9] contrasts the 1935 Silver Jubilee celebrations in east London with working-class poverty and the drift towards war. The pressing, waving crowds, the bunting, the procession of mounted cavalry and the arrival of the royal family are seen. A phalanx of commercial newsreel cameramen are shown at work recording the celebrations and then more scenes of people waving and cheering. Titles appear, 'The National Government Celebrates . . .', scenes of flags being waved and the royal carriage, '25 Years of Progress'; immediately followed by shots of slum dwellings, and the people who live in them. A title, 'Progress?', precedes shots of unemployed, lines of men outside an employment exchange, and a sign, 'No hands wanted'. 'Progress?' again precedes shots of disabled war veterans singing in the street. A placard advertising for recruits to the army is then followed by 'Progress . . . Towards . . . War', and the film ends with warships at sea and military planes in formation. Ironical titles are used in combination with rapid montage sequences of bunting, flag-waving and ceremonial scenes, to gradually expose the contradictions between the Jubilee jamboree and what is happening in the real world. The film's producers attempt to convey the impression that the National Government is using the Jubilee celebrations to divert attention away from the miserable realities of everyday life, and in so doing continue with its rearmament programme unchallenged.

By far the bulk of workers' films produced by the League, Kino and other groups were either of the newsreel type, or of a documentary type, portraying in particular various aspects of the Spanish Civil War. A very small number of short fiction films were also made. The appeal of their productions was mainly to the workers' movement, and several attempts were made by these film groups to build up close relationships with trades councils, local Labour Parties, co-operative guilds, etc., both to establish new outlets for their films, and generally broaden their basis of support within the working-class. Both Kino and the League, while completely independent of the Communist Party, derived the bulk of their support from Party branches, its auxiliary organisations and left-wing groups such as the Left Book Club. Kino in particular also derived much support from left-wing intellectuals, cultural figures and artists, and one of the most remarkable films of British origin distributed by Kino, *Hell Unltd*, was made by two left-wing artists based in Glasgow, Helen Biggar and Norman McLaren. *Hell Unltd* is a silent anti-war, anti-arms trade film which lasts 15 minutes, using documentary, fiction and animation film, and employs techniques such as pixillation, graphics, stop-frame photography and elaborate montage sequences. The film portrays an arms dealer, Mr Hell (played by Ian Fleming), and his part in world history since 1900. Each point in the film is conveyed in simple but multiple images, using imaginative combinations of actuality footage, animation, titles, etc. The film is addressed, as the opening titles explain,

> . . . to all who are made to pay each day for their own and other people's destruction/. To all who are taxed just now to pay for the future murder of millions of men, women and children, / and especially to those who sit back and say 'We can do nothing about it'.

Animated graphs reveal the growing proportion of the British budget spent on armaments. The colossal scale of the death and destruction of the First World War is described, and post-war attempts to achieve disarmament ridiculed. Mr Hell is seen selling arms to both Britain and Germany, and amassing a great fortune as taxes are levied by governments to pay for their rearmament programmes. The horrifying effects of a future war on civilian populations are then portrayed. The film ends by advocating three measures for stopping the arms trade, the drift towards war, and the mass destruction which would ensue: writing to one's MP; demonstrating, if that has failed; and, should that fail, the mass strike. A hand is seen turning off a machine. A city is shown at rest, with smokeless chimneys, pit-wheels at a standstill and stationary trains. 'No government can contemplate war with things at a standstill.' In the form of models, people join together and push armaments off a world chess board, the arms dealer collapses, and the people join hands and dance in a circle.[10]

An important source of films for Kino was the Progressive Film Institute (PFI), which produced several documentaries on the Spanish Civil War. The PFI was the principal distributor of 35mm Soviet and 'progressive' films in Britain in the 1935–9 period, and was, like Kino, politically associated with the Communist Party. Its leading figure, Ivor Montagu, led two expeditions to Spain to film resistance in Madrid to Franco's forces, the International Brigade, the educational work of the Republican Government and evidence of German and Italian intervention in the war. The first PFI production. *Defence of Madrid*, released by Kino in December 1936, was used extensively to raise funds for two relief organisations, Spanish Medical Aid and the National Joint Committee for Spanish Relief. These films, presenting events in Spain in terms sympathetic to the republican cause and covering aspects of the war largely ignored by the commercial newsreels, were extremely popular with left-wing and liberal audiences, enabling them to visualise what was happening.[11]

Support for the republican cause was a central element in the 'popular front' strategy of the Communist Party, and while the popular front never gained the support of the bulk of the working-class movement, within those working-class, intellectual and artistic circles which did subscribe to this strategy the use of films of the kind produced by the PFI and distributed by Kino became common practice as a regular part of their political, cultural and social activities. There was moreover a correspondence of production and distribution work within the workers' film movement with the broad policies of the Communist Party, greatly facilitated by the close co-operation between the two main workers' film groups, Kino and the PFI.

In early 1939 Montagu and a number of film technicians produced an election propaganda film at the request of the Communist Party, which was then distributed by Kino. The 25-minute sound film, *Peace and Plenty*, was probably the most expensive of the productions of the British workers' film movement, and is certainly the most accomplished of those which have survived. Released in March 1939, *Peace and Plenty* is based on the Party Secretary's report to the 15th Party Congress held in September 1938. Harry Pollitt's two main themes had been the fight against fascism by means of an international peace front, consisting of Britain, France, the USA and the Soviet Union, and the struggle against the policies of the National Government by means by a British popular front, consisting of a broad alliance of all who opposed the Chamberlain Government and its foreign policy. Focussing exclusively on the latter theme the film uses a variety of techniques, including compilation, animation, graphics and stills, and a sound track consisting of a factual narration backed by a disquieting musical score. A series of statistics and charts explain scenes of rural and industrial poverty, showing that despite the election promise of the National Government in 1935 it had made little improvement in problem areas such as nutrition, housing, education, agriculture and industry. Using readily identifiable symbols and stills of individual ministers, the film explains their wealth and landowning backgrounds and their connections with big business. 'This government is a government of rich men.' A single, high-pitched percussion beat derisively introduces each cabinet minister, and Chamberlain is portrayed as a mannequin brought jerkily to life with marionette strings. Widely disliked policies in Chamberlain's career are recalled, such as his reduction of relief scales in 1926, and lead on to a discussion of his foreign policy. The commentary accuses him, 'Friends with Hitler, friends with Mussolini'. 'They give us this', is followed by images of gas masks and air raid shelters, 'to send against this', and shots of the destruction caused by aerial bombardment. Finally, 'This government has done enough – how can we get rid of them?', precedes a short speech by Pollitt direct to camera urging the British people to unite against the National Government. Pollitt declares,

> The defeat of the Chamberlain government is the supreme task of the labour and democratic people in Britain . . . the time has come . . . for all opponents of the Chamberlain govern-ment to get together and elect a government which . . . will defend the British people from fascist aggression . . .

The didactic expository tone of *Peace and Plenty* has much in common with documentaries of the period such as *Enough to Eat?* Its abrasive political analysis and technical proficiency make it outstanding among the workers' films of the period. However, the general election anticipated in 1939 never materialised, and the film was probably never shown widely beyond the audiences which the Communist Party and its auxiliary organisations could command.

With the outbreak of war in September 1939 Kino continued its distribution work on a greatly reduced scale, operating mainly as a library for the Workers' Film Association (which had been established by the Labour Party and the TUC in late 1938), and closed down in 1941. The Progressive Film Institute suspended operations for the duration of the war, but never resumed its work in 1945. The Film and Photo League had been periodically on the point of collapse since 1936 and finally disintegrated in early 1939, with most of its active members resigning, or simply losing interest, in view of the government's preparations for war.

The activities of the principal agencies of the British workers' film movement came to a premature end therefore in 1939. Its achievements are difficult to assess because firstly its primary work, with the exception of the Film and Photo League, was the distribution and exhibition of imported films, mainly of Soviet origin. Such material was shown to audiences consisting largely of people with left-wing or liberal-progressive views, and mainly to supporters of and sympathisers with the Communist Party, whose national influence within the workers' movement, though far greater than its minute membership would suggest, never seriously challenged that of the Labour Party. The use of film by the Communist Party and its auxiliary organisations, as with that of other sections of the workers' movement, was distinctly within the context of cadre work. There were no 'mass' audiences, although audiences of between 500 and 1000 were not uncommon for meetings in large halls where a leading Party member was to speak. The workers' film movement never aimed to achieve the support enjoyed by the commercial cinema. Its concern was with employing the medium to promote the class struggle, by using film specifically for agitation and propaganda, and by providing sustenance for the workers' culture as the essential basis of the consciousness of class needed for this struggle. As the decade progressed, and the 'popular front' strategy assumed precedence within the left wing of the workers' movement, the 'influence' of the activities of the workers' film movement was almost certainly greater than during the 'class against class' period of the late 1920s and early 1930s when the Communist Party posed as a revolutionary organisation. As is usually the case, however, 'influence' on a national scale cannot be reliably assessed.[12]

Secondly, the achievements of the workers' film movement are difficult to assess because many of the films produced by the various film groups have not survived; and not all of those which have are in the condition in which they were originally shown, with material taken out of some for use in other productions. Furthermore, it is difficult to judge how these films were received. There are many reports written by Communist Party organisers and Kino or League publicists of films being well liked or making a substantial impact on audiences attending political meetings, but there is a noticeable shortage of evidence indicating in what terms these films were judged by the ordinary person in the audience – the trade unionist who had to sell the *Daily Worker* every day at the factory gate or on the street corner – or whether such films had any influence on their political work.

Much more research needs to be done in the area of film and

the workers' movement before any satisfactory survey can be made. Particular attention needs to be paid to clarifying the relationships between these various film groups, and to their connections with the Communist Party and other sections of the workers' movement in different parts of the country. More information is needed on the numerous local production and exhibition groups which sprang up. Given that they often had connections with amateur cine groups (whose interests were usually cinematic rather than political) careful research and no small amount of luck may lead to the rediscovery of missing films and ephemera, such as publicity leaflets, which provide details of local activities otherwise so difficult to find.

NOTES

1 For a more detailed account see B. Hogenkamp, 'Film and the Workers' Movement in Britain 1929–39', *Sight and Sound*, Spring (1976).
2 See B. Hogenkamp, 'Arbeidersfilm in Belgie, 1914–39', *Skrien*, no. 66, July/Aug. 1977. See also, W. Muenzenberg, *Erobert den Film! Winke aus der Praxis für die Praxis proletarischer Filmpropaganda* (Berlin, 1925); *Zur Theorie and Praxis gewerkschaftlicher Medienarbeit* (Hamburg, 1975).
3 See B. Hogenkamp, 'Workers' Newsreels in the 1920's and 1930's', *Our History*, no. 68 (1977); 'Workers' Films in Europe', *Jump Cut*, no. 19 (Dec. 1978).
4 As a result of his experiences with the Film Society, Montagu published the pamphlet *The Political Censorship of Films* in 1929.
5 *The Worker*, 22 Oct. 1929, p. 7.
6 R. Bond, 'The production of working-class films', *Experimental Cinema*, no. 4 (Feb. 1934) p. 42.
7 See M. Baker, 'Film Conference', *New Theatre*, Sept/Oct. (1933) pp. 24–5; *Daily Worker*, 3 Aug. 1933, p. 4.
8 The films of the League have recently been rediscovered. See Victoria Wegg-Prosser, 'The Archive of the Film and Photo League' *Sight and Sound*, vol. 46, no. 4 (Autumn, 1977).
9 *Daily Worker*, 8 Oct. 1935, p. 4.
10 After producing this film Helen Biggar became a key figure in Glasgow Kino, Kino's principal agent in Scotland. For details see A. Shepherd, 'Helen Biggar and Norman McLaren', *New Edinburgh Review*, no. 40 (Feb. 1978).
11 See B. Hogenkamp, 'Interview met Ivor Montagu over het Progressive Film Institute', *Skrien*, no. 51 (July/Aug. 1975).
12 Useful perspectives however may be derived from comparisons with similar movements in other countries. For the USA see R. Campbell, 'Film and Photo League: Radical Cinema in the 1930's', *Jump Cut*, no. 14 (Mar. 1977).

7 Political polarisation and French cinema, 1934–39

ELIZABETH GROTTLE STREBEL

Jean Renoir's *Le Crime de M. Lange* (1935) was one of the most politically charged films of the thirties. It was executed by a team largely composed of members of the leftist cultural Groupe Octobre and was deeply inspired by Popular Front consciousness. Its narrative centered on a workers' co-operative formed to take over a bankrupt publishing company run by the deceitful and slippery capitalist Batala. Perhaps even more remarkable than this readily accessible dialectical narrative is a parallel dialectic of Renoir's cinematic language. Here fragmentive editing and use of Hollywood découpage classique[1] defines the world of Batala, whereas long takes, a highly mobile camera that tracks and pans, and depth of field photography produces a sense of organic binding that characterises the artistic/proletarian alliance sparked by Lange. In both form and in content, *Le Crime de M. Lange* can be seen as a metaphor for the dramatic polarisation of French society in the mid-thirties and more specifically for polarisation within the film industry, epitomised by Renoir's own personal artistic and ideological struggle against a certain film industry 'establishment'.

In an earlier study,[2] I have sketched the contours of leftist cinema in this period. This included the extensive involvement of the French Socialist and Communist Parties as well as various syndicates of the CGT in film making and distribution, the active interest of the Popular Front government in the film industry, the far-reaching social legislation which was enacted for cinema workers along the lines of the Matignon Agreements, the promotion by the Left of films like *La Marseillaise* financed by popular subscription, and the role of the leftist press, for example

Regards, in fostering a preferential rating of films on the basis of their social consciousness. The other dimension of political polarisation, the right-wing influence, both traditional and pro-fascist, has thus far been neglected in the literature and it is this dimension that I would like to begin to explore.

There has been a neglect of the right-wing influence for a number of reasons. There is the traditional popularity of left-wing topics. There is the fact that the political parties of the French Right had neither the resources, nor the organisation nor, most importantly, the insight to produce their own films of propaganda at this time. In addition, much has been made of the 1934/5 collapse of the large conglomerate film companies of Pathé and Gaumont, which had previously dominated the production market churning out escapist 'dream factory' films, which emphatically avoided topics of social relevance.[3] However, the eclipse of these companies in the field of production hardly precluded the influence of vested interests of a conservative ideological orientation. Just as Batala in *Le Crime de M. Lange*, though presumed dead, returns in the guise of a priest, so did the essentially conservative impact of Pathé and Gaumont extend itself in a more politicised form by a plethora of new, smaller film companies.[4]

Unfortunately, there are few financial records and business documents available for this period for Pathé and Gaumont, much less other production companies, some of which were so small that they were legally constituted for the sole production of a single film. Thus, one of the best sources for the views of the conservative vested interests of the corporate establishment of the film industry, better than the rightist press, has been various weekly cinema trade journals like *La Cinématographie Française*, *La Critique Cinématographique*, and *L'Action Cinématographique*.

Probably the single factor which rallied right-wing opinion in the cinema industry more than any other was the enactment of the social legislation of 1936, the Collective Contract for cinema workers and technicians. Especially singled out for attack by the Producers Association was the 40-hour week. Praised by a director like Renoir for providing 'time for reflection in the midst of the sets enabling us to eliminate useless scenes',[5] the 40-hour week was denounced by film industry heads as militating against the free flow of artistic creativity. Never before had industry

heads voiced such concerns over artistic integrity. Yet in a letter
to the Minister of Labour, spokesmen for the Producers Association warned that the introduction of the 40-hour week would lead
to the collapse of French film production.

> It seems, a priori, that it would be paradoxical to want to
> extend to the artistic professions the principle of a limitation of
> labour, because until now this limitation has only been applied
> to those professions which have little to do with personal
> creativity. One would never think of regulating the maximum
> number of hours that a writer, painter, sculptor or composer
> could exercise his profession.[6]

In the perennial debate over whether the cinema was essentially
an art or an industry, the film industry, in its own interest, was
arguing for the cinema as art.

Still another objection of industry heads to the new social
legislation was directed against the salary increases. It was argued
that such an augmentation of salaries would lead to an increase in
prices. The public would turn its back on the cinema, and the
film industry, already in a precarious state of affairs because of
the depression, would be unable to survive. Still, the industry
managed to fare extremely well, exhibiting a marked upturn
after its nadir of 1935.

Certainly the biggest fear evoked by the new social legislation
was the threat of imminent nationalisation of the film industry.
As Charles Le Fraper, editor of *Le Courrier Cinématographique*,
mouthpiece for industry heads, expressed it:

> I confess, that for the first time in my life, I no longer know
> where to direct the survivors of the raft of the Medusa, and I
> wonder whether or not this is leading us straight towards the
> nationalisation of the cinema against which we have cautioned
> our readers for so long.[7]

Throughout the thirties, Le Fraper served as a Cassandra figure,
furnishing the industry with the most dire prognostications for its
future in the most graphic of languages.

In March 1936, the review *L'Action Cinématographique* was
founded with the express purpose of girding the film industry
against the possibility of state control. In attempting to bolster

the arguments in favour of a total absence of governmental interference in the cinema industry, *L'Action Cinématographique*
called upon noted political figures who were wont to plead such a
cause. One such figure was Pierre Taittinger, founder of the
proto-fascist league 'La Jeunesse Patriotes', who declared,

> If I was head of government, I would leave the cinema industry
> in private hands. State management in France has only given
> pitiful results. Cinema propaganda should never be put in the
> service of governments . . . but in the service of a national
> ideal. France is collapsing from doubt, indifference and
> weakness in the face of countries which are resolute, impreg-
> nated with a powerful national mystique. It is high time to
> regenerate her if we don't want her to die and to give her faith
> in herself. The cinema, better than any other means of pro-
> paganda, can help us.[8]

The editors were perfectly delighted with this analysis. 'M.
Taittinger, we see, speaks like the great majority of cinematographers of our country. Sentinels, beware!'[9]

Fearing as they did the encroachment of the Popular Front
government, the corporate establishment of the film industry
vigorously objected to the formation of political cinema groups
like the 'Directeurs de Cinéma du Front Populaire'. On the other
hand, it was a totally bogus assertion for industry heads to claim
neutrality when it came to political issues. There was a blatant
inconsistency evident when Charles Le Fraper could in one statement maintain, 'the primary condition to be respected is one of
strict neutrality', and in the very next statement rail against the
freely elected French Government, 'They have to be completely
blind and deaf to observe the reactions and protests of the more
healthy elements in this country who are fed up with the Popular
Front and its dictatorship'.[10]

If the film industry establishment took clearly defined stances
regarding the domestic scene, it was hardly less reluctant to
define its position on foreign issues. Indeed, there is a close cor-
relation between its domestic and foreign positions, the common
denominators being deep seated anti-Bolshevism and a desire to
maximise economic self-interest which led to a flirtation with
fascist Germany and Italy.[11]

To illustrate this proposition, the attitude adopted *vis-à-vis* an

Italy that had just violated the Charter of the League of Nations by invading Ethiopia was indeed very cordial, since Italy constituted a prime market for exported French films. The sanctions imposed on Italy by the League of Nations were looked upon as an anathema by the film industry establishment.

> The censors have just banned a remarkable Italian film: 'The Truth about Italy', and one which shows the renaissance of our Latin sister, impoverished by the war, under the inspiration of its leader Mussolini. In effect, this banning is due to the sanctions which have been applied to the cinema since 18 November 1935 and not because of the film's political nature. At the same time, films from the U.S.S.R. are polluting the country . . . and we are losing ten million francs in business with Italy! Down with the sanctions![12]

In the same vein, film industry heads generally favoured a close rapport and the exchange of films with Germany. They appeared to be particularly supportive of Germany's cinema pavilion at Expo '37. When Leni Riefenstahl came to Paris for the projection at the 'Pavillon du Cinéma' of her powerful propaganda film *Triumph of the Will*, she was feted royally by the corporate establishment. One incident which marked her visit perhaps illustrates better than anything else the extent to which the French film industry was polarised at this time.[13] Riefenstahl was invited to tour the Pathé studios on the Rue Francour. As she mounted a stage followed by a whole entourage of admirers and officials, from the bottom of the set a chorus of cinema technicians broke forth with the 'Internationale' as their own personal greeting to the German film directress. Corporate leaders were very embarassed by the incident, as testified by the editorial comment in *La Critique Cinématographique*, 'To think that a guest, a foreigner, most especially a woman be subject to such an affront from a handful of rowdies, is inexcusable and unworthy of French manners'.[14]

Still, when its vested interests were threatened, for example when its own films were censored abroad, the French film industry could be less than enthusiastic about the German Reich. Early in 1937, through the intervention of the German consulate, five French films were banned in Yugoslavia, among them the widely acclaimed film of Jean Renoir *La Grande Illusion*. *La*

Critique Cinématographique was quick to express its shock and dismay over the incident, 'this must not pass without a word or two against this arbitrary intervention of the German authorities from whom we expect more "fair play" '.[15]

How did the polarisation within the film industry manifest itself in terms of the type of film which was made and how it was distributed? To investigate this question thoroughly, one would first of all in principle have to analyse the total French production which amounted to some 110 to 130 films each year. Unfortunately, it has been estimated that 70 per cent of the production is no longer extant.[16] However, recently Raymond Chirat of the Royal Cinémathèque of Belgium has published an invaluable catalogue of all the French feature films of the thirties, providing synopses of each film's scenario as well as a filmography based on articles in film magazines and journals of the period.[17] The significance of this catalogue for filling in gaps can not be over-emphasised. Another aspect of production and distribution of course is the popularity of films, which can be measured by consulting surveys periodically published in *La Cinématographie Française*.[18] Finally, in terms of strict distribution, to ascertain what films different social classes were going to see, working class *vs.* bourgeois audiences, I have taken as one index the weekly listings in *Cinémonde* of film showings of Parisian cinema houses.

One of the most striking aspects of French film production and distribution in the second half of the thirties was the extent to which it reflected and undoubtedly influenced the whole pacifist/militarist debate, which was so closely tied to domestic political affairs. It was a critical point in French history when, as Charles Micaud emphasises, both the French Left and the French Right were in the process of re-evaluating their traditional positions on the question of military preparedness and Franco – German relations.[19] The French Left was beginning to evolve from a traditionally-pacifist, pro-German stance to a more militarist, anti-German position in the light of domestic and international signs of fascism, whereas the French Right was deviating from its characteristically militarist, anti-German stance largely in reaction to the victory of the Popular Front. What role did French cinema have to play in terms of these re-evaluations?

Certainly one of the most important films of the period was Jean Renoir's *La Grande Illusion* (1937). Its pacifist message was strong but subtle. How much more poignant empty chairs and tables in the German peasant woman's cottage and her need for male companionship even if it be French, than gory scenes of trench warfare. How effective Renoir's unique approach to the filmic language as he underscores organic bonds of fraternal camaraderie across international boundaries through panning, tracking and shooting in depth. Today of course *La Grande Illusion* has become a great classic. But what is significant is that it was by far the top film in terms of box-office receipts, not to mention cinematographic prizes for 1937, and that this success was true for the provinces as well as Paris. Publicity pages in *La Cinématographie Française* boasted that *La Grande Illusion* had broken all time box office records in Le Havre, Dieppe, Mulhouse, Rennes, Marseilles and Bordeaux.[20] Naturally, some of the film's success had to be attributed to its famous stars, particularly Jean Gabin, who was a tremendous box-office attraction at the time. On the other hand, Gabin also appeared in another Renoir film *La Bête Humaine* the very next year, but this did not have much commercial success at all.

La Grande Illusion was an extremely well-made film with a particularly moving narrative, but its pacifist message must have also had a powerful appeal. The very experience of physically attending a showing of Renoir's film could be a bit awe-inspiring. A number of cinema houses had huge sets at the entrance patterned after the film's fortress prison, guarded by larger than life cardboard figures of Prussian soldiers, through which spectators had to pass to enter the theatre.[21] This undoubtedly made a dramatic impression on a populace rooted in the realities of 1914, obsessed with its demographic 'classe creuse'. Probably the most revealing aspect of *La Grande Illusion* is the fact that Renoir and his team, highly politicised and linked to the far Left, were still opting for traditional leftist pacifist solutions in the winter of 1936/7 when the film was shot, however illusory that may have been.

Despite the success of *La Grande Illusion*, there were relatively few other pacifist films at this critical time. There was Abel Gance's *J'Accuse* (1937), a remake of his 1918 film of the same name. The narrative begins on 10 November 1918 and runs to some undetermined date in the 1940s when on the eve of a major world conflagration, the hero of the film Jean Diaz (played by Victor Francen) calls up the nine-million dead of the First World War, who rise up hauntingly from their tombs at Douaument in striking cinematic superimposure. Gance is a master of images, of crowd movements, of dramatic, baroque effects like the clouds passing eerily behind the lighthouse at Douaument. But perhaps the impact was a little too frightening, too overpowering on a subliminal level. The film did not have a particularly noteworthy career in terms of box-office popularity.

Yet another pacifist film was *Paix Sur le Rhin* (1938), directed by Jean Choux. Set in 1918, it involves two brothers, one of whom has fought in the French army, the other in the German army, who return to their native Alsace. The first brother marries a Parisian and the second a German. The father chases the latter from his home but finally comes to comprehend the inanity of nationalistic hatreds. Here again is a film that was not particularly successful.

Films like *La Grande Illusion* and *J'Accuse* which are well known today give the impression of a heavy pacifist slant to French cinema of the period. In fact, the exact opposite was true. Between 1937 and 1939, there was a whole spate of traditionally conservative militarist films which quantitatively far outnumbered the pacifist films and which, although they have long been forgotten, did extremely well at the box office when first released.[22]

The prototype for this genre was *La Double Crime sur la Ligne Maginot* which was released shortly after *La Grande Illusion* and which had a rival career in Parisian cinema houses.[23] It was first presented at a gala on 23 September 1937 in the Salle Pleyel in Paris, in the presence of 'high military and civilian officials', as a benefit for the EPSOR of the Artillery and the Railway for their propaganda coffers and for work on the Maginot Line.[24] The film was made in direct co-operation with the French Army and has some rather remarkable footage of the Maginot fortifications.

La Double Crime sur la Ligne Maginot is a direct antithesis of *La Grande Illusion*. Whereas in the latter love and passion are able to transcend international boundaries, in the former patriotism and duty to France triumph over the love bond. In *La Double Crime*, Captain Bruchot (Victor Francen), who has had a brilliant career in the First World War, is ruined by his marriage to a German and is relegated to some distant colonial outpost. Alcoholic and ailing (undoubtedly the German influence), he is accused of murdering the Commandant d'Espinac. He suspects the real murderer to be one of three officers attached to his unit.

Bruchot lays a trap and exposes a German spy who has managed to infiltrate the French army through false papers. The latter happens to be the brother of Bruchot's own wife, whom of course he now must renounce. Somewhat melancholy but proud and now hale in body and spirit, he rejoins the marching feet of his unit, the Franco – German bond having been ruptured decisively.

La Double Crime sur la Ligne Maginot was produced under the auspices of the 'Compagnie Française Cinématographique' (CFC).[25] An examination of other films financed by this company at the time shows a similar anti-German, militarist, chauvinist thrust. A subsidiary of the CFC was the 'Société des Films Véga' which began to put out a spy thriller series known as the Captain Benoit series in 1935. The first film of the series, *Deuxième Bureau* (1935), served as a model. In this film Captain Benoit manages to seize the plans for a new German aeroplane. German counter-espionage gets one of its agents, the beautiful Erna Flieder to seduce Benoit. But the two spies fall in love and in the end Erna saves the captain by dying in his place.

The film was highly successful[26] and German agents, stolen documents and Mata-Hari like intrigues were to constitute the ingredients of a recipe that would repeat itself in the next couple of films in the series, *Les Loups Entre Eux* and *L'Homme à Abattre*, both of which were made in 1936 by Léon Mathot, as well as in a number of films produced by other companies. There was *Marthe Richard au Service de la France* (1937) again a very popular film[27] about the famous First World War French spy and her relationship with the head of German counter-espionnage; G. W. Pabst's *Mademoiselle Docteur* (1936) about the well-known German spy Anne-Marie Lesser and her love for a young French officer; and *Soeurs d'Armes* (1937) directed by Léon Poirier about Louise de Bettignies and Léonie Vanhoutte, who during the First World War organised the information service in the north of France and Belgium for the Intelligence Bureau.

A common feature of these spy films, as with *La Double Crime sur la Ligne Maginot*, is the prevalence of a Corneillian ethic over a Racinian approach, duty above passion. This was true, however, only when it concerned French men and women. For the Germans of these films, the exact converse held. Invariably they would abandon all thoughts of the Fatherland, so caught up were they in passionate involvement with the French.

Throughout the thirties, but with the pace dramatically

stepped up between 1936 and 1939, there was an attempt to glorify the French military on the silver screen. In this vein there were films like *Un de la Légion* (1936, Christian Jacques), *Nitchevo* (1936, Jacques de Baroncelli), and *Trois de Saint-cyr* (1938, Jean-Paul Paulin). Government and military officials actively encouraged the production of such films. In an interview published in *La Critique Cinématographique*, Francois Piétri, Minister of the Navy under the Popular Front, revealed that it was his objective to 'encourage, aid, inspire and guide the production of such excellent documentaries as *La Marine Française*, *Branle-bas de Combat*, *La France est Une Ile* and other feature films like *Veille d'Armes*, *La Porte du Large* and *Nitchevo*.'[28] Even the military comedies, or farces set in the barracks, epitomised by the highly popular *Trois Artilleurs au Pensionnat* (1937)[29] can be said to have served the cause, keeping uniforms visually prominent and in a positive light.

Some of the so-called militarist films were very explicit in their message. Such was the case with *Sommes-nous défendu?* (1938) a feature length documentary by Jean Loubignac which lauds the Maginot defence and boasts the unforgettable line 'France can close its doors and shut up its security bolts'. With other films, the influence of the traditional, conservative approach was more subtle. For example, in still another film put out by the CFC in 1937 *Tamara la Complaisante* the Corneillian ethic is under-scored without the military context. Moreover, films which focused on individualistic heroism, high adventure, aviators breaking records, as with *Anne Marie* (1936) with a script by Saint-Exupery and the CFC's *Aloha, le Chant des Iles* (1937) made a similar more subtle contribution.

The imperialist, colonialist films which abound in the thirties, also had a special upsurge between 1936 and 1939 linked to that of the militarist films. One particularly noteworthy film of this genre was Léon Poirier's *L'Appel du Silence* (1936). In essence this film was the biography of Charles de Foucauld (1858–1916) a missionary explorer in Algeria and Morocco, who was assassinated at Tamanrasset by a band of rebels from Tripoli. Rather remark-ably, the film was financed by popular subscription, by no means a unique innovation on the part of the French Left.[30] More than 100,000 Frenchmen responded to Poirier's call for aid in pro-ducing the film. *L'Appel du Silence* did extremely well, ranking second to Pagnol's *César* as the most popular film of 1936,

according to the popularity poll of *La Cinématographie Française*. It must be noted that Poirier was also director of the spy
film *Soeurs d'Armes* as well as having made two rather sober
commentaries on the battle of Verdun in his *Verdun, Visions
d'Histoire* (1928) and *Verdun, Souvenirs d'Histoire* (1931). Thus,
in the work of one director, we have a case of militarism, im-
perialism, anti-German and anti-revolutionary sentiments, all
inextricably linked in the traditional right-wing Weltanschauung.

In terms of distribution, both militarist and pacifist films were
shown to a fairly broad cross section of the population. Films like
La Double Crime sur la Ligne Maginot and *La Grande Illusion*
could be seen in nearly every arrondissement of Paris. However,
whereas *La Grande Illusion* was universally popular, most of the
militarist films seemed to have been more popular in bourgeois
quarters, in the 8th arrondissement or the 'grandes boulevardes',
than in strictly working class areas like the 18th, 19th or 20th
arrondissements, judging from the length of runs.[31]

If, as we have seen, the militarist, chauvinist influence was so
strong in French cinema, why did it not have a stronger impact
on French society? There are a number of reasons. First of all,
most films that alluded to the contemporary military situation
tended to foster a certain complacency, a Maginot mentality.
Secondly, even the more serious films of the genre, supported by
governmental and army circles, presented a highly romanticised
view of military life or merely a military backdrop for the perennial conjugal triangle. In this regard, a vituperative article by
Francois Vinneuil appeared in *Cinémonde* bemoaning 'senti-
mental idiocies under the tricolor' like *Veille d'Armes*, *Nitchevo*
and *La Porte du Large* and pleading for more 'viril' tales
enabling the spectators to 'participate more directly in the
dangers of a colonial soldier or transatlantic aviators' as American
cinema had done with films like *Lives of a Bengal Lancer*.[32]

Still a third reason for the failure of militarist cinema to have
more of an impact, was the dramatic reversal of attitudes towards
Germany which was apparent in some of these films in 1938. The
Captain Benoit series and other films of the CFC, as we have seen,
were full of German spies and explicitly anti-German propaganda
between 1935 and 1937. Then suddenly in 1938 the 'Société des
Films Véga' came out with two films which in a striking fashion
called for co-operation with Germany. One of the films was
Alerte en Méditerranée, which received the Grand Prize for

French Cinema in 1938 and was fifth on the list of most popular films for that year in *La Cinématographie Française*. Raymond Chirat has summarised the film's narrative.

> In the waters of the Mediterranean, marked by the wakes of ships from many naval powers, a suspicious vessel appears. French, German and English commandants unify their efforts, which are fortunately successful after some dramatic events.[33]

Given the anti-Leftist views of the film industry establishment, of which the CFC surely had to be a cornerstone, the 'suspicious vessel' could only have come from the Soviet Union.

Yet another film showing the complete reversal of opinion was *La Capitaine Benoit* of 1938. Here Captain Benoit saves the life of Prince Joachim (this can only be a German) who has just purchased some hydroplanes in France on behalf of a friendly nation and whom a band of spies has just tried to assassinate.

The reversal of attitudes towards Germany must be linked to fears on the part of the film industry establishment regarding the Popular Front and its actual and potential impact on film production. Having already documented these fears at the beginning of the paper, it is not without significance that Léon Mathot, who had earlier directed *Les Loups Entre Eux* and *L'Homme à abattre* for the 'Société des Films Véga', directs a film in 1938 called *Le Révolté* about an anarchist who joins the navy and who, under the influence of a woman becomes 'worthy of his new profession and the flag under which he serves'.[34]

In every possible way, French cinema of the period contributed to a defeatist mentality, to a psychological acceptance of the Munich agreements and to the 1940 defeat. One of the most popular films of the thirties *La Grande Illusion* was a strong pacifist statement which effectively pushed the line of fraternal class solidarity across international boundaries. A substantial number of films championed the militarist, chauvinist cause. But these films were more often than not escapist rather than realistic and fostered a Maginot mentality of self-complacency. As the French Right, responding to the accession to power of the Popular Front, began its flirtation with its fascist neighbours, so did German spies and villains disappear from the French screens. They were to reappear in dramatic fashion in 1939 with a whole spate of anti-German propaganda films that came after the outbreak of hostilities, just as *La Grande Illusion* was banned outright. But by then it was too late.

NOTES

1 This is the old Hollywood style of seamless narration. In dialogue sequences it involves an establishing two-shot followed by a montage of one-shots for each speaker in the dialogue.
2 Elizabeth Grottle Strebel, 'French Social Cinema and the Popular Front', *Journal of Contemporary History*, July 1977, pp. 499–519.
3 French film historian Georges Sadoul was probably the first to dwell upon this collapse in his *Le Cinéma Français (1890–1962)*, (Paris: Editions Flammarion, 1962), and Paul Léglise has fully documented and analysed this major crisis of the French film industry in his *Histoire de la Politique du Cinéma Français, Le Cinéma et la IIIe Republique* (Paris, Librairie Générale de Droit et de Jurisprudence, 1970).
4 By 1935, 115 films were produced by 83 different production companies and no one company produced more than 5 films.
5 Jean Renoir, 'La Production Française Veut Vivre, Il Ne Faut Pas l'Assassiner', *Regards*, 5 Nov. 1936, p. 11.
6 Letter published in *La Cinématographie Française*, 26 Sept. 1936, p. 58.
7 Charles Le Fraper, 'Au Seuil du Paradis', *Le Courrier Cinématographique*, 12 Sept. 1936, p. 3.
8 *L'Action Cinématographique*, 10 Apr. 1936.
9 Ibid.
10 *Le Courrier Cinématographique*, 12 Sept. 1936.
11 This phenomenon is a reflection of a larger trend in French society at the time, described in Charles Micaud's *The French Right and Nazi Germany, 1933–1939* (Durham, N.C.; Duke University Press, 1943).
12 *L'Action Cinématographique*, 25 April 1936, p. 8.
13 The whole incident is described in *La Critique Cinématographique* of 15 July 1937.
14 Ibid.
15 'Cinéma et Politique', *La Critique Cinématographique*, 10 June 1937, p. 25.
16 This is the figure of Raymond Borde, Director of the Cinémathèque of Toulouse, cited in Eric Losfeld, *Deuxième Cinécure. Les Français et leur Cinéma 1930–1939* (Creteil: Maison de la Culture, 1973) p. 6. It may be a slight exaggeration, but nonetheless, the percentage is quite high.
17 Raymond Chirat, *Catalogue des Films Français de Long Métrage, Films Sonores de Fiction 1929–1939* (Brussels: Royal Cinémathèque of Belgium, 1975).
18 Various popularity polls were taken by *La Cinématographie Française*. They were mostly local results based on box office receipts earned by films in the first seven days of showing, as for example with the poll of 1 Feb. 1936, which gave the last quarter results for 1935 for the city of Marseilles. Then there were a couple of national polls taken on the basis of a survey of some

600 French cinema houses. Such was the poll of 31 Mar. 1939 which recorded film popularity for 1938.

19 Micaud, op. cit.

20 *La Cinématographie Française*, 21 Jan. 1938, publicity pages.

21 Ibid.

22 Five militarist films *Le Double Crime sur la Ligne Maginot, Trois Artilleurs au Pensionnat, Marthe Richard, Nitchevo, L'Homme à Abattre* were sixth, ninth, twelfth, fourteenth, and seventeenth respectively in the list of the top 20 films of 1937, according to *La Cinématographie Française* (1938) p. 1170.

23 See *Cinémonde*'s listings for Parisian cinema houses for the month of December 1937.

24 'Le Gala de *Double Crime sur la Ligne Maginot*', *Cinémonde*, 23 Sept. 1937, p. 830.

25 A complete list of films shown in France in 1937, both French and foreign and according to production company, can be found in the Anniversary Issue of *La Cinématographie Française*, 31 Dec. 1937, pp. 86–7.

26 It was sixth in terms of popularity in 1937, although it polled a mere 2,280 points compared to the points of the top three films *La Grande Illusion* (12,500), *Ignace* (9,810) and *Un Carnet de Bal* (12,500).

27 The film was twelfth in terms of popularity with 715 points.

28 'Interview chez M. Francois Piétri, Ministre de la Marine', *La Critique Cinématographique*, 5 Jan. 1937, p. 7.

29 In terms of popularity, it was ninth with 1540 points.

30 Chirat, op. cit., no. 65 (numbers are according to film listings).

31 Based on an analysis of the distribution listings of *Cinémonde*.

32 François Vinneuil, 'Le Triomphe d'un Genre Faux, le Mélodrame Héroique', *Cinémonde*, 28 Jan. 1937.

33 Chirat, op. cit., no. 23.

34 Ibid., no. 1046.

PART III
Film propaganda in Britain in the Second World War

8 The news media at war

NICHOLAS PRONAY

The work of the documentary film movement during the Second World War has attracted much more attention from film historians than the newsreels. Those divisions of the Ministry of Information which were engaged in the conduct of positive propaganda have also received more attention, so far, than those in charge of negative propaganda: censorship or 'control'.[1] The reasons for this emphasis are not hard to find. Documentary films like the posters, books, pamphlets and other tools of positive propaganda are artefacts which museums and archives have collected ready for the historian. Moreover, since they were designed in the first place to be noticed by the public, there is a good deal of contemporary discussion of them to be found in the press and elsewhere. By contrast, secrecy and not publicity is the essential mode of operation for news-control and censorship. The more it relies on informal means invisible to the public, and the less on using its legal and police powers, the more effectively it is done. Its aim is to persuade through affecting the balance of information which reaches the public through omissions and the better its work is done altogether the less it is noticed and discussed by contemporaries. There are also intellectual reasons: documentary films were not only a part of the art of the cinema but they were also supposed to be dealing with 'larger issues' in a manner calculated to appeal to educated people. The newsreels, and the popular press, dealt with day-to-day news, employed a style which was deliberately tailored to conveying news and views in the entertainment context of the popular cinema and on a level which was calculated to appeal to an audience which did not possess sophisticated literacy. Paul Rotha, who was as influential as a film historian as a practitioner of the art of the documentary, cast the newsreels into the outer darkness as 'an elementary form of the cinema, without joy'[2] – a dismissive sentiment with which many historians, as intellectuals themselves, were apt to agree.

The actual structure of the Ministry of Information, however, does not justify the great deal of attention given to its productive divisions at the expense of its control work. The Press and Censorship Division had been given the first priority in planning the Ministry and throughout the war it employed the largest number of officers.[3] Its task was to control the output of news and as Lord Reith wrote while Minister of Information: *news is the shock-troops of propaganda*.[4] The newsreels were regarded as part of the news media, together with the press and the BBC, and received the mixed blessing of top priority in the matter of stock and personnel allocation coupled with a far greater degree of attention and control than was given to the more artistic products of the Films Division. News control was indeed the crux of the work of the Ministry of Information. What had excited most the admiration of contemporary foreign observers, including Dr Goebbels, and what was undoubtedly the most vital contribution in Britain to the war on the front of morale, was the way in which the press, the BBC and other organs of 'news' managed to maintain the trust of the British public at home and gained a reputation for Britain abroad for having even in wartime an honest, free and truthful media, yet which gave practically nothing of significance away to an ever-vigilant enemy. The newsreels played their part in that successful story of 'propaganda with facts' and it may be argued that their role was the most difficult. The innate realism of the newsreel camera for detail and the extensive development of news reportage in Britain long before the war, made the newsreel a weapon of propaganda which could either be used with virtuosity or not at all.

The story of the use of newsreels in that role, however, can only be told as part of the overall control of news media, for the most essential aspect of successful news control is that all the different and apparently independent instruments must play the same tune. Virtuosity consists of producing as many different variations on the common theme as possible. The reason for the success of British news-propaganda during the war derived from the firmness with which this point was grasped and the skill with which it was put into practice.[5] Yet at the outbreak of war the outlook was grim. In the crucial area of newscontrol the Ministry of Information in the Autumn of 1939 was deficient in detailed planning and organisation. Above all its newly appointed officials were raw recruits who lacked a clear understanding of either the structure or the mode of operation of the news media, and had little idea of its true potential. The gradual transformation of this dangerous situation, just in time for the testing months of Dunkirk and the Blitz, is perhaps one of the most interesting stories of that period.

By the time war was declared in September 1939 it was generally accepted that civilian morale was going to play a crucial role in the outcome. The Committee of Imperial Defence had given much worried thought to the likely effects of aerial bombardment. Overall military strategy, in as far as it can be said to have existed at all as a coherent plan, looked to blockade, Bomber Command and propaganda to achieve victory by bringing about a collapse of the German people's will to war, as it had collapsed in 1918. The Foreign Office, and to some extent the Cabinet, realised that there would also have to be a propaganda campaign for the support of the uncommitted nations of Europe, and to a lesser extent even for those of the Commonwealth and that it might well be necessary to wage a crucial propaganda and diplomatic battle for persuading the United States to come to the rescue once again.[6] The ostentatious use of propaganda by Nazi Germany had been already demonstrated fully in the case of Austria and Czechoslovakia and no persuasion was needed to accept that Germany possessed a powerful and technically advanced propaganda machine geared to war. The resources available to Britain in this field were however formidable, if only they could be properly mobilised and led. Britain possessed the most sophisticated and highly developed modern system of mass-communications at home and still occupied a good position in the centre of the international network of news-communications through Reuters. But, as we shall see, the reality of news-power had been passing to the USA since the palmy days of the First World War, when Britain controlled the cables of the world and the wireless was still in its infancy.[7]

On the home front, the most important asset was the fact that by 1939 the news media in Britain had achieved a greater degree of social penetration than anywhere else in the world, except for the USA. Daily newspapers reached some 14.5 million sales, there were some 9 million radio-receiving sets and the newsreels could count on a regular audience of some 20 million people each week. With the coming of the cinema and the growth of newspapers, such as the *Daily Mirror* under the editorship of Guy Bartholomew, Britain possessed a medium which reached for the first time not only the relatively large British middle class but also the great mass of the working classes. The cinema in general and the newsreels in particular were conscious of being the medium of the working classes and by trial and error learned to be highly effective in that role. No other country in Europe possessed such a degree of social penetration and thus such powerful means of influencing all sections of the population equally. A further asset in the coming war for credibility was to be found in the structure of the media in Britain. Unlike the United States, where, alone, a roughly comparable penetration had been achieved, Britain had a mixed system which combined the advantages of plurality with those of a centralised national medium. While in the press there was infinite variety and a cherished absence of government direction, in the BBC there was a single national medium, which had been carefully built up as the 'Voice of Britain', the organ of the 'governance of the realm', so to speak, as opposed to being the organ of the party in power at the time. This was a distinction baffling to foreigners, but well understood by the British. The newsreels were the third major component of this communications system. They occupied a middle position between the over-a-thousand-strong plurality of the press and the one BBC. There were only five newsreels for the whole country. Even the smallest of these, Universal (Talking) News reached an audience larger than the circulation of the largest national daily newspaper, the *Daily Express*. On the other hand the newsreels which were very definitely privately owned, stressed this fact publicly through a personalised approach and competitiveness, in clear contrast to the national monopoly of the air exercised and emphasised by the BBC.

What was not realised by the public was that all the media were in fact linked together at one point. By the 1930s the newspapers depended almost entirely for their basic international news-coverage on the information provided by the newsagency tape-machines. The expansion of the political 'world', from a handful of European capitals and a few Imperial centres of the nineteenth century, made quite impractical the maintenance of Special Correspondents by each newspaper at each of the main centres of news around the world, once the pride of nineteenth-century British journalism. Even in the few places where they were still to be found, they were hardly more than a gimmick for circulation purposes. Their place as providers of 'hard news' had been taken by the 'agency journalists' who supplied the real newscoverage for all the papers equally. Thus the art of the news-editor largely deteriorated into the skill of serving up in as different a form as possible the same 'copy' provided by an agency journalist through the 'tickertape' to all the newspapers. They developed great skill in padding-out the 'story' with tit-bits of general information culled from their 'libraries', devising special 'angles' for presenting it and by juxtapositioning it with other news items on the page appropriate to the newspaper's own characteristic approach. They maintained thus the appearance of individual reportage and variety as the outward characteristic of the British press. Roving 'special correspondents' could also be directed to follow up the agency stories and add spice, but the *basic* sources for all the national papers were essentially a few centralised agencies.

As far as the provincial press was concerned, there was in existence since the 1860s, a cable network, run from the Press Association in London directly to the offices of provincial papers, and which had long been their chief source of national news-stories as well as international news. In 1931, after a great deal of thought, Sir John Reith took the decision to reject the idea of an independent news-gathering organisation for the BBC, and instead to rely on the agency tape services. In the case of the newsreels, although agencies did not as yet supply newsfilm, as they do now, (thus the newsreels were independent in their sources of *pictorial* news), yet they too were subscribers to the agency tape-services and depended upon them for the interpretative element of the commentary, and for deciding where to send their camera crews in the first place: what was or was not to be 'the news' on the screen.[8]

As part of the preparations for a possible war before 1914, the Post Office had re-routed its cables to permit the location of both the Press Association and Reuters in the same building. Thus if the cable-centre in the heart of London could be controlled, as it was possible to do in wartime, it was possible to censor and control the flow of news *at source*, and to do so unobtrusively and without reducing the reassuring variety of its presentation. This system allowed the news editors of the press as a whole, as well as the BBC, to exercise to the maximum effect their long acquired skill in giving a great variety of form to what in fact was centrally released and thus reinforce their credibility through the illusion of many apparently independent presentations. An additional source of strength was the fact that the same news could be presented to the public at three different times by three different media. Members of the public could reassure themselves by comparing what they took to be instantaneous – hence uncensored – communication over the radio, with the variegated and elaborated version in the newspapers next morning and then with the newsreels supplying it for the public to see 'with their own eyes'. Ably handled, this system worked so well, for the censorship was practically invisible under it, that it became a source of national pride and hence a boost to morale. Rear Admiral Thomson, who perfected the system after a shaky start in 1939, recalled with justifiable pride after the war:

> Many people had an idea that BBC broadcasts went out uncensored. This is quite incorrect though it might seem at first sight an extraordinarily difficult problem to cope with. The BBC were broadcasting throughout 24 hours over their various services ... fortunately for censorship however, although the BBC sent war correspondents to the fighting areas and also had correspondents resident in one or two important places, such as New York, they depended entirely for their *news* bulletins on the agency tape machines. And this news had, of course, already been submitted to and passed by the censorship.[9]

When Sir John Reith was appointed Minister of Information, after 4 months of war, this potentially quick, flexible but highly sophisticated system was still hardly working at all. Yet something like it had been developed during the First World War and was well understood by the press world and 'control' or censorship had already been given priority over 'publicity' during the 4 years planning of the Ministry of Information. The declaration of war was followed by a wholesale choking of the flow of news, both in the direction of the British public and abroad. As far as the press was concerned, the chaos and desperation caused by the initial attitude of the censors, considering their prime duty to be to pass nothing at all, is well known and needs no rehearsing here. The reason for this was thought to be the unsuitable personnel chosen to be censors – mostly retired brigadiers and admirals – who took

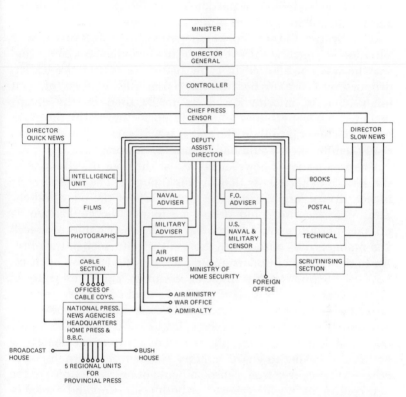

FIGURE 1 British Press Censorship Organisation in the Second World War (from G. P. Thomson, *Blue Pencil Admiral* (London, 1949)).

the sort of blanket view of security prevalent in the middle ranks of the military and reflected a similar attitude on the part of the service departments themselves. What made matters worse apparently was the ignorance and confusion about the needs and working of the press amongst the officials of the Ministry of Information including in particular the elderly Scottish lawyer, Lord Macmillan who, to universal astonishment, had been chosen by the Cabinet to be the Minister of Information. A situation in which a baffled American correspondent could find that he was not allowed to cable home the text of the leaflets dropped on Germany because the censors' 'list of stops' of what might contain information likely to be used by the enemy included the leaflets, and who could not be moved by the argument that several million Germans, it was earnestly hoped, had read them by then, could hardly have been worse.[10]

The reasons for it however lay less at the door of censors or of the service departments than it was thought. The censors were indeed drawn largely from the retired lists of the navy and the army – where else could people be found who could identify military hardware and terminology? – and their habits of speech and manners did conflict with those of the gentlemen of the press. An initial failure of understanding was inevitable. Most of them, however, learnt quickly. Sharing common character traits of aggressiveness, patriotism and a love of ritualised roguery, they got on well with pressmen in a remarkably short time. Much the same applies to the service departments: it was inevitable that it would take some little time before they could adapt from the peacetime position of having to guard military secrets from journalists and others basically free from censorship and other restrictions, to the new conditions in which there was both censorship and a need to supply the public with far more military information than in peacetime. Initial shambles were inevitable: liberal countries at war with autocracies pay for their privileges by being apt to lose the first battles on any front, notably that of propaganda. Ignorance and inexperience on the part of the newly appointed officials of the Ministry of Information were also to some extent inevitable. The Ministry of Information was being planned under the Committee of Imperial Defence and thus in conditions of secrecy. The sophisticated system envisaged for the control of news called for close co-ordination and co-operation involving both the civilian and services section of Whitehall as well as

Wardour Street, Fleet Street and Broadcasting House which under the limitations of official secrecy could not be done. The personnel required to provide the political and civil service hierarchy of the Ministry of Information; competing as it did with the demands of a vastly expanded officialdom required by the wartime ministries, inevitably meant that the majority had to be recruited at the outbreak of war from outside, which also meant outside the circle allowed access to official secrets. Where the government can be directly blamed for the extent of what in any case would have been an inevitable period of initial confusion, is in the appointment of Lord Macmillan in place of Sir John Reith, the man regarded since 1926 as the expert on propaganda in general and news propaganda in particular and who had been expected to lead the Ministry. Reith was a difficult man, his success in building up the BBC went to his head and gave him some illusions of grandeur and his behaviour in May 1939, when he rejected the post of Director-General Designate of the Ministry of Information and probably Minister upon the outbreak of war in September 1939, was both eccentric and unacceptable, culminating in his departure for an extended holiday overseas in August 1939 and thus his absence from Britain at the outbreak of war. Nevertheless, he was, and was known by the government to be, the only man of sufficient standing and experience for heading a department of state who also had an intimate knowledge of the planning of the Ministry of Information as well as an unparalleled command of the intricacies of modern mass-communications. He was the man for the job and the Prime Minister should have put aside the lesser considerations relating to Sir John Reith as a person and summoned him to take charge of the Ministry of Information. The new organisation with totally inexperienced personnel, planned in secrecy, above all needed a man who knew the job.

Translating the plans into practice in these circumstances would inevitably have led to a period of extensive confusion; the reason however why it proved to be not only so extensive but also so long, lay in the failure of the planners themselves to think through one particular aspect of the system which had been devised. Neither the planners themselves, nor Whitehall or Westminster had come to understand one basic principle without which such a sophisticated and elegant system for controlling the flow of news at source without interfering with the outlets, could

not operate at all: there *had* to be an ample and regular flow of
news fed through the cable system. If a large quantity of newsworthy information was to be withdrawn from that flow because
of the needs of war, it was important to ensure first that as little as
was absolutely essential to suppress was in fact withdrawn and
equally vital to ensure that at least an equivalent quantity of
newsworthy information came to be fed into the system. Newsworthy information in wartime means primarily news 'from the
front' and there are limits to journalistic ingenuity in dressing up
other news as from the 'home front' or the 'kitchen front'. The
Ministry and most of all the services had to be made to learn to
operate as news generating as well as news suppressing agencies
and to co-operate with the censorship in balancing the needs of
security against the propaganda disadvantages of appearing to
restrict the amount of information available to the public. No
evidence, in the surviving papers relating to the planning of the
Ministry, has been found to indicate that any serious consideration had been given to this need at any time prior to the autumn
of 1939. The sheer volume of news handled by a sophisticated
modern system of communications at home and abroad appears
to have been overlooked.[11] The 'voracity', in Duff Cooper's
phrase,[12] of the news machine was not anticipated and came as a
total surprise when the Ministry sprang into life in September
1939.

The result was that under frantic pressure from the press in
general and since the Minister of Information himself was manifestly ignorant, from Lord Camrose in particular, the censorship
division was removed from the Ministry of Information and as
from 1 October 1939 an independent Press and Censorship
Bureau was set up under Sir Walter Monckton. To begin with Sir
Walter was not very clear himself about the ends and means of
effective control of the press but he appreciated that some news
must be released or else rumours would take its place.

To Sir John Reith the willingness with which the Ministry of
Information agreed to the removal of Censorship exposed how
totally those in charge of the Ministry had failed to understand
propaganda. He wrote: 'But this was the Ministry of Information
and information surely means *news*. We were responsible for
propaganda at home and in neutral countries and news is the
shocktroops of propaganda.'[13]

If the first Minister of Information, Lord Macmillan — an

elderly Scottish lawyer whose experience in matters of propaganda was confined to a brief spell in the Ministry of Information at
the end of the First World War – found it difficult to comprehend
the use of the press in modern propaganda war, it is not surprising to find that the use of newsfilm was even less understood.
Newsfilm held additional terrors to the military censors installed
in the 'photographic' section of Censorship, for were they not
bound to show *something* recognisable by the enemy?

The results were predictable though if possible even more
farcical than in the case of newspapers. The newsreel companies
had laid good plans for combating the expected German propaganda offensive and were not a little taken aback to discover
that they too were covered by the initial order banning all photography of military subjects issued by the War Office, on 10
September 1939. One immediate result was that they were not
allowed to film the departure of the British Expeditionary Force.
When on 12 September the Head of the Films Division (Sir Joseph
Ball) demanded that the censors think again and fast, for as he
pointed out 'the event would soon be history and not news', he
received a reasoned answer from the Chief Censor Vice-Admiral
Usborne; he regretted but: 'Newsreels of troops departing for
overseas or preparing to depart overseas are absolutely
forbidden'.[14] He explained that the reasons were firstly, that as
far as the Admiralty was concerned ports were naval installations
which may not be photographed and secondly that the War
Office could not permit films showing any military equipment.
So, while the Germans flooded the cinema screens of neutral
countries, such as Holland, Belgium and Norway, with images of
vast armies moving east and vast armies taking up positions in
magnificent looking fortifications in the west, the only image of
the British Empire at war, available for counterbalancing
German propaganda, was that of a platoon of Royal Engineers
marching through a suburban street, carrying shovels and
pickaxes. This image was not enhanced by the choice of the
accompanying music-track (the newsreels being also forbidden to
say what the troops were or where they were marching): '*Wish
Me Luck As You Wave Me Goodbye* . . .'.

The first round in the propaganda war went to the Germans.
By the time the ban was lifted, the BEF had long departed, all
Europe had been already treated to convincing pictures of
German strength and, since new film about the arrival of the BEF

in France was equally under ban, the German campaign in France on the twin themes of 'Where ARE your British Allies?' and 'Britain will fight to the last Frenchman' had been allowed to take a strong foothold. In the case of the press there was at least some general understanding about the need to balance the needs of security against credibility for the independent Press and Censorship Bureau to be able to restore a measure of effectiveness, even if at the cost of destroying any chance of a unified propaganda policy. This was however no great loss for the time being since there was not one in existence.

In the case of the newsreels the situation was much worse. Very little was known about them outside their own circle. They were new, brash and had no prestige amongst the educated, largely middle class, Civil Service or academic personnel of the Ministry of Information. As far as one can discover no thought had been given to their precise role during the planning of the Ministry, largely because the cinemas were expected to be closed during the aerial bombardment which, it was assumed, would be launched by the Germans immediately after the outbreak of war. The cinemas, and the newsreels, were expected to re-open once the 'knock-out blow' had been survived, but the planners did not – and realistically could not – plan for the conditions and needs created by the devastation. When the Luftwaffe refused to come, there were no plans ready for that situation. So to begin with, the Films Division spent the month of September thinking lofty thoughts about producing their own newsreel which, they all agreed, should be a much more high-class product 'something like the March of Time' as one memorandum put it.[15] The *March of Time* was a curious American invention which mixed actuality footage with re-enactments, in order to produce, in effect, political pamphlets in the medium of film, somewhat similar, in approach and vocabulary, to the products of the Left Book Club.[16]

In its attempts to supplant the newsreels the Films Division found an ally in the War Office, who wished to produce their own news footage because they preferred to have their own well-drilled cameramen around rather than those brash and disrespectful 'newsreel-boys'. The War Office did in fact deliver some 6200 feet of material shot by their own cameramen – of which less than 150 was proved usable so amateurish was the quality.[17] In the meantime Sir Edward Villiers had been put in

charge of the newsreel problem in the Films Division with instructions to prepare a memorandum on the question of distributing
the planned, national and prestige newsreel. By the time he
concluded his inquiries in that direction news of the War Office's
own filming fiasco had reached the ears of Lord Strabolgi –
probably from one of the newsreel editors who, not unnaturally,
were greatly alarmed by all these developments. Villiers' report
concluded that, however much he was in favour of replacing the
newsreels with something better, he was bound to state that there
appeared severe difficulties in the way of distributing the proposed
new product. When Lord Strabolgi followed up a mild sounding
question in the Lords with energetic behind the scenes pressure
disclosing the mess which had been made of supplying convincing
newsreels about Britain's war effort abroad, and point out
that we were wasting golden opportunities to make use of the
wide connections and expertise of the Newsreel Companies,[18] Sir
Edward Villiers was commissioned again to find out just who the
newsreel companies were and what they were in fact doing. The
report presented by Villiers on 23 September 1939 was full of
mistakes.[19] He failed to realise for example that British Movietone
was not wholly owned by 20th Century Fox – and what is worse,
that it was editorially controlled by none other than Lord Rothermere. (Movietone's editorial policy has been summed up by one
of its staff as 'when in doubt, ring up Rothermere, the Mail'.)[20] It
also failed to realise that Pathé might well have been 'an insigni-
ficant company' in Britain, but it was a major supplier of
newsfilm in the strategically important American circuit. It was,
however, the first attempt on the part of the Films Division to find
out some of the basic facts about the newsreels. It is indicative of
the attitude and planning of the Ministry that such an inquiry
had to be made 3 weeks after the outbreak of war, and that the
demarcation lines between 'Films' and 'Control' were so unclear.

Sir Edward Villiers, like many other permanent or temporary
officials of the Ministry of Information, was however learning
quickly about the new world of communications and propaganda. By 16 October he informed the General Policy Committee
that 'Germany appeared to have realised for some time that the
newsreel was by far the most efficient form of propaganda, by
virtue of feeding a somewhat hectic appetite in somewhat hectic
times'.[21] Before long, he was also beginning to realise that
whatever might be said in favour of producing a more sophisti-

cated newsreel by the Films Division, it could only be distributed anywhere in the New World by courtesy of the US parent companies of the newsreels who controlled distribution arrangements all over the American hemisphere. The arrival of Reith put paid to any further thoughts of supplanting the newsreel companies. On 19 January 1940 it was stated that:

> We need the co-operation of the newsreel companies more, possibly, than that of any other part of the film industry. We are actively seeking their co-operation at the moment, because without it the distribution of favourable news is almost impossible.

It was also recognised that this co-operation could be obtained without 'leaving the editorial control of the newsreels to the newsreel companies'.[22] After 4½ months of war, the Ministry of Information learned the first lesson: that in the news war Britain was not an independent power any longer, she depended on the goodwill of American companies, not only in the newsreel field, but equally so in the news agency and broadcasting field. This recognition within the Ministry coincided with the establishment of Sir John Reith as the new Minister of Information who had known it all along and from then on the mobilisation of the existing news media became first priority. This could only be done, however, as Reith realised, by an intelligent and *politically* sophisticated use of the machinery for censorship. This point was also grasped by Sir Walter Monckton, the head of the Press and Censorship Bureau, and the two agreed at once to work towards bringing the Bureau back into the Ministry. After some difficulty with the Cabinet, mindful of the effect of so many changes of policy, the Press and Censorship Bureau, followed by Postal and Telegraphic Censorship, came to be incorporated in the Ministry of Information. Monckton took the position of Deputy Director General combining it with a liaison position in the Foreign Office, as an additional Under Secretary. These posts reflected the central importance of 'Censorship' within the structure.

From April 1940, at last, the unification of censorship and positive propaganda in one organisation, with news control recognised as the first priority, the shock-troops indeed, a workable administrative framework had been created for carrying into practice the British approach to propaganda: with facts, if not *the* facts, truth, if not the *whole* truth.

It was not only in foreign distribution that there was a compelling case for giving newsreels top priority. At home the
position was, quite simply, that as long as the cinemas remained
in the hands of private owners it was only the newsreels which
could reach significantly large audiences. For various reasons,
hotly debated at the time, cinema owners would not take the
alternative, the so-called documentary films, whatever intellectual
or artistic merits they possessed.[23] Owners and managers claimed
that only force would make their patrons sit through most of
them. It was not propaganda they objected to, but to documentaries, as a form of film-making. Only later and under pressure
were documentaries introduced in modest numbers into ordinary
cinemas. The non-theatrical distribution department, or rather
the able people who dedicatedly served in it, Lady Helen Forman
and Thomas Baird in particular, worked miracles but audience
figures could not be compared with those of the newsreels. The
13th Select Committee on National Expenditure of 1940 was told
by the Films Division that non-theatrical distribution might reach
as many as one million people a week, a figure accepted by the
Committee. Nevertheless it came to the conclusion that the production of documentary films for non-theatrical distribution
should cease altogether. The Committee agreed that while it was:

> not unmindful of the educational and artistic value of docu-
> mentaries, an audience of one million a week made it difficult
> to justify the expenditure incurred in the course of their pro-
> duction, in time of war, since audiences fifteen to twenty times
> as much could be reached through the cinemas.[24]

If the Select Committee had known that it had been greatly
misled about the actual audience figures, its recommendation for
winding up the production of non-theatrical documentary films
could hardly have been subsequently ignored, as in fact it was.
Although the Committee repeatedly asked for actual figures as
opposed to a statement of 'approximately one million', it had to
conclude its deliberations without them. The figure which the
Films Division adroitly avoided supplying, was nothing like 'one
million' – it was a mere 130,000 a week. Even 4 years later the
figure was still under 350,000 viewers per week. It may be noted
that a figure of '12 million' is claimed for the non-theatrical
distribution system both in Lady Forman's contribution in this
volume, and invariably, by accounts written by members of the

Documentary Movement. It is in fact the same figure representing 350,000 per week, but involves a nice example of 'propaganda
with facts' applied in this case by John Grierson's disciples. '12
million' was the total number of admissions to non-theatrical
film-shows *in a year*. By the same mode of calculation, the newsreels may be said to have had an audience of 1248 millions! The
proportions, and their significance, remain the same, however.
The newsreels reached 20 million people each week by 1940 and
reached 24 millions in 1944. Thus the non-theatrical distribution
system could not exceed a mere 1.8 per cent of the audience
penetration of the newsreels.

The conclusion of the Select Committee was that 'It is generally
conceded that the newsreel is the most important for propaganda
purposes of the three principal kinds of film, that is features,
newsreels and documentaries'.[25] It recommended that they should
be given full co-operation by the Ministry and that they should be
extensively used abroad as well. While its recommendation concerning the discontinuation of non-theatrical film production
was ignored, their recommendations concerning newsreel, were
accepted and not challenged during the war. From the summer
of 1940 the newsreels were left alone by the Films Division to carry
the main burden of the propaganda war, and they were assured
priority in film-stock and personnel.

By the time the 13th Select Committee presented its report in
the summer of 1940 the first experiments in issuing foreign
language versions of newsreels had also been carried out. The
Germans had of course been making extensive use of newsreels
with commentaries in foreign languages since 1936 and succeeded
in making Hitler and Nazism the idol of many young men in
Central Europe, Scandinavia and the Low Countries. Here, as
elsewhere, the cinema belonged to the young in general and to
the working class and petty-bourgeois young in particular.
Nazism could convey its beliefs by sound and vision much more
easily than in the cold light of the printed word. It is therefore
barely creditable that it was not until 1940 that it occurred to the
Foreign Office, the Colonial Office and the Ministry of Information to issue British newsreels not in English but in the language
of the countries to which they were sent. In 1940 however serious
effort was at last being made. The Select Committee helped it by
urging unequivocally that every effort should be made to extend
and co-ordinate the use of newsreels overseas. As so often in the

story of British propaganda, a slow beginning was followed by intelligent and rapid development commencing after the invasion of Norway.

This was just as well, for as a result of the loss of France and the beginning of the much-heralded German aerial offensive a great deal came to depend on what the world thought about Britain's ability to resist the onslaught. In the event, the handling of the Battle of Britain, a subject singularly adapted to sound and vision, proved to be the first real success for the Ministry of Information as well as for the Foreign Office and the British Council. Britain emerged with a reputation not only for unshakeable resolution, which the outcome of the battle would have ensured in any case, but also as an honest and credible source of news about the war. This was a considerable propaganda achievement considering the poor repute Britain had before the Second World War as a result of the atrocity propaganda excess of the First World War.

The increasing degree of sophistication and understanding of what Reith meant by calling 'news the shocktroops of propaganda' amongst the officials of the Ministry of Information, the Foreign Office and the British Council, partners in foreign persuasion, was well demonstrated by a lengthy and salty, correspondence between them concerning the presentation of the Battle of Britain. It was conducted by R. A. Bulter and A. W. G. Randall for the Foreign Office, Sir Maurice Peterson for the Ministry of Information, himself former ambassador in Madrid, and Lord Lloyd of the British Council.[26]

The specific issue was the way in which the bombing was handled by an apparently independent newsreel, called 'Olympic News' distributed in several languages abroad. It was, in fact, made by British Paramount News and was controlled and financed by the Ministry of Information, as opposed to another similar production compiled under the aegis of the British Council and the Foreign Office, appearing under several names of which 'British News' came to be the most common.

The problem arose from the belief of the Ministry that it was a good idea to show at least some of the devastation suffered by London. The Foreign Office held that while such realism might work in some countries such as Sweden, it gave the impression in other countries, such as in Latin America, that Britain had had more than she could take. As A. G. Randall put it:

The policy of emphasising the horrors of the bombardment of London in order to excite admiration for the people who are capable of standing up to these horrors, is likely in some foreign countries, to have the effect of exciting admiration for the efficient way in which Germany is laying London in ruins.[27]

The Foreign Office accordingly requested, on the evidence of Embassy officials, that shots of extensive damage should be omitted from newsreels going to 'soft' as opposed to 'hard' countries: the former group included all of Latin America, while the latter included Turkey. The debate soon widened to include film propaganda in general. According to the Foreign Office, the Turks responded to seeing devastation and casualties by admiring the toughness of those who took the punishment but did not wish to see what Mr Kemal at the Turkish Foreign Office was pleased to call 'the insipid type of documentary such as *Night Mail, Men at Work* and *Study in Steel*'. Sir Maurice Peterson on behalf of the Ministry of Information was prepared to concede a reduction of the number of shots showing air-raid damage in films going to 'soft' countries, but felt that the Foreign Office ought to be aware,

> . . . that such scenes were bound to appear in American reels since it was not in the interests of British Propaganda to ban the export of all air raid damage scenes. Any Cuban who first sees a British reel and then an American one would at once doubt the honesty of our reels and wonder what we were concealing.

He also wished to have further evidence for the rejection of documentaries by the Turks for he took the view that the copies of telegrams sent on to him by Randall were merely evidence that the Foreign Office 'had primed their YESmen to submit the telegrams expected of them'. Despite the spirited defence, the Ministry of Information conceded that newsreels should be substituted for these documentaries in view of reports from Embassy officials that 'Turkish audiences actually applauded at the end of some of the Paramount reels, which is most unusual in Turkish audiences'.[28]

In the course of this long-drawn-out correspondence, described by Peterson as 'this battle of Whitehall' the arguments came to centre on the approximate 'balance of shots' showing damaged areas and shots of undamaged areas and on 'balance of stories'. It was felt for example that the story *Carry On London* provided just the right 'off-setting effect showing as it did smiling Londoners'. It was eventually agreed that there should be a committee working with a British Council official 'selecting the appropriate stories for balanced issues' and that 'information officers of the Embassies, or British Council officers where appropriate, should in addition themselves edit the reels if the particular locality makes it desirable'.[29] By November 1940 the market for newsreels had grown to such an extent that 'dupe negatives' were specially flown to New York to ensure that all 19 South American countries received their reels as quickly as possible.

By the winter of 1940 the Foreign Office, and their officials serving abroad, British Council officials and the 'amateurs' of the Ministry of Information thus spoke a language which would have gladdened the heart of any newsreel editor. They could refer to the 'Library' for creating 'stories' where no actual 'footage' happened to have been shot, in the best newsreel 'fakes' tradition.[30] In fact the correspondence shows the high degree of understanding of the techniques of news-propaganda permeating through the departments which these kinds of officials in Britain a year earlier would have regarded as gobbledegook and black art with which they would not wish to meddle. Indeed one can detect a certain relish with which its technical terms were being flourished.

The same came to be true of those handling news-propaganda in the medium of print. Admiral Thomson, the Chief Press Censor, in fact also in charge of books, newsreels and radio, got on so well with the press and other 'media' people eventually, that it was suspected by some of his colleagues in the Censorship Bureau that he must have been looking for a job in Fleet Street after the war. (He did indeed move to Fleet Street. As soon as his job as Chief Press Censor was abolished, with much publicity on 3 September 1945, he took over the post of Secretary to the Services, Press and Broadcasting Committee – the peace time (and until 1961) secret body which issues the 'D Notices' – remaining in the job for another decade!)[31] Once the point was firmly grasped that the real function of the censorship was not so much the removal of particular shots but the creation of the desired 'balance' within an apparently unimpeded and unguided flow of information, the full potential of the British news media could be mobilised for war service.

At the beginning of the war, censorship consisted chiefly of lists, of what must not be referred to, must be 'stopped'. The list of 'stops', issued for example on 22 September 1939,[32] contained 38 items:

1) Location of children evacuated to be treated with discretion. 2) No mention of I.R.A. activities in Northern Ireland. 3) No mention of movements of Royal Family without prior authori-sation. 4) No mention of Russian complaints of British economic measures. 5) No messages to the effect that Hitler asked Mussolini to make a peace demarche and that Mussolini had agreed to do so. 6) No strong anti-Italian bias in articles etc. 7) No reference to King Farouk's visit to the Western Desert until his return to Cairo. 8) No mention that Soviet Union recalled ships bound for Britain. 9) All references to Bremen. 10) Position of ships sunk never to be mentioned with-out authority.

The remaining 28 stops covered just about everything in which the press and public was interested. They included 'No mention of RAF in action in France.' (no. 37), 'No mention of Balloon barrage; whether 'many' or 'few' or whether 'up' or 'down' (no. 33), and one which should be specially noted: 'No suggestion should be made that the Allies would have declared war against Russia had she launched her attack earlier and that collapse of Polish resistance had to be taken into account'. (no. 29) The list highlighted particularly clearly the problem of trying to control the media by merely negative 'stops'. Something more positive was needed.

By the summer of 1940 the nature of the censors' stop-list instructions themselves had considerably changed. Rules now contained provisions such as: 'No still photographs of air-raid damage may be published which do not contain at least 50% of non damage within the area published'.[33] There was, however, still a certain amount of 'stiffness' in the system. The order containing this provision appeared on 13 August 1940 and for some time the censors were required to ensure in the case of moving pictures that each individual shot in a newsreel should conform to this rule; it must have made very heavy weather of the viewing sessions, even though by this time a Moviola (a viewing machine with facility for viewing single frames) had been supplied for the censors as well as normal projection facilities. Exactly one month later, 13 September 1940, this order was amended. The rule from then on was that each 'pan must start from an undamaged building and must conclude on an undamaged building, and it must not linger over the damaged building'.[34] Instructions as to the precise proportions varied with policy as it changed and developed in response to the reports from Home Intelligence and other sources. For example when the City of London was devastated at the end of December 1940 it was decided by the Cabinet itself that it should be played up as much as possible instead of toning it down. Some interesting, though not fully convincing, reasons for this decision were recorded in Sir Alexander Cadogan's diaries.[35]

A year later, in the summer of 1941, Director's Order S.13 (23 July 1941) spelled out specifically that: 'The translation as far as practicable of the Minister of Information's wishes in regard to propaganda into terms of moving pictures and commentaries is to be regarded as a proper part of the Censor's duties'. It also provided a clear description of the practical working of the by then fully developed system for the control of newsreels. There were three stages:

1. 'One or more censors' were to go to the offices of each company and there to view 'all pictorial material proposed to be included in the newsreel.' The censors were instructed to view each item as a whole and also to view it, if in doubt, frame by frame on a Moviola.
2. 'Commentaries proposed to be given with the newsreel must be submitted in writing but if pressure of time does not permit that, they should be dictated over the telephone to a typist in the Censor's Office.'
3. 'Between Ten and Eleven in the morning on each Monday and Thursday the completed newsreels are to be brought to Malet Street and there submitted to a final Scrutiny Viewing.' It was pointed out that further alterations might still be ordered.[36]

The possibility of alterations ordered at the final scrutiny meeting was the spectre which haunted all newsreel editors. It did

not happen often, but one does occasionally come across melancholy entries in the books of the newsreel companies, such as this
for 19 June 1941: '131 reels were printed at 776 feet but were cut
by censor to 733 feet'.[37] Not many in the cutting rooms of
Gaumont British News could have had lunch that day.

So how voluntary was 'voluntary censorship'? Were the newsreels submitted to more censorship than the newspapers? If so
why?

In the light of the surviving lists of 'stops', instructions to
censors and Director's Orders it seems clear that the term 'voluntary censorship' as confined wholly to matters of 'military security'
needs to be approached with semantic caution. Caution is also
appropriate in view of the fact that after the 'sorting out' process
which occupied the last six months of the existence of the Ministry
of Information, no minute book, no 'stops' lists and no instructions to censors or editors found their way to the Public Record
Office, at least to the proper decisional records of censorship.
This was in spite of the fact that censorship employed over 400
persons, was directed by daily meetings of a committee, including
the highest officials of the Ministry, produced daily issues of
instructions and confidential notes for editors and held daily
briefings for them. The evidence which we have been able to cite
appears to have survived entirely owing to the blessed habit of
bureaucratic organisations in the age of the typewriter of dissemi-
nating 'carbons' to the most unlikely files.

As far as the press was concerned, the point is that the British
system was a system of *pre*-censorship as opposed to *post*-censor-
ship, and that it sought to achieve its aims in the first instance by
co-operation rather than confrontation with those who produced
the newspapers. It was the information upon which the actual
stories could be written that was censored rather than the finished
article after it had been written. In theory, therefore, it was
indeed possible for an editor to print something undesirable in
wilful defiance of the censorship – provided, of course, that the
control of the agency cable system had not in fact kept him
ignorant of it in the first place. It was indeed possible – but only
once. There were ample legal powers to ensure that he would not
be in a position to do it again and there were also powers for the
police to collect and confiscate newspapers after issue, as was
done, for example, in the case of the famous muddle when the
departure of the BEF was reported prematurely.[38] In fact, in

addition to pre-censorship, the censorship also had a section whose task it was to scrutinise printed newspapers and to deal with lapses on the part of the editors. But in the sense that a determined editor was in a position at least once to get on to the streets a newspaper containing something which he knew would land him in gaol (for nobody stood guard between the editorial offices of a newspaper and its printers), historians may, if they wish, call the censorship of the press 'voluntary censorship'.[39] If we do, however, wish to perpetuate the use of this happy wartime phrase, so widely publicised at the time, we should be aware that the same opportunity, in the physical sense, for actually printing anything forbidden, also existed in Germany. No doubt the consequences of availing himself of the opportunity would have been vastly more brutish for a German than for a British editor, but it is nevertheless the fact that it was editorial 'voluntas' not the control of the means of printing which determined what *might* get into a newspaper.[40] To understand the system of press censorship in Britain, it is more meaningful to regard it as a system based on the pre-censorship of information, buttressed and elaborated by regular and confidential guidance given to editors in matters of interpretation, separating as far as possible national interests, that is security and high morale, from party-political interests, and relying on that patriotism and responsibility which could be expected in wartime of the vast majority of the people including journalists. Adequate machinery for detection, as well as ample legal and police powers for swift action were available, however, should anyone prove not to possess those qualities.

The Daladier government in France opted for the alternative, the post-censorship system. French newspapers had to submit their printers' plates to censorship before the presses could start rolling and unacceptable items were struck out. Under the French censorship system it was indeed physically *impossible* to get anything the censors objected to into print and the French repeatedly tried to pressure the British Cabinet into adopting their total security system. Total or post-censorship, however, results in white gaps in newspapers and it is possible, indeed natural for the public to read the most awful rumours and fears into those white spaces. Whatever may be said for post-censorship in terms of keeping military secrets, in terms of propaganda it is the worst possible system. It not only actually aids the spreading of rumours, the first task of the black propaganda sections of the enemy, it also constantly reminds the reader of the fact that he is reading only what the government intends him to read. Its worst effect, however, is that it irritates and alienates the very propagandists on whom the government has to depend. Journalists grumble if they are told not to use a particular piece of information, but they are used to it because that is an occupational cross for all journalists to bear, whether due to the laws of libel or to the proprietors' whims. They hate to see, however, their finished piece cut about and are apt not to see the point of the cuts. Moreover, post-censorship is also very expensive and requires a very large staff: a point much used in stiffening the resolution of the Cabinet in resisting French demands for adopting it in Britain.

Why, then, were the newsreels, unlike the press, subject to post-censorship as well as pre-censorship, for as we have seen, the finished reel as a whole also had to be subjected to scrutiny before it could be printed. In fact, to a certain extent broadcasts were also subject to both pre- and post-censorship, a censor being installed in the broadcasting studios with his finger poised on the 'cut-out' button. The reason lies in the difference believed to exist between communication through the medium of writing on the one hand and through newsreels (and broadcasts) on the other hand.

In the case of newspapers neither the make-up of the pages nor, within reason, the style of the writing up of the permitted information, matter a great deal. At any rate it does not matter sufficiently to throw away the very solid propaganda value of appearing to have a 'free press' even in wartime. In the case of newsreels the make-up of the reel is the crucial element. The juxtaposition of pictures, and of words with pictures – *montage* – is the essence of audiovisual communication, of film and television alike.

The real art of the newsreel editor lies in the conveying of that overall message – 'the sediment left on the mind' as Sir Charles Grant Robertson once called it[41] – to which audiovisual media of persuasion are so singularly adapted. The overall impression left by the newsreel could only be judged and thus controlled, when the final make-up of the reel was done.

The importance of the newsreel from the point of view of the propagandist lay in the fact that what it actually communicated was an over-view of the events of the period it covered, while at the same time appearing merely to show actual pictures of them. Newspaper reports were manifestly merely the word of a particular reporter, and editorials evidently argued a case. Argument in a sophisticated society used to newspapers was an invitation to examine the case, to argue against it. Shots which did not appear in a newsreel were not missed any more than what had been omitted by newspapers, except by the handful who might have been present on the actual scene, but the shots which did appear carried an interpretation by virtue of their mere order and juxtaposition. So did the *order* of the sequences made up from them and even the order of the 'stories' in the reel as a whole. Here was another fundamental difference from the newspapers. In the case of a newspaper it is the *reader* who determines in which order he should read the items; whether to read the whole of a piece or just the first line, and even whether he should read it over again looking between the lines. He can do all this at his own leisure. In the case of both the newsreel and the news broadcast, however, it is the editor who determines the sequence-order and the time available to the viewer to scrutinise it. The viewer or listener cannot stop it or repeat it for himself. Putting items in a newsreel into a particular sequence is tantamount to imposing an order of relative importance and indeed of imposing an interpretation on them, without openly stating that interpretation. It was for this reason that a tighter and much more elaborate control was exercised over both news broadcasting and newsreels, and why the final product was also more closely scrutinised. In the case of the BBC there came in the autumn of 1940 the intrusion of a 'Home News Adviser' a 'Talks Adviser' and a 'Foreign Adviser' (who were to have weekly meetings with the Minister of Information) in order to reinforce the splendid system of precensorship operated by Admiral Thomson. And it was for essentially similar reasons that the only newspapers which really rattled the government were the tabloids. They developed in fact a montage-like system of communicating viewpoints by the juxtaposition of pictures with captions, rather than by reasoned, written, arguments. The famous *Daily Mirror* episode, when the government seriously considered suppression, exploded eventually on the juxtaposition of a perfectly unobjectionable drawing of a shipwrecked sailor, with a perfectly unobjectionable sentence by way of a caption under it which merely reproduced the official announcement that oil-companies would raise the price of petrol. It was but the latest in a series of juxtapositions and 'headlinings' which implied that the government lacked vigour and leant towards the rich. As far as 'security' censorship was concerned the *Daily Mirror* had the best record of all the papers for never making slips – unlike the *Daily Telegraph* which, however, was never thereupon threatened with suppression.

The elaborate and very expensive system of treble checking which on occasion extended even to the physical cutting of each newsreel print reflects the importance which came to be placed on newsreels as weapons of the home front. The almost as elaborate additional system of selecting again from the newsreels a composite foreign edition (British News) with provision for special tailoring for particular countries and even the provision for editing it again on the spot, reflected the importance placed upon the newsreel in the foreign field. It was a tribute to the system of pre-censorship and guidance, that little cutting of actual footage had to be done. The archives of the Paramount Company, now preserved in the library of Visnews show that between 1940 and 1944 there were only 166 cuts ordered in material filmed by Paramount.[42] About one-third of the cuts were ordered on grounds of military security – the shot identified a unit, a locality or a piece of equipment. About one-third were cuts on the grounds that they would have had a depressing effect on morale – such as a shot of a British destroyer blowing up. About another third were cuts made on grounds which, owing to the lack of surviving Ministry of Information records, can only be guessed at, such as a whole story showing the help received by the Eighth Army from Italian guerillas, or a German flag being trampled on in Burma, or one mysterious item which showed 'American soldiers in German uniforms doing German drill'. Ninety-eight of the cuts were eventually given back to Paramount at the end of the war, while 68 were held by the censor for good, including the last item. Only 166 cuts out of some 1500 stories originated by Paramount show a remarkable degree of harmony and understanding between the companies and the Ministry and between the censors and the newsreel men.

The companies of course knew that they were up against an impregnable system of censorship. There was no point in wasting celluloid on stories which could not be shown, and not even kept for 'future reference' in their libraries, because the supply of celluloid was controlled too. It was also impossible to make more money by producing a scoop, as it used to be in peacetime, there being also imposed upon them a compulsory sharing or 'rota' system, run by the Ministry and bitterly resented by the newsreels.[43] Nevertheless the evidence indicates that though they complained at times the companies acted in a thoroughly patriotic fashion, obeying their orders and seeking to anticipate them.

It was on the level of the 'newsreel-boys' however that willing co-operation with the Ministry really mattered. What happened on that level was simply that they acted like patriotic, straight forward and relatively unsophisticated Englishmen tend to act when 'there is a war on'. They knew they had an important job to do and they carried out what they understood to be expected of them, without too much arguing. They knew all there was to know about the particular newsreel form of communication and they carried out their jobs with resource and intelligence.

The description given in the memoirs of Ronnie Noble, one of the 'newsreel boys', of a meeting at the headquarters of Universal News illustrates their attitudes and approach:

In early July 1940 Universal News held a war conference in the small offices in Wardour Street. The future coverage of the War had to be discussed – where should our cameramen be positioned to ensure maximum coverage? There was the invasion – should we have our men stand by on the South and East coast and wait for the Germans to land? Would the Germans precede their invasion by blitzing the airfields? We must have a man stand by for that. We must have a man in Egypt because the Italians might well attack Egypt. We must have a man with the Navy. And London may get bombed and we must have a man standing by for that. We must show our anti-invasion preparations, we owe it to the nation! The conference went on for hours. There were only eight camera-men, at the time, we were going to be busy. My first assignment was to boost the nation's morale. 'I don't care what you do. But bring back a story on the nation's strength' said the Editor. I went to Leatherhead in Surrey to film a tank demonstration. There were only a handful of tanks. They deployed this way and that way but I was not satisfied. As a child I saw a picture of an elephant pushing a huge tree with its trunk. And then leaning its immense weight against it until it cracked, and slowly crumpled under the slow-moving heavy body. I looked

at first at the tanks and then at the trees close by. I said to the
Major, 'Sir, if we cut one of those trees half way through would
one of your tanks be able to push it over?' The Major turned to
the men and shouted 'Corporal, knock that tree down!' 'THAT
tree, Sir?' 'That tree.' The tank moved up to the tree, revved up
the engine and then slowly climbed up the tree. When it was
almost vertical it stopped and backed away. The major
bellowed: 'Idiot!' The tank rushed again at the tree and with a
great thud, stopped. The Major turned to the Sergeant:
'Sergeant, return to camp and bring a saw. A great big saw!'
And so it was done.[44]

This story hardly needs a comment. It tells almost all one needs
to know about the nature of newsfilm and indeed of the reality of
any form of audio-visual news communication. But there is
perhaps one additional point which should be noted. Tank
demonstrations have long been one of the staple items of the
newsreels, in fact almost as long as there have been tanks, for the
cinematic attractions of that machine of war were discovered
even by the Official War Cinematographers of the First World
War. Ever after, any editor short of a 'story' would ring up the
War Office Publicity Department to see if a 'tank-demo' could be
arranged. And each time he would pray that something
unexpected, spectacular and unusual, (and given particular
British conventions, preferably also 'funny'), that is 'news', should
happen. A year earlier cameraman Noble would have rushed
back triumphantly with that shot of the tank stuck in the tree and
he would have been sure of a bonus from his editor, but not now.
He knew the shot would not now be used and indeed he had
something different to convey. News values were replaced by
propaganda values. Instead of the *real* story, that 'there was a
grave shortage of tanks and their quality was weak, which shots of
the few tanks 'deploying this way and that way' and one of them
getting stuck would have done, he manufactured a propaganda
story, using the camera which appeared merely to convey pictures
of actuality.

This tale illustrates the way in which the individual 'stories' of a
newsreel were created to convey the desired perceptions to the
public. We should now consider the techniques used for conveying larger perceptions of how things were going by the composition of the whole newsreel, through the order, juxtaposition and

simply by the selection of stories which should go into the reel. This may be best illustrated by comparing a British and an Irish newsreel of the same date. The Government of Eire did not wish the idea to be brought home to Irishmen that Britain was engaged in life or death struggle, or indeed that there was in fact a gigantic war fought over fundamental issues going on in Europe. Of course there were the Irish newspapers, with which it would have been impolitic to interfere but which could safely be left to argue amongst themselves as much as they liked about the precise degree to which Irishmen should feel involved in the war. But the Irish Government was determined that the particularly compelling realism with which film can portray war should not dominate Irish screens, and above all that it should not bring it home to the great mass of the people of Ireland through their cinemas. The newsreel companies had no option but to respect the government's wishes: the importation of film depended on government licence.

So here is how the news of the past three days appeared in the cinema in Ireland and in Britain on 23 May 1940, at the height of the battle for France:

Eire
1. Italian royalty received by Pope Pius.
2. Australian boat race.
3. Sultan of Morocco at the Mouland Festival.
4. Madame Chiang Kai Shek inspects air-raid damage in Chunking.
5. Kentucky Derby.
6. Dublin Great Spring Show at Ballsbridge.

Britain
1. The Navy on guard in the north.
2. The fleet at Alexandria.
3. War zone special: Belgian towns attacked. Bombed hospitals. BEF tanks blow-up bridges. Refugees hide from machine guns. Belgian Army on the road. Parachute troops prisoners guarded. German wounded and prisoners arriving in England.

Join the Ambulance Brigade! (Trailer).

The two newsreels were the largest circulation newsreels respectively of Eire and the United Kingdom. The manifest difference in the coverage, almost as if they projected different worlds, had nothing to do with the availability of materials, 'security' or technical differences. They were both produced in London, by the same company and the same editor, Gaumont British News and Mr E. V. H. Emmett; they were the Irish and British 'Editions' of the same newsreel.[45] Only the brief to which these skilled communicators had to work was different. Editorial policy was in neither case any longer that of the company, but was dictated by the conflicting propaganda policy requirements of the two countries. Precisely for that reason they illustrate exceptionally clearly the techniques of communicating through the selection and juxtaposition of factually/pictorially 'true' items: each in itself accurate. The difference in the overall impression left in the minds of their respective audiences is however self-evident. In terms of detail we should also note in the British edition the manufactured 'media' or 'non-news' sequences showing the Fleet in unsullied strength (nothing actually happened) used for opening the reel, and also the sequences made of the arrival of wounded German prisoners in England used for concluding the reel. Led from the Naval images, the customary symbol of British power, through the hell of land war in Belgium and ending with wounded Germans in unaffected England, to the viewer the reel conveyed an impression of strength rather than weakness, without producing an argument or presenting a case for it.

The newsreels bore the brunt of the propaganda war in Britain. This was partly because of the illusion of completeness which a well-produced newsreel created (as does its modern television news equivalent), so that what had not been included at all did not appear to be missing by the time the customary length of a newsreel had been reached and the reel concluded by the also customary 'light' story. It was also partly because the cinema was so completely controllable by the authorities and unverifiable by the audience. One could not be prevented from listening to an alternative foreign broadcast or catching sight of an allied or neutral newspaper but the importation and exhibition of foreign films could be, and was, completely controlled. The weapons the newsreelmen contributed to the propaganda war were the perversion of the rules of their art, the transmutation of news values into propaganda values, the deliberate altering of the rules of 'balance' and also the undeclared transmission of direct government messages dressed up as though they were their own. They also contributed much skill, dedication and bravery in order to supply the flow of realistic combat material which was needed for effective propaganda. The Ministry of Information, especially its Press and Censorship Division contributed a modicum of generalship and a growing understanding of their techniques, at any rate from the summer of 1940. As a result of the arduous and dangerous work of the newsmen at home, the matching dedication of the censors, the printers and the film-laboratories, the newsreels, like the BBC and the newspapers, never closed, never failed to appear at the accustomed times. That was no mean feat during the Blitz and no mean contribution to morale by itself.

The contribution made by the newsreels – and indeed by the press, feature films and departmental publicity – to the perceptions, stereotypes and expectations of the British public, of themselves, their government, their enemies, their allies and their future role after the war, cannot be attempted here. Indeed much detailed work needs yet to be completed before the larger picture can emerge: a major subject of considerable importance.

The impact on the newsreels themselves of being drafted into the war does however seem to be clear. The newsreels had the hardest job within the trinity of the news media. Their job was to present the news in the realistic form of film and they could do little else. Unlike the BBC, they could not also provide entertainment, religion, or any other solace during the dark early years. Unlike the newspapers they could not hide amongst the multiplicity of the press, or provide the many little services which foster liking and loyalty for a newspaper. Newsreels always had to report from the frontline – and there was no good news to present from the fronts for almost three years. People hate bad news and the bearer of bad news is never popular. The newsreels knew they were losing some of the popularity which they had built up with hard work before the war. They asked time and again to be allowed to 'lighten the reel'. But they were the most closely controlled of the news media and the Ministry would not let up. There was perhaps no choice in the matter. Britain was at war and the war had to be presented. It was bad luck on the newsreels that there was nothing to cheer about in the cinemas, whose public used to cheer and boo with the newsreels. They were however also pushed into providing a constant barrage of talk and exhortation – every script had to be discussed and agreed with the Ministry.[46] To some extent they themselves lost some of their zip and light touch. Two issues a week were a hectic enough task to produce in peacetime; the strain became too much in wartime. There was no room in their peacetime schedule for including both the time-consuming processes of censorship and the distractions provided by the Luftwaffe. It was no mean task to keep working in a cutting room in Soho, surrounded by large quantities of fiercely combustible cellulose during the day and fire-watch on top of those very buildings during the night. As it happened only Universal News burned out. But as the war went on they lost some of their fine timing, their light touch and under endless lecturing from the intellectuals of the Ministry, something of their common touch too. They had always depended very heavily on these showman qualities and now they paid a price for that dependence. At the end of the war the newsreels were the only part of the news media to emerge as net losers from their war effort. They never recaptured their popularity, for by the time victories could be featured it was a little too late for them, and within a few years, they fell to television, more easily perhaps than they might.

NOTES

1 This was written originally in 1974. However neither Dr Ian McLaine's *The Ministry of Morale* (London, 1979), nor Professor M. L. Balfour's *Propaganda in War, 1939–1945* (London, 1979) deals with British newsreels at all and only deal with censorship in broad generalisations, in a few pages. Both books in fact concentrate almost totally on the work of the production divisions, including of course the BBC, but hardly at all with the operation of newscontrol.

2 Paul Rotha, *The Film Till Now* (London, 1967) p. 400.

3 Report of the CID Sub-Committee to prepare plans for the establishment of Ministry of Information, PREM1/388.

4 J. C. W. Reith, *Into the Wind* (London, 1949) p. 341.

5 The point was also grasped by Goebbels: he compared it to an orchestra, in which instruments played different notes but all followed the same score and beat. The difference was that Hitler detested the Press as a remnant of the liberal age and would not back Goebbels against the more flat-footed Dietrich, the Reich Press Chief. See Balfour, op. cit., pp. 34–5 and the

excellent discussion of the work, organisation and problems of the German press and newscontrol in R. E. Herzstein, *The War That Hitler Won* (London, 1979) chap. 4, which largely supersedes O. J. Hale's *The Captive Press in the Third Reich* (Princeton, 1973).

6 On the remarkably effective work of the News Department of the Foreign Office in preparing for propaganda needs of the next war, see P. M. Taylor, *The Projection of Britain*, unpublished PhD Thesis, University of Leeds 1978. Pt. 3 'Psychological Rearmament: Preparations for War'.

7 For British use of cable-communications for penetrating into the American, neutral and even German, press, see J. D. Squires, *British Propaganda at Home and in the United States* (Cambridge, Mass., 1935); H. C. Peterson, *Propaganda, For War* (New York, 1939). Already, seeing the operations of cable-control and Reuters during the Boer War, the French took the view that, 'Britain owes her influence in the world today more to her control of cable communications than to her Navy' – preamble to the French Telegraph Act of 1904.

8 For the development of news agencies and the co-operation of the Post Office as well as the Admiralty in their strategic use, see G. Storey, *Reuters' Century 1851–1951* (London, 1951); Sir Roderick Jones, *A Lifetime in Reuters* (London, 1951); C. E. Cook, *The Press in Wartime* (London, 1920).

9 Admiral George P. Thomson, *Blue Pencil Admiral* (London, 1949) p. 165. See also chap. V for an excellent summary of the working of the 'voluntary' system and the role of the news agency cable network within it. The working rule for the censors concerning information originating from abroad, thus constituting no security risk in itself, perhaps best explains the extensive and complex criteria applied by the censors: 'Agency messages received from overseas (including Germany) and submitted to censorship (the reader will remember that all the newsagencies serving the British press had agreed to submit such news to censorship) were to be passed unless they were completely untrue and would *at the same time* have a depressing effect on the morale of our people'. (Thomson's italics) op cit., p. 45.

10 Nigel Nicolson (ed.), *Harold Nicolson Diaries and Letters 1939–1945* (London, 1967) p. 32. It should be added, that the Censor *did* refer the matter higher-up.

11 In fact, the original plans assumed that a central office located in the Malet Street headquarters of the Ministry of Information could receive through teleprinter all the agency material – and retransmit it as well after censorship. Sir Edward Wilshaw, Chairman of Cable and Wireless Ltd., amongst others pointed out in vain that this system was bound to break down. Thomson, op. cit., p. 5.

12 Lord Norwich, *Old Men Forget* (London, 1953) p. 285.

13 Reith, op. cit., p. 341.

14 PRO INF1/178 A, 'Censorship'. Letter of Sir Joseph Ball to Admiral Usborne, the Chief Censor, 11 Sept. 1939; reply by Admiral Usborne, 14 Sept. 1939.

15 PRO INF1/195 'General Policy Committee'. Sir Edward Villiers to Sir Joseph Ball, 16 Oct. 1939.

16 See, Raymond Fielding, *The March of Time* (New York, 1976) – a highly sympathetic account!

17 PRO INF1/194 'Government Policy and the Film Industry; Questions by Lord Strabolgi'. This file contains a series of memoranda prepared by Sir Joseph Ball which give a detailed description of the events of the first 6 weeks of the war as far as the relationship between the Ministry of Information and the newsreels was concerned with some pre-war background as well.

18 Ibid.

19 PRO INF1/195. Report by Sir Edward Villiers to Sir Joseph Ball.

20 Information by Mr Raymond Perrin, Picture Editor Movietone News, interview, 27 May 1972.

21 PRO INF1/196 'General Policy Committee' Sir Edward Villiers to Sir Joseph Ball.

22 PRO INF1/196. Sir Edward Villiers to Sir Kenneth Clark.

23 On the question of newsreels *versus* documentary films and the debate about why the cinema-managers so steadfastly refused documentaries, see my Introduction to F. Thorpe and N. Pronay, *British Official Films in the Second World War* (Oxford, 1980).

24 *The XIIIth Report of the Select Committee on National Expenditure*. 21 Aug. 1940, par. 26.

25 Op. cit., par. 18.

26 I am indebted to the Librarian of the British Council for allowing me to see this correspondence in 1973 before the papers were transferred to the Public Record Office.

27 A. W. G. Randall to Sir Maurice Peterson, 25 Oct. 1940.

28 Sir Maurice Peterson to A. W. G. Randall, 19 Dec. 1940.

29 Lord Lloyd to Mr A. A. Haigh, Foreign Office, 6 Jan. 1941.

30 See in particular Lord Lloyd's letter to Haigh, cited above, and the reply to it, 14 Jan. 1941.

31 *Report on Security Procedures in the Public Service*, Cmnd 1681, (1962).

32 PRO INF1/178 A. Commander Powell's File.

33 PRO INF1/178 A – 'Instructions of Chief Newsreel Censor to Commander Powell'. Cmdr Christopher Powell, a retired Naval Officer who long specialised in constituency propaganda working for Central Office, became Head of the Photographic and Film Censorship, Quick News Division.

34 PRO INF1/178 A.

35 David Dilks (ed.), *The Diaries of Sir Alexander Cadogan, 1938–1945*, (London, 1971) p. 344.

36 PRO INF1/178/3.

37 Visnews Library, Gaumont British Issues, MS. Catalogue with notes. *GB 678*, 19 June 1940 (Misdated in Catalogue to 27 June.)

38 10 Sept. 1939: the police occupied the newspaper offices, stopped the presses, went to railway stations and confiscated the bundles on their way to the provinces and swooped on news vendors and even took newspapers off astonished commuters the following morning.

39 The phrase appears to have been the brainchild of the Joint Select Committee of the House of Lords and House of Commons on Stage Plays (Censorship) 1908. They suggested that the Lord Chamberlain's Office might be replaced by a system of 'voluntary censorship' whereby authors could voluntarily submit stage plays to a State Censorship Board. If not submitted *and* performed, because in the opinion of the author and

producer it did not fall within the prohibited subjects, they could be prosecuted if, in the opinion of the Board, it did. The Chairman of Committee, which published its Report in 1909, was Sir Herbert Samuel.

40 In comparing the work of German 'security' censorship with British, Professor Balfour concluded 'The Division was responsible for military censorship, which was run on somewhat the same lines as in Britain, although more material was sent out pre-censored, submission was compulsory on more subjects and penalties for mistakes more drastic.' Balfour, op. cit., p. 105.

41 'It is not merely a question of whether this or that is artistically bad, whether some incident in a film is repugnant. The extraordinary potency of this instrument is in the kind of sediment which it leaves on the mind.' Speech to Conference on *The Cinema and its Influence Today*, 17 Nov. 1930. British Board of Film Censors, Verbatim Transcript, 1930–31, pp. 10–11. Grierson called it 'the hangover-effect of the film'.

42 Visnews Library, British Paramount News Files: 'Censorship'. Contains full list of all Paramount material censored and whether or not it was released subsequently, from 1939 to 1946. It also contains several Censors' Instructions to Newsreels, none of which appear to have survived in the Public Record Office.

43 Paramount tried in fact to test the legality of the rota system in 1942. After three months and despite much support from the press, it learned that there was nothing it could do about it. See account of the episode in *Manchester Guardian*, 30 Oct. 1942, by Paramount's own chief, E. T. Cummins. The Labour Government which was far from unanimous in the view that they had acted wisely when, as junior partners in the Wartime Coalition Government, they had pressed to have the Ministry of Information abolished, and had used the COI for purposes much beyond its agreed role, also kept the rota in being. It was not until 1 Oct. 1950 (!) that the newsreels were freed altogether.

44 Ronnie Noble, *Shoot First, Assignments of a Cameraman*, (rev. ed.), (London, 1957) pp. 30–2.

45 Visnews Library, Gaumont British Issues, MS. Catalogue. GM 665. This is a typical rather than the most remarkable example. The previous week which saw, for example, the arrival of the Dutch Government as refugees in London; the bombing of Rotterdam; the bombing of Canterbury, as well as Churchill's new Cabinet, amongst other events, was represented on Irish screens thus:

1. Models in New York's World Fair
2. US polo stars play for charity
3. Feria Fete in Seville
4. Carnival in Zurich
5. Baseball season opens in US
6. Torrential floods and storms in America
7. Pope proclaims Saint in Rome

46 Writing in *Reynold's News* Joan Lester sums up both the work of the newsreels under 'guidance' and the attitude of intellectuals to it: 'One section of film-fare which is rarely mentioned in columns such as this is the newsreel.

This week I made it my business to see a current newsreel and had a surprise. As a journalist I believe that news is news and a matter for straight, fair and accurate reportage. The news bulletin seems to me to bear a close relationship to the news-story. The place for political comment and deduction is in leaders or feature articles. ... But the commentary to this newsreel was far from being just straight reporting. It had a very definite political line of its own. Here were remarkable and most interesting pictures of the work of allied bombers. With them, was a commentary to tell us that this *was* the second front in Europe ... and much else, hardly unbiased reporting ...' 3 Oct. 1943.

9 The Crown Film Unit, 1940–43

IAN DALRYMPLE*

My main contribution to British war films was not as a maker. From my appointment in midsummer, 1940, to the then Ministry of Information's Film Production Unit I organised film-making by others: myself only occasionally commenting on content and execution. However, we must go back a little further, to the opening of the war in Europe in 1939.

Apart from the enterprise of the GPO Film Unit in spontaneously going out into the streets to cover what was going on in those first days, initiative in Great Britain for the use of the film medium for war purposes came from private enterprise, in the person of Alexander Korda.

A few days before 3 September, some of us working at the Denham Studios – a fortuitous gaggle of directors and writers of various ages and origins, all of sadly unbellicose aspect – were summoned to Alex's office. He told us that we were to make a film to reassure the public of the power of the Royal Air Force, and that a liaison officer from the Air Ministry was on his way to assist us. Almost immediately the door opened and a fair young

---

*Ian Dalrymple graduated from Cambridge and joined the film industry in 1927. He worked until the war as a film-editor, screen writer and director, as head of the Crown Film Unit, 1940–43, and on feature productions and helped the Army Film Unit, 1943–45. He was responsible for the inception of many of the wartime propaganda classics, such as *Fires Were Started*, *Western Approaches*, *Coastal Command*, *Wavell's 30,000* and *London Can Take It* amongst others. He has been an independent producer since the war and his post-war work includes *The Royal Heritage*, *A Hill in Korea*, *The Boy and the Pelican*, and the series *The Changing Face of Europe*, amongst many others. He was Chairman of the British Film Academy 1957–58.

god in sky-blue with the rank of squadron-leader appeared. There was an odd happening. All of us rose to our feet as one, in dramatic salute to this representative of our potential guardian-angels. The squadron-leader, named appropriately H. M. S. Wright, was quite taken aback.

Those among us geared to undertake the film promptly set to work: though with little conviction that we would complete it before the Germans blew us to bits. Michael Powell dealt with Fighter Command, Brian Desmond Hirst with Bomber; the GPO Unit supplied material from factories, it seemed overnight; Alex himself inserted one or two staged scenes with Merle Oberon and Ralph Richardson; and our skilful American film-editor, William Hornbeck, and I compiled a rude opening sequence denigrating Nazism. I fear that we gave an optimistic impression of the strength of the RAF at that time; but if, like poets in Flecker's play, we could be classed as telling lies, we could reply, like his poet Ishak, 'Yah, but we tell excellent lies'. And, a year later, we were to be exonerated by events. Anyhow, after five or six weeks, with Henry Cornelius' energetic help in the cutting-room, we projected a show copy of a feature-length film to the inaugural chiefs of the Ministry of Information, to their stupefaction as to how it had come about.

To historians invited to apply to films the same criteria as to written media, *The Lion has Wings* may not aid them on the road to truth: and I refer to it for these reasons. Whether it was Alex's own idea or whether he had been unofficially prompted to make it, I do not know. What I do know is that he had no financial help from the government; that, stalled by the closure of cinemas, he had to pawn his last life policy to complete the film, as his normal finance was tied up in a major product awaiting exhibition; that those working on it received token fees; that it was released to exhibitors on minimal terms; and that, apart from technical guidance, the content was spontaneous – nothing was imposed by the authorities.

While in charge of this film for Alex, I had become interested in the whole use of film for war ends; and with naive enthusiasm I composed an exhaustive paper which I submitted to the Ministry through a friend in the Films Division. This evoked no response whatever – it was the period of the Phoney War, though perhaps the Poles might have disagreed with the *nomer*.

It was not until the Germans attacked west that, with a new

Minister and Director-General and with the late Jack Beddington, with Sidney Bernstein as adviser, in charge of the Films Division, a stirring of activity became perceptible in the Ministry of Information. A series of 5-minute films to illustrate the war-effort, to be given away to cinemas (now re-opened), was embarked upon under the energetic supervision of Dallas Bower. Persons prominent in feature production were invited to make these at their own risk and allocated £500 per film. Makers were free to choose their subjects and, once these were adopted, there was no pressure nor interference. I was allotted two slots and chose for my first an off-shore fort, then manned by Territorial Army gunners. *Sea-fort* was in a way symbolic of Britain, which we liked to regard as our sturdy island-fortress now that, with the fall of France, we were alone against the Germans. This film was duly released but I ran into trouble with my second, although the subject had been accepted by both the Films Division and War Office PR.

The Army Pioneer Corps had been formed from First World War veterans too old for combat, and refugees anxious to serve, such as Czechoslovaks: and units of the Corps were the last British troops out of Calais at the time of Dunkirk. I thought that their performance warranted some notice; and I put together a composition of factual shots and personal interviews in which men told of their ordeal. The result was considered crude and inartistic by a high official in the Ministry and the film was suppressed. I mention it as being the only case in *my* experience of the official silencing of a film-maker's freedom of expression in the war.

While I was sulking in my suburban tent over this rebuff but, unlike Achilles, wondering how to get *into* the war, my problem was happily solved. Simultaneously I received a request to call at the Ministry, and an invitation to lunch from persons unknown to me.

The purport was the same. The Ministry had now decided on the energetic use of the GPO Film Unit in connection with the war effort and I was invited to manage it. The Unit's history went back to the days of the Empire Marketing Board; and when the Board ceased to function the Unit had been rescued and lodged within the GPO. This was an adroit device for the continuance, and indeed expansion, of its social filming, in that the Post Office's services touched all activities. Following upon Grierson, the Unit had been brilliantly supervised and guided by the Brazilian, Alberto Cavalcanti; and the only reason for his replacement in its wartime role was that he was not a British subject.

My hosts at lunch were the senior members of the Unit – Harry Watt, Jack Holmes and Humphrey Jennings. I am ashamed to confess that I knew nothing of their work: but when afterwards they took me back to their austere headquarters off Soho Square and showed me samples, I was so impressed by the imaginative handling and technical skill that I was scared to accept appointment. I had little experience of non-fictional production, apart from a pious silent film on HRH the Prince of Wales made in the thirties from newsreel material; and obviously I had nothing to teach these resourceful young men about film-making. Photography and recording were superior and I was amazed to learn that their two leading cameramen had, not so long ago, been post-office messengers. There was a truth and vitality in their product which might be vitiated by my fictional mentality; and I felt that these zealots, with their art and aims, must have qualms about accepting a supervisor from the commercial industry. However, if such was their feeling, they concealed it under cordiality; and, as the intention now was to make films for public cinemas as well as for 16mm outlets, I decided to have a go. But I made up my mind on my function: the Unit could get on with *making* the films, while I would fight for facilities, conditions and opportunities. This was to lead in time to my difference with Harry Watt, who felt that I should be in the field at the film director's elbow and not lounging in an office chair; but, with several projects in hand at once, with the need to act as buffer between the Films Division and the Unit, and with my nocturnal rambles as a Civil Defence warden, my attendance continuously on locations and sets was not practicable.

On joining I found that the Unit, even without a producer, had been far from idle. Holmes was completing his *Merchant Seamen*: Jennings had made a pictorially arresting tribute to land workers, *Spring Offensive*; and, with the Germans bombing our Channel ports and shipping and southern airfields in the preliminaries to the Battle of Britain, Watt was down at the coast covering what was now our *Front Line*. I was mostly at the Ministry discussing practical changes, some of which were far from popular with the Unit. 'GPO' seemed to me now an inappropriate name and I asked for the change to 'Crown'. Secondly, I wanted the base moved out of central London, partly because the Soho premises and a mini-studio at Blackheath would prove inadequate; and partly because, in those first days of air attack, every time the sirens sounded, orders were to go to shelters or basements, which made a nonsense of the working day. Fortunately the enemy favoured my wishes, for both of the Unit's sites were soon affected by the bombing; and, by courtesy of Arthur Rank, we were accommodated first in outbuildings of Denham Studios and, later, more adequately at Pinewood. Thirdly, we would need more equipment and at least some secretarial provision; and here I came up against the nucleus of permanent civil servants at the Ministry who dealt with personnel, supplies and expenditure. One official could not take in why lamps might be needed for photography; another, what possible need I could have for a secretary. However, when I explained that I must have a girl to take to Brighton at weekends, I got my secretary (who later developed into the most efficient production manager I could have wished for, one Dora Wright); and there was one civil servant who contrived always to get us what we needed in the long run, the incomparable Fletcher.

Events were now hotting up; the Night Blitz was upon us; it was an obvious subject for an official film-statement in addition to haphazard newsreel shooting; and most of the Unit were turned on to *London Can Take It*, under the direction of Harry Watt and Humphrey Jennings. Good as the pictorial material was, the film's composition and impact were due largely to the American journalist, Quentin Reynolds, to Stewart MacAllister, the editor for the eventual cutting of the film and to Humphrey Jennings for the commentary which was not spoken to the edited film. I think we had Lord Bernstein to thank for Quent Reynolds; and Quent, for his subtle delivery, had to thank Harry Watt's direction. Lord Bernstein also arranged the exhibition of the film in the United States through Warner Brothers; and undoubtedly it awakened American understanding of, and sympathy with, our resolute prosecution of the war, though alone, and perhaps counter-balanced the prognostications of Ambassador Kennedy.

Not many Crown war films may interest current historians, as I shall explain. But *London Can Take It* is of value in conveying the atmosphere of those days. Some may laugh it off as an instance of our British *penchant* for being sorry for ourselves when in trouble, and for parading our woes for devious ends. This brings us to the difference between the ranting Nazi film-propaganda and our . . . shall I say gentler disseminations, for in our case 'propaganda' was officially eschewed as a dirty word. The Nazis would trumpet their might and mercilessness and glory in it as a grim warning. Remember their film *Baptism of Fire*, with its lingering and gloating over a blasted Polish column: and the ratiocinating commentary – shame that Poles should have been condemned to this fate through the stubbornness of false leaders and their trust in treacherous allies! We, on the other hand, plaintively piped our weakness in those first years. But after all this was of a piece with the facts and contrasting attitudes. We had not wanted the war or any war and naturally were unprepared and powerless.

The Blitz evoked other films from Crown. Harry Watt followed *London Can Take It* with *Christmas Under Fire*, which he now regards as spurious. But we were not to know that the Germans would suspend their attacks for the festival. And the film included in picture and sound part of the carol service in King's College Chapel, Cambridge. This was deliberately done in case the building were destroyed, which it well might have been in the later, so-called Baedeker air-raids on precious heritages. And it also contained that marvellous shot of people settling down for the night on an underground station platform which, Heaven knows, was a commonplace sight at the time.

For his follow-up, Humphrey Jennings pursued the Blitz to the Midlands in *Heart of Britain*, to which I refer later. But it was Jack Holmes who truly captured daily life in London during the Luftwaffe attack in *Ordinary People*, a film made only for overseas use but which should have a permanent place in our archives.

With the Nazi abandonment of the Battle of Britain after that last fierce raid in May, 1941, in which RAF night fighters at last made substantial kills, we could turn our attention to counter-activities. Harry Watt had his idea of *Target for To-night* accepted by the Air Ministry and Bomber Command: and from this time for the next 2 years much of the Unit's energies were devoted to 'dramatic documentaries' of routine service activities. This is why I said that many of our films in that period may not be of interest or value to the general historian. It was inevitable that the government film production Unit should be used for this work, with access being desirable to operations rooms and other security-graded premises. The records of our personnel had been carefully checked, and they were subject to the Official Secrets Act.

Several films were devoted to the RAF until they formed their own Unit, and this gave us a chance to bring forward a new set of young directors. While it was Jack Holmes who took charge of the over-elaborate (not our fault) *Coastal Command*, Arthur Elton's younger brother Ralph made *Air Communiqué*, which explained the care taken in estimating enemy losses and the difficulties of securing accuracy. Jack Lee, who had helped Holmes on *Coastal Command*, made *The Pilot is Safe*, featuring the Air–Sea Rescue Service; and Pat Jackson, the pictorially delightful *Ferry Pilot*, which commended the civilian men and women who ferried new aircraft from factory or assembly-point to airfields.

The army from the start of the war had operated a Unit to make training films, but only gradually recruited a second for publicity and information to back up what had been the solitary work of their heroic cameraman, Harry Rignold. Consequently it fell to Crown to commemorate the first North African campaign against the Italians, in *Wavell's 30,000*. John Monck, who had been Robert Flaherty's chief assistant and film-editor on *Man of Arran*, took charge of this, which again could only be a compilation of newsreel-type material with commentary and interviews. And when the Prime Minister came to the Ministry of Information to inspect it, I heard the Old Man growl sultrily 'Why can't they get their facts right?' The reason was the impossibility of learning them. One or two young officers did come back to enlighten us at home, but they knew nothing outside their immediate sector. But at least the film was the first example of the three fighting services co-operating with each other and with our Ministry on a joint information project, which, in the early days, was an achievement in itself.

At last it was realised that the RAF must have its own filming unit, and a strong one, not merely for publicity but for Intelligence, sending cameramen on operations, for instance, to record the accuracy and results of the bombing; and at the start I served the new Unit also in an honorary role, partly to help in the selection of personnel, and partly to continue Ministry liaison. At the same time the three official Units, Army, RAF, and Crown were all lodged together at the Pinewood Studios, sharing office and production facilities. Brendan Bracken was by then our Minister and showed personal interest in the new development, visiting the studios to inspect the composite set-up and view samples of the product. For, as the RAF were now looking after their own affairs, Crown were finding other users of their services.

The Royal Navy were always complaining that they lost out on publicity. This had been partly their own fault through their PR Films Officer's preference for using commercial channels, but was due more particularly to the difficulty of their providing shooting facilities. At a late stage ships were equipped with 16mm cameras but, as their operation was mainly in amateur hands, I doubt if much was gained. Crown now made a feature-length production for them – *Close Quarters*, a documentary in dramatic form of a submarine on patrol. For this, ordinary studio craftsmen constructed a large and elaborate half-section of part of a submarine interior in wood and plaster, to the drawings, and under the supervision, of a woman art director, Peggy Gick. This was so well-made that, on completion of the filming, the Admiralty took it over and re-erected it elsewhere for training use. Jack Lee directed the film which was notable for Lieutenant-Commander Gregory's performance.

Another of our young directors, Julian Spiro, dreamed up a project for the Ministry of Supply, *We Sail at Midnight*, telling of the urgent despatch from a factory in America of a vital machine-tool for Britain. This crafty idea called for a trip to the USA for himself, cameraman and assistant director, and seemed to me a crazy dream. But incredibly it was sanctioned and realised, despite the wartime problem of sea-passage and the even greater teaser of securing permission from American Trade Unions for foreign technicians to work on their manor. Our cameraman, Chick Fowle, used polaroid lenses for the first time; and the spectacle of an American truck hurtling through illuminated Broadway to jazz-type music by Richard Addinsell provided an enlivening change from our black-out, and normally austere production.

Not all Crown films were for the services or civil departments. We were required by our Ministry to commemorate the first *United Nations Day*; and also to record the meeting at sea between the Prime Minister and American President, for the Former Naval Person to present to the latter. To mark the Russian alliance we made *A Tale of Two Cities*, a cross-cut of scenes in London and Moscow under duress. But the films with most impact continued to come from Humphrey Jennings. He followed *Words for Battle*, spoken by Laurence Olivier, with *Listen to Britain*, told without any words at all, in sounds and music, and the making of the film performed a service in itself. It included a lunchtime concert at the National Gallery – a feature of the time – at which Myra Hess was to play with orchestra, and which HM the Queen was to attend. The National Gallery had suffered bomb damage but, with so much work on hand, its repair was not a priority. The proposed filming somewhat accelerated reconstruction.

But there was another quite different and even more valuable film from Humphrey Jennings in my period at Crown. He had the artist's gift of setting up his camera at what might be called the *angle juste*; but his films until now had tended to be a series of static images of places and persons, their effect depending upon symbolic, enigmatic or sometimes epigrammatic juxtapositions of image and sound, worked out by himself and MacAllister in the cutting-room. It was Harry Watt who got me to allot him an action-subject, for the good of Humphrey's soul and the widening of his scope. With qualms I followed his advice: and when the chance came to devote a feature-length film to the Auxiliary Fire Service, I offered it to Jennings. The result was *Fires Were Started* which, despite arguments over the final editing to meet the distributor's views, emerged as a happy blend of realism with poetry. And it proved that Humphrey, who was a marvellously well-organised person, was as able to handle the active as he was the static.

The last feature-length film, the shooting, but not the editing of which was completed in my time was Pat Jackson's masterly *Western Approaches* in colour, inspired by the Battle of the Atlantic. In this case there was more latitude than usual in the casting, for Pat had access to the pool of seamen awaiting ships; and the men 'playing' the torpedoed survivors in the lifeboat provide a cross-section of the kind of men who saved Britain from starvation and paralysis. Moreover, the Unit spent many weeks making the lifeboat sequences in the open sea. The film was widely exhibited in cinemas and in later years was shown on both television channels.

With the clearing of the enemy from North Africa we had reached what was described as 'the end of the beginning' of our prosecution of the war; and I felt that events were now taking over from our sort of action films. They had served as a temporary substitute and had a value apart from any historical aspect. They raised the morale of home audiences: the making of them brought a relief and interest into the lives of servicemen and civilians who appeared in them; and they were reassuring to troops overseas, as, even more so, were the less matter-of-fact subjects. *Listen to Britain* was particularly popular with those serving in Egypt and North Africa, with its nostalgic scenes (including the appearance of Flanagan and Allen), and the visual proof that the spirit at home remained high and resolute.

But now, on the production of the Beveridge Report, I suggested that the Unit should return more to their old role, and prepare films which might be of use in the period of re-construction: but I was told that it was too early. I suggested also that we should assemble selections of the material amassed by ourselves and others into a first rough draft for a Film-History of the War. But after a few days the reply came from Beddington, 'I'm sorry, Dal, but they don't like history'. There were other disappointments. I had the idea of 'A Day in the Commonwealth War Effort', on the lines of the Russian *A Day in the Life of the Soviet Union*. But it was impossible to get the co-operation of many Units of the various dominions which would be essential. Then, as a record of our invasion of North Africa, I planned a film to show it as the total military and civil effort which it was; and indeed we shot a considerable amount of material covering the industrial and organisational preliminaries which made the landings and campaign possible. This material was handed over to the Army Film Unit who were to undertake the actual film production. But, in the event, they ignored it and confined the film to the Services' operations. I began to feel superfluous. I had been over three years in my job and was exhausted. Consequently, when Korda aimed to re-start commercial film production in England and asked for my release to join him, I did not contest it, but was miserable for the rest of the war.

There had been one pleasing development – the attention paid by the Americans to the work of our official Film Units, after their entry into the war. William Wyler for the USAF and I think it was Darryl Zanuck for the US Army, both came over and spent time at Pinewood inspecting what had been done before planning their own operations. With their vast resources in personnel, equipment and money they could do so much better. Our difficulties in making ambitious and sustained products had been severe. Though our technicians were skilled and dedicated they were few and poorly paid. New equipment was almost unobtainable and what we had was subjected to hectic use and somehow had to be kept serviceable. Personnel and equipment in Crown were somehow juggled around by the resourceful Dora Wright who served not only as production manager, but also as a sort of Unit mother. Finally, it must be remembered that, although our major films were in dramatic form, they were denied the depth of a playwright's scenes of interplay of characters. They contained no dialogue not precisely to do with the functional duties of the 'actors', who were all servicemen or servicewomen or ordinary civilians, allotted as available, which gave directors little chance of careful casting. Arising from all this, there was an ingredient which became of vital importance to us – music.

Since our modest budgets did not run to a tithe of normal fees, we came to an arrangement with composers whereby they received a token payment of £50 or £100 according to the length of film, and retained copyright and the right to further use. The impact of our films was thus greatly strengthened by the work of the most thoughtful composers of the day, some of whom, such as Vaughan Williams, had never written for films; and Muir Mathieson was invaluable in guiding and conducting the scores. For *Malta G. C.*, a film which we made as a tribute, even the formidable Sir Arnold Bax contributed the music on Myra Hess's insistence. And when a copy of the film was presented to the island through the then Governor, Lord Gort had the unusual experience for a soldier of being presented also with a musical score, Sir Arnold's original manuscript, which presumably now resides among the rest of Malta's miscellaneous age-old muniments.

Humphrey Jennings made powerful use of music; though I fear that in his *Heart of Britain*, devoted to the Coventry blitzing, his use of the Hallelujah Chorus might have startled Handel. Far from a paean of praise, it sounds like a savage war-cry, for the

English were fed-up with Nazi bestialities. One hears an echo of
'The Sword of the Lord and of Gideon'. And one recalls Kipling's
lines composed in the earlier war:

> It was not part of their blood,
>   It came to them very late
> With long arrears to make good,
>   When the English began to hate.

10 The non-theatrical distribution of films by the Ministry of Information

HELEN FORMAN*

I joined Films Division in June 1940 to work on the re-organisation and expansion of the 16mm mobile film units which had been taken over from the GPO, given hereafter the name 'non-theatrical distribution'. I was therefore not involved in the phoney-war period or as some would say the phoney Ministry of Information period as well. In 1943 I moved over to non-theatrical production and stayed till the end of the war. Throughout the war we enjoyed a great deal of creative freedom. We were not told what to do from on top or plagued with theories about morale. The Ministry of Information had responsibility for enforcing security regulations and issuing 'D' notices and we were aware when it was necessary to check on these. There were, too, many specific home-front campaigns on collecting scrap or digging for victory which were co-ordinated centrally as far as

---

*Lady Forman graduated, as Miss Helen de Mouilpied, from the University of Oxford. After working with S. C. Leslie, one of the pioneers of modern public relations and a major sponsor for the Documentary Movement, joined the non-theatrical distribution organisation of the Documentary Movement at the Imperial Institute, from where she transferred to the Ministry of Information, rising quickly to be a Specialist, and second in charge of the non-theatrical distribution section of the Films Division. From 1943 she worked in the production of documentary films becoming Chief Film Production Officer in 1945 and later contributed a great deal to the development of the British Film Institute as governor.

timing went, through all production divisions and in the regions
by the Chief Information Officers, when films, photographs and
exhibitions were called for at the same time.

Apart from these factors, Films Division and the producers,
directors and writers outside it, generated their ideas for films, or
a whole series of films, by constant debate, argument, our own
research efforts, contact with subject experts, and other
government departments. I will return to the importance of this
below. The Crown Film Unit, which for a time had its own
programme of production, which was not tied in with that of the
Films Division, did the same, though both reported to Jack
Beddington, the Director. I am refering throughout to films
made for showing in Britain.

There was no positive policy imposed on us from above. Films
Division put up its programme. If some project fell down it was
likely to be because the script was not good enough, or events
overtook it, or the right directors and writers were not available,
or because the cost was disproportionate to the theme. Part of this
creative freedom was due to the character of Jack Beddington. He
was a man interested in people and the specific things they
wanted to do. If he was taken with an idea for a film, he would
back it hard. He hated committees and minutes and general
theories. He knew instinctively that it was no good any
administrator saying 'Let there be more of X or Y' – instead you
had to find and build up teams of film makers who felt *themselves*
that X and Y were important and actively wanted to make films
about them.

There were two other factors which should be mentioned.
Films could not be produced as fast as photographs, although
there were instances of films being put together by people
working night and day, in 10 days. Events and people's needs
changed fast and it was necessary to have an alert and
imaginative sense of the next phase. I remember, during 1943, on
one of the rare occasions that I read the minutes of the Ministry
Policy Committee, writing in the margin against some suggested
new policy statement the titles of three films which had already
reached script stage.

The other factor which needs stressing is the constant consultation we had with other government departments. A member of
Films Division, or an outside producer, would spend a great deal
of time discussing immediate problems and future plans with the

Information Officers of the Ministry of Agriculture, or Health or Education and so on. These discussions not only produced ideas for specialised instructional films for non-theatrical distribution, but also much wider themes. For example, for the Ministry of Agriculture we made *Breeding for Winter Milk Production, Silage* and many other instructional films for farmers, but also Green Parks' *Pattern of Britain* series came out of these talks. The Ministry of agriculture reported that the National Farmers' Union felt that the efforts of farmers and farm workers to produce more food at home and indeed to revolutionise farming, were not known, or were taken for granted by the rest of the community. So a series of films about different types of British farming were made: *Fenlands, the Grassy Shires, Cornish Valley Crofters, North East Corner, Downlands.* Some of these were shown in the cinemas – others to large audiences in the factories.

This is only a brief note of some of the processes which led to the production and distribution of films. It bears very little relation to the picture which would be presented by the 'policy' documents which remain in the official files. This reminds me of Kingsley Martin's remark that 'historians are obsessed by written documents and the motivation of statesmen'. Historians have laid much stress on the morale boosting function of the Ministry of Information, as expressed often in papers written, some before the war and others before the blitz. But I must emphasise that as from the end of 1940, Films Division and film makers did not think of their jobs in the simplistic terms of 'raising morale'. We all felt that people were determined to win the war (we all lived in London during the blitz), that exhortation would be impertinent, and what was needed was more information on how to do it.

'Theatrical distribution' was through the cinemas and reached a massive audience in a short time, with 5 minute films, monthly 15 minute releases, newsreels, trailers and features and shorts booked on a commercial basis. For instance a short on how to handle a new type of fire bomb would obviously need to go into all the cinemas at once, and agreements were made by which it could.

'Non-theatrical distribution' was a convenient label for films shown other than in the normal cinema programmes. In August 1940, a Select Committee had judged that the 16mm mobile film units taken over from the GPO were showing films that were 'too educational'. *Documentary Newsletter* ridiculed the idea that it was not proper to educate people in wartime. In fact so united were we all in believing that only by giving people the maximum amount of information and instruction or, if you like, education, could they possibly re-orientate their lives in wartime and understand the changing society around them, that the scheme went ahead, with only a small initial cut in the budget. It expanded so vigorously that by 1942 there were 130 16mm units on the road whereas we had started with only 76 in 1940.

An item in *Documentary Newsletter* of February 1942 gives an idea of the size of this operation. They printed in full an official report, of which I wrote the greater part myself! The figures were based on reports sent in by projectionists to the Regional Film Officers and correlated by them. I can not think now of any reason why we should have wanted to exaggerate the size of the audiences, since the case for the mobile units lay, not in the large numbers of people they would reach, but in the flexible and selective way they could be used.

It was estimated that in the 12 months ended August 1942, an audience of 12 million was reached in three ways:

1. By mobile 16mm units – 6½ million. Later on about one dozen 35mm units were added which could show films to much larger audiences, up to 1000 at a time.
2. By loans of films from the Central Film Library to borrowers with their own projectors – 4½ million. The Central Film Library also supplied all the prints for the mobile units.
3. By shows in cinemas out of ordinary hours – about another million.

What was the purpose of this operation, and how was it run?

There were three main objectives. Firstly, it aimed to show to people in villages who could not get to a cinema, and to workers in factories where shifts and overtime made it unlikely that they would go to a cinema, films like *London Can Take It* or *Target For Tonight* which had already been given theatrical distribution. Secondly, whenever there were specific home front campaigns, like 'Dig For Victory', the campaign film would certainly be included, even if it had already been shown in the cinemas.

Thirdly, it was possible to make and show films with far more detailed information in them than would have been possible to a

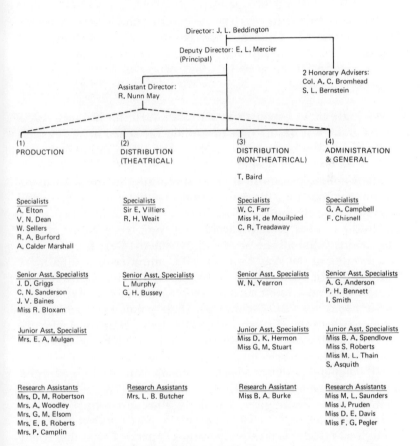

FIGURE 2   The structure of the Ministry of Information Films Division, Summer 1941

Note: This structure changed during the Course of the War.

cinema audience. Subjects could be dealt with at greater length and in greater depth. To quote again from the *Documentary Newsletter* report on non-theatrical distribution.

> It is not their business to provide entertainment. It is their task to provide a constant background of knowledge and inspiration. ... It supplies a continuing education ... The aim behind all the work is to put people in possession of the facts.

What are facts, especially in wartime? Well, for instance *A Job To Be Done* was an attempt to explain the schedule of reserved occupations. It was a good example of a detailed, rather technical film, as was *Control Room*.

The whole approach to non-theatrical production and distribution was based on the assumption that the same people were interested in different things at different times. A man taking his girl to the cinema probably would not want to see *Silage* even if you assumed that all the people in the cinema were farmers. But at a meeting of the War Agricultural Committee or in a Farmers Club, he might be interested and discuss it afterwards. Even films of more general interest such as *Keeping Rabbits for Extra Meat* or *Six Foods for Fitness* could get their points over better at a Womens Institute meeting, it was thought, than in a cinema programme designed primarily to entertain. There was, however, a lot of protest from women's organisations about our programming. They did not want 'special women's films' and I see from a report from one Film Officers Conference in 1942 that I announced we would give up making films on cooking!

Looking back on it, what the official report does not bring out enough was that this diverse operation depended as much, if not more, on the work of the Regional Film Officers as on London. In each of the eight regions into which Britain was divided for Civil Defence purposes, the Ministry of Information had a Chief Information Officer. Under him, Films Division selected and appointed a Film Officer. Our attitude to 16mm distribution was defined by the sort of people we chose as Film Officers. We did not, for example, choose people from advertising or Wardour Street. We looked for people from the *educational* field, university lecturers, teachers, Workers' Educational Association organisers. To give two examples. Austin Duncan-Jones was a lecturer in philosophy at Birmingham. He was Film Officer for the Midlands. Roger Manvell, in charge of the south west, had been lecturing on film at Bristol University. Interest in film, through film society work, or in some other way, was an added qualification.

Film Officers were responsible for all the contacts in their regions which could lead to film shows being booked. We in London would agree on the type of audience we should try to reach, make arrangements with other government departments for back-up help, such as lists of factories and construction sites from the Ministry of Supply, and by supplying the names of organisations in which the departments like Fuel, Food etc. were interested. Or to give another example, we would negotiate in London a new system of showing films for Civil Defence units and the National Fire Service. In 1942 both these services agreed that apart from direct training films, they wanted a more general information programme and they wanted it during the daytime as part of their welfare and educational programme. This was an important decision because it meant that the mobile units could do a whole series of extra shows in the mornings or afternoons, and not only at peak demand time in the evenings. We would send out a note of this new agreement to our Film Officers and the Civil Defence and Fire Services would do the same to their regional organisers.

The existence of the mobile units was vital when considering production, not only of instructional films like the gardening series (not much use showing gardening films to people living in flats in the centre of London), but especially all the instructional films made for specialist audiences. This was true of a whole series of medical and farming films. The audience for such films would usually be small, but I see from a report written by John Maddison, Film Officer of the North Eastern region, that he organised shows of medical films for doctors and nurses in cinemas in Leeds and York, to audiences of 800 to 1500 for each show. The object was to give them some idea how film was being used for popular instruction in social and preventative medicine and to indicate the potential usefulness of film in medical teaching.

The more general programmes for villages and factories were spooled up in London at the Central Film Library, but first there would have to be regular conferences of Film Officers with Films

Division and they would be asked to comment on the programme we suggested *before* it was sent out.

It is very difficult to put together a programme of shorts. Nowadays I would not want to look at more than an hour of one or two reelers. Whether the films are on one theme or not, whether contrasted in style or not, it is easy to get mental indigestion. We did I believe over-estimate the amount of information that could be projected at any one time and made up programmes lasting up to 1½ hours. For factory workers they *had* to be shorter – 25 minutes – allowing time for the meal break.

If, however, any Film Officer found that the general programme did not go down well in his area, he would report it and be told to change the order or leave out a film whose style or commentary was not liked or understood, whether in Yorkshire, Wales or Scotland. The whole operation was flexible in this way.

At the same time there were many reasons, apart from unfamiliar dialect or style, which made films unacceptable. There were formidable technical difficulties in showing 16mm film on the projectors of the day. One was constantly being reminded by Film Officers and by one's own visits that maps and diagrams which looked fine on 35mm in the Ministry cinema, were unintelligible under some conditions in the field. Remember too, that nearly all films were shot on 35mm and reduced to 16mm by the laboratories. This led to people in Films Division on the production side and the film makers themselves visiting factories and other shows to see how films were received and also studying the often appalling conditions under which they were shown – background noise, inadequate blackout and so on.

Uncomplicated soundtracks, clear commentary without music, bold diagrams, these were some of the things we kept nagging on about. Whether we were successful in dealing at the film making end with some of the problems of 16mm projection, it is difficult to say. There was also the problem of those films which were not necessarily aimed at non-theatrical distribution in the first place – films, for instance, which had already been shown in the cinemas or which were planned for cinema distribution but did not get it for various reasons. Also it must be said that at the beginning some film makers were reluctant to make any concessions to 16mm projection.

If the technique of making films for 16mm distribution improved, the 16mm projectors themselves were getting steadily older. John Maddison in the North East claimed in 1945 that four out of five of his original projectors (he had twelve by now) had been in continuous use since 1940. There was a team of travelling inspectors and headquarters maintenance staff but spares became increasingly difficult to get. Remember that the quality of 16mm projectors 30 years ago was not what it is today.

There is no doubt at all that there were technically inadequate shows. I have been to many myself and very embarrassing they were. An issue of *Documentary Newsletter* for 1943 claimed that the following was a description of a fairly typical show to a rural audience:

'Lights please', shouted a voice over the babble of laughter and children's voices. 'Listen children', said the man operating the movie projector, 'for the second time I must remind you that this is a free show given by the Ministry of Information. If you cannot keep quiet you will have to leave. Alright everybody, lights out ... With considerable concentration we could only get a few words in every sentence. The hall was ice cold, and the chairs were hard. The projector squeaked and rattled ...

That, is a fairly typical generalisation. If the majority of shows were like that one can only assume that people had gone out of their minds. But would the demand for shows have increased and for shows at the same places like factories and villages, which were on a regular circuit, if that had been the case? Above all would the Film Officers, who were not remote people in London, but very closely in touch with all local government and voluntary organisations in their areas, have been able to sustain their role in the community? I think not.

What sort of audiences were they? The report published in *Documentary Newsletter* for November 1942 gave a breakdown of audiences of 1224 shows during one week in November, as follows:

408 in factories and construction sites.
230 classified as general shows which probably means villages.
226 for Civil Defence, Fire Service and Home Guard audiences.
78 specialised shows for other departments, agriculture, health, food, fuel.
114 to women's organisations.

84   to schools.
46   to youth organisations.
22   to service and US Army and 16 miscellaneous.

Into broader categories, it worked out that one third of the shows each week were in factories, the majority of which had a show a month. One third were to women's organisations, villages and groups in small country towns, where the aim was to give a show every two months. The rest were much more specialised and not organised on a regular monthly or two-monthly basis.

If you go through the lists of films made specifically for non-theatrical distribution, you will find that a great many were concerned with reporting either on what other parts of the community were doing, for instance *Coal Front, Air Operation, Coastal Defence*. Or they were attempting to show the wider implications of a routine job which the audience watching the film was doing, such as *Worker and Warfront*. One of the NT films under the heading of 'general' in our jargon which was liked and applauded was Humphrey Jennings' magical *Listen to Britain*. All sorts of audiences felt it to be a distillation and also a magnification of their own experience of the home front. This was especially true of factory audiences. I remember one show in a factory in the Midlands where about 800 workers clapped and stamped approval. Films got very short shrift if they touched any area of people's experience and did not ring true. Except for factories, 800–1000 would be an exceptionally large audience. The average was estimated at 100. Between 1940 and 1943 more footage of film was produced for non-theatrical distribution than for cinema showing.

But did we know what audiences made of these films and what effect they had on them? The answer I believe must be no, in the sense that no scientific audience reaction research was carried out.*

---

*Tom Harrisson subsequently said in his talk at the Conference that this was not true and described the work of Mass-Observation. But I was not referring to films made primarily for distribution in the ordinary cinema programmes, which were the only ones Mass-Observation reported on. Further, it should be noted that the reports quoted were predominantly about films made or planned very early on in the war, before various upheavals in film making took place.

Our only clues were:

(a) The Film Officers who attended many more of the shows than we could from London, and who reported when films were not liked and also when people wanted more films on a given subject. These reports were supplemented by our own visits.

(b) The fact that they were asked to show films regularly. There was no *compulsion* on anyone to book shows or attend them, except possibly in Civil Defence and the Fire Service, when the shows took place in duty time as part of what was called their welfare and educational programme, fire and blitz permitting. Films in schools would also be shown in working time. People who went to the cinema to see a feature film *had* to see the short, whether they liked it or not, whereas the organisers of film shows made up of documentary films would not re-book unless the audience liked them. Very often films were pre-viewed by the organiser before booking.

(c) The specialised shows were often attended by a speaker, which meant there could be more discussion on the subjects. In the winter of 1942/3 I went with Jack Beddington and Austin Duncan-Jones round a number of farmers' shows, where the War Agricultural Committee speaker led a debate afterwards.

You could only get farmers together in the winter, of course. It was incredibly cold and uncomfortable and Jack Beddington was bored stiff. It was not his line, but the fact that he agreed to come, shows the importance attached to these small gatherings. Twenty would be a good audience.

No-one can possibly say whether more milk was produced as a result or whether children's eyes, ears and teeth were better looked after when those admirable films by Margaret Thompson were shown in clinics. You may well say that as far as the general shows in factories were concerned, the people stayed there because they had nothing else to do. May be. But is there any evidence about how many of the 25 million a week who went to the cinema in the thirties went because they had nothing else to do, or went because the cinema was warm, had thick pile carpets and you could make love to your girl there? Our audiences had no such comforts. If the factory audiences not only stayed to watch, but came back again to the next monthly show, if the village audiences turned out in the blackout to sit on very hard chairs to watch prints which were often not in mint condition, they must have got something out of it. There are probably, in the sacks of documents about the Ministry of Information, reports from Film Officers on the reception of individual films and someone should hunt them out. These are the real clues to the effect of these films.

I think the thing that shines through all this activity is a belief, which was universal during the war, that more information about the working of our society, more education on health, welfare, industrial jobs, country jobs, was a good thing. This was what we all believed before the war. The war added a new sense of urgency to the task, and greatly increased the amount of public money which was made available for production and distribution.

The Select Committee of August 1940 has described the existing non-theatrical scheme as 'too educational'. It was continued in spite of this and to the best of our ability continued to be educational – if by that is meant giving people the why and wherefore on all subjects within the limits of the security regulations. The desire to know more about the present and to speculate about the future was not an invention of Films Division, or of the film makers. It was basically a response to the needs of a people at war to know the why and how of things as never before. There were few rhetorical appeals in these programmes. It was asssumed anyway from the autumn of 1940 by Films Division and by the documentary movement that ordinary people had determined to finish the job of winning the war. What they wanted was some practical information which would help them to do it. This was reflected in our own activities and in the huge demands made by other government departments for information film.

There was also a nationwide feeling that all the effort and the killing must lead to something better. There was much debate about the social problem, which the war itself had laid open to public view, abruptly and dramatically. This debate went on also in government departments and in the Coalition Government itself. For example, evacuation. For the first time it came home to many people that a lot of children could not read, that their health was not good, that they ate the wrong foods; and there was also the problem of illiteracy among conscript soldiers. The blitz had revealed some appalling housing conditions in the cities. The documentary films which looked to the future, in education, housing, employment, town planning were projecting this public concern. The 'never again' theme was not invented by the documentary film makers and Films Division, it was recorded by them – and also recognised in part by the Coalition Government which published the Beveridge Report in 1943 and put through the Butler Education Act of 1944.

It was a belief held then and which I hold now, that by more information and education a democratic society can survive a war and make a peace. For those too young to remember Britain in wartime, it is difficult to re-create this atmosphere. Perhaps films that can be studied, good, bad and indifferent, but especially the good ones will help to do so.

11 Films and the Home Front – the evaluation of their effectiveness by 'Mass-Observation' *

TOM HARRISSON[†]

I am in a slightly difficult position here and I should like to explain myself a little before coming to my subject. In the nature of things what I am talking about always tends to be critical; and, further, it is based on material collected by Mass-Observation 30 years ago – since when I have spent 25 years living in South-East Asia. I have come back from the jungle to this old vomit, now housed in the University of Sussex as a separate archive. It is not always easy to interpret it properly today. So I am going to rely mainly on a long series of typewritten documents (what we call

---

*Transcript. Tom Harrisson died before he could prepare this paper for publication. The editors thought it appropriate to include it as delivered, with only a minimum of alterations.

†Tom Harrisson, DSO, OBE, after graduating from the University of Cambridge, explored Borneo and other areas as an anthropologist before returning to England in 1937. Co-founder of Mass-Observation, a research organisation studying the social habits of the natives of England and publishing the results in a racy and popular form. Served in the Ministry of Information, 1940–2, thereafter in the army as a parachute officer on special service behind the Japanese lines in Borneo and Sarawak. Taught in several universities as a visiting professor as well as conducting research into a wide range of subjects. Died 1976. His publications include *Savage Civilisation* (1937), *Living amongst Cannibals* (1937), *Mass-Observation* (1938), *Britain by Mass-Observation* (1939), *War Begins at Home* (1940), *Home Propaganda* (1941), *People in Production* (1942) and *Britain Revisited* (1959) and 17 other books. Produced with Hugh Gibbs the award-winning film series *The Borneo Story*.

file reports in our archive) done principally for the Ministry of Information. Curiously enough, I have never been able to find my letter of employment from them. But Dr Ian McLaine has discovered it in the Public Record Office. It is so typical of the whole Ministry of Information set-up that it was signed by Leigh Ashton, later distinguished Director of the Victoria and Albert Museum. I did not even know he was in Bloomsbury's war-time Tower of White Words.

I want to begin by emphasising one point about Mass-Observation. It was started in 1937 with Charles Madge, poet and reporter, and Humphrey Jennings, whose films we have seen much in this conference and who, on our audience responses, was one of those whose films were most effective public-wise. As well as Humphrey Jennings we were deeply mixed up from the very beginning with Stuart Legge, Arthur Elton, Basil Wright and Jack Holmes; those especially. So from the beginning film was of the highest interest to us, we were film-minded. I am also interested in film myself, though terribly out of touch – with film in this country since the war having lived in Borneo. The 12 films I made myself have all been about South-East Asia.

So, already before the war and partly because of Humphrey Jennings, who to my mind was one of the real – I do not think it is too strong a word to use – intellectual geniuses of our time, we started a lot of film observation, working out techniques for observing people's responses and behaviour in cinemas. Already by the beginning of the war we had a quite considerable experience – and, incidentally, our first customer in this field was then Sidney Bernstein, here today as Lord Bernstein.

When the war came we immediately started diagnosing films in this sort of way. We did, or tried to do, two things. First, we always tried to preview the film that we were going to study. In the case of the Ministry of Information films that was easy, because they showed them to us. (I was surprised that Helen Forman seemed to say, earlier in the Conference, that there was really no good intelligence in the Ministry of Information about film reactions. Several of our Mass-Observation reports ran to many pages.) What we did was in the first place to preview the film and break it down into a series of sequences, usually in a longish film 60 or 70 – it depended on the film of course. We had a standard set of reaction patterns, of how the audience responded in the cinema, such as applause, hissing, booing and so on to each of the sequence patterns and we sent this out to our investigators. You may think that slightly academic; but built up over a period of time it told us a good deal. Basically, of course, the approach was mildly academic. We did not try to please the Ministry of Information: we tried to satisfy ourselves, like any good research workers must, in any academe.

Secondly, we recorded conversations, we recorded people coming out of the cinema, and we talked to people. We did not normally believe in direct interviewing, but we did talk to people coming out of the cinema about the films they had just seen, then spontaneously criticised.

Thirdly, we had a national panel of voluntary observers, a self-selected panel, of about 2000 who would report on film or anything else we wanted in their district.

The response sheet we used listed along the top the sequences of the film. In the case of *The Lion Has Wings*, for example, this came to 50 sequences. We attached to it the summary of the investigators' reports – 25 in the case of *The Lion Has Wings*. In each column we tabulated all the responses to one sequence.

We were then very much in the same position, incidentally, as was the film industry at the beginning of the war. We also were nearly bankrupt and almost out of business. It was a very difficult time. But on 4 April 1940, Leigh Ashton wrote that letter and started us working for the Ministry of Information specifically. We continued to do that solidly for nearly two years and had many *ad hoc* jobs for them right through the war, as well as for other government departments too.

The government's Social Survey did not tackle this sort of problem. First, it did not get going until late in 1940; and, secondly, it was a highly technical and efficient statistical questionnaire survey machine, with a different sort of approach, very important but separate functions. They did some major surveys of film *audiences* (not responses) in wartime, the most important of which are published in a book by Kathleen Box, whom they recruited from us to work on this project for several years, with Leonard Moss. There are two books by them; the main one is *The Cinema Audience*.

I should like to distinguish, from the present point of view, three sorts of film: (1) war 'features'; (2) newsreels; and (3) the Ministry of Information documentary material, the Ministry shorts and such like.

If I may dash briefly over war feature films. They were important, some of them very important. We have not really had very much about that in this conference. We started by studying *The Lion Has Wings*: if you remember, Ian Dalrymple wrote the story and was associate producer with Alexander Korda. Merle Oberon starred. It was our first opportunity thoroughly to study a war situation on film in the war. We found, very broadly, a considerable body of favourable response, but a lot of detailed criticism. The criticism was largely of the commentary, which was by E. V. H. Emmett of the newsreels. As I shall point out in a minute, people were already beginning to have an awful lot of that sort of peppy talk, and there was a disappointment with it. The sort of remark one got on *The Lion* – something that from now on kept emerging more and more as the war went on – was a woman saying, 'It was all propaganda. Nobody wants to see that sort of thing – you get enough of it on the newsreels'. Or a middle-class woman of 25: 'Rotten – too much propaganda.' Or a young unskilled worker: 'I think it's un-British to shove propaganda down your throat like that.'

Well, people soon learnt to be un-British. In a certain way, the whole war was that. We concluded that *The Lion Has Wings* really misfired rather badly and I think that most people would agree. I had very much hoped to get hold of a copy to show here what I mean, because it is a very good case of hamming, under-estimating the intelligence of your audience, plus a sort of mock heroism which comes into a great many films about the war, including some of the documentaries. No copy is available, alas.

A contrast at that time was a film George Formby made, *Let George Do It*, a comedy in which he became a secret service agent, went to Norway to crack a code, captured a German submarine and much more. This film was well received. From the start of the war, we find comedy getting across again and again, putting the stuff over; Will Hay likewise. Looking back with hindsight, one is rather surprised that so few seriously motivated films sufficiently used comedy – though a few did very well that way. The George Formby film *Let George Do It* got at people much more than *The Lion Has Wings* and yet did not try to, whereas *The Lion Has Wings* did try – too hard, perhaps. We also made an analysis of Press criticism of films at the same time as we observed. The Press was rapturous about *The Lion Has Wings*; it was a perfect Establishment picture. There was very little unfavourable criticism. But the Press was far from rapturous about *Let George Do It*. A considerable section – 5 out of 24 of the main critics – actually wrote that the film was in bad taste. But that was not mentioned in audience response reports. For the mass audience largely had that same taste.

Incidentally, the joke that people most liked in *Let George Do It* – we analysed from those sheets, among other things, the biggest laugh, the biggest applause, the biggest boo, and so on – was when Formby knocked out Hitler and suddenly all the stormtroopers cheered like mad – a terrific cheer. This was one of the big laughs of the year in films. About that time the *Sunday Dispatch* (now defunct) held a competition for the best joke ever on a film; people had to remember and send it in. We got 1865 response letters from the *Sunday Dispatch* and analysed them for the paper. The biggest laugh was for Charles Laughton as the butler in *Ruggles of Red Gap*, made in 1935, so it had been long remembered in 1940. It was rather the same situation – I do not know if anyone will remember it – as Charles Laughton is drinking away steadily, silent deadpan, soaking the stuff back, then suddenly he lets out a terrific 'Yippee'. This convulsed people.

There were a lot of other feature war films at that time that I have not time to go into here. Thorold Dickinson told the story that there was a change of government policy about all Germans being bad, which is no doubt correct. It is interesting to note in that context that there was a whole series of feature films in 1940/1 dealing with Germany in one way or another, such as *The Mortal Storm, Pastor Hall, I Was Captive in Nazi Germany, Hitler: Beast of Berlin, Night Train to Munich*, and so on. Except in one film, which was made in Russia, the main German characters were always simply misguided people who got lured into Fascism. There were black Germans, really bad, such as heads of concentration camps, but they were never the *major* German characters. This is another subject. But at no stage in the war, according to our Mass-Observation archive material, did people ever stop thinking that there were a great many good Germans, despite the violent emphasis of many newsreels.

Let us come secondly to the newsreels. Nicholas Pronay has put the broad picture there very clearly. But perhaps I could take very briefly the results of studying 190 newsreels in the first 9 months of 1940. The thing that showed most strikingly as a trend over that period, was a tremendous decline in esteem for the newsreel. It went down from about 60 to 65 per cent of general liking for newsreels in January (the value is only comparative, recording the same thing in the same cinema in the same way on the same day week after week) to only 25 per cent by September 1940. A form of positive distaste, which the English do not easily express in public (especially to an interviewer or somebody they have never met before) rose from 15 to 50 per cent, a very high figure – especially in wartime and especially as the newsreels evidently thought they were being super-patriotic and perfectly expressing the public mood. The newsreels, on our evidence, gravely over-played the war emphasis. People just got fed up with that.

'Fed-upness' is always a factor in going to a cinema or anywhere else, even in going to a cinema on purpose to see something and sit right through it; you will accept it even if in the end you do not like it. But there was an extra capacity developed during the war to switch yourself off pretty completely from something you did not like. It was part of the whole 'thing' of morale. The idea of morale as people going round cheerfully and putting their thumbs up, the official view, was very superficial. Part of good morale, *the ability to endure in any circumstance*, is the ability to switch yourself off completely. It was a very necessary quality, which a great many British were and still are rather good at anyway, (e.g. in politics).

The thing that I think put most people off with newsreels (and we got this again and again) was that the material was stuffed with over-commentary, too much talk, the inability to stop spouting heavy words. As one can see from the war newsreels shown since, when they are not talking, they are putting words on the screen, as if nobody can see anything or can understand anything for themselves, you have to keep on telling them, over-telling them what it is. Emmett and Leslie Mitchell eventually ended up producing a sort of phonetic nausea in people – which is also rather pleasant in itself, of course.

We had some interesting experiences with 'faking' in newsreels, incidentally. Our investigators, would pick up the same shots differently presented in two different newsreels. There is a nice example in one of our reports. On the evacuation from Dunkirk, Paramount showed British Tommies landing in Dover, and the momentarily depressed commentary goes: 'One look at them shows what they have been through.' But Gaumont-British had almost the same shot at the same place, of cheerful English Tommies, all carefully coached, with commentary. 'These shots, all taken *at random* show laughing faces.' On the same day in two different cinemas.

We reported such faking to Home Intelligence, then run by Mrs Mary Adams, who played a major part in setting up Home Intelligence and made a major contribution to the Ministry of Information. She was from the BBC. She brought several things into being, such as the Social Survey. She had good relations with Jack Beddington in the Films Division and was feeding information in all directions.

One of the best cases of faking was in the Finnish War. At one stage they were showing villages burning and the bombing of Helsingfors with no snow on the ground, whereas that same day the radio had announced it was impossible for the Russians to bomb Helsingfors because there was so much snow falling. We suspected these were shots from the Spanish Civil War. There was a weird correspondence with Sir Edward Villiers on that.

Enough about newsreels. Now I come to the third group, which will probably get me into some trouble here this morning, – the Ministry of Information official shorts and documentaries. As I have said, we covered many of these, we have boxes of material on these films. I think that I am right in saying that except for *The First Days* nothing much really came onto the screen until about May or June 1940. We then covered 15 Ministry shorts plus separate GPO Film Unit releases (before the GPO Film Unit was brought into the Ministry) as they were coming out. These films were initially received with great enthusiasm, partly because the newsreels had done themselves much harm – and incidentally, they were realising it, by this time and had become interested in our researches. They were starting to put out their own news documentaries, one of which for example was an erratic report about the Fifth Column in July 1940, with Attlee at the end of it talking heavy.

The Ministry of Information therefore came in on a very good wicket there, and a high level of potentially favourable response was directed to their films at the beginning, rebounding off newsreel distaste. Constantly, all through our material, Ministry shorts and pictures were liked. People were ready to be on the side of these films. They started with goodwill, they produced some very nice pictures to begin with and then – this is very important in marketing or anything else – they kept this kind of image. Even the bad films, the films that were not liked were never subject to the level of dislike that the newsreels were, and such as *The Lion Has Wings* to some extent, along with some of the other feature films.

Having said that, the people would then often show, (a) by their reaction to a film, which would be a very low threshold indeed compared with what one might expect, or (b) in their verbal discussions afterwards, that they were not satisfied with this one or that one. There was soon a lot of criticism. Already by the middle of 1940 people had become extremely conscious of this thing called propaganda. I could give you hundreds of quotations from people, of the sort I gave you just now about propaganda. It was not exactly that they did not 'like' it but that they were uncomfortably detecting it, and this was where the switching off came in. Many were disappointed that there was more visible 'propaganda' in the Ministry films than they at first expected.

Secondly, the criticism mounts and continues, on over-use of words and commentary. In some ways official documentaries took over a great deal from the newsreels and previous forms; there seemed to be an almost compulsive necessity to keep talking in many of the pictures. Much of the public did not really want that; they were more interested in the pictures themselves.

In the latter part of 1940, we thought we would try to do something different from mere observation, and we asked our national panel all over the country to tell us which of the films they had seen so far they liked the best. We established, of course, that they had seen them. Most of these people anyway went to the cinema regularly. Easily first on the panel list came *London Can Take It;* a very good second came Thorold Dickinson's *Miss Grant Goes to the Door,* third, a film I had completely forgotten called *Dai Jones;* fourth, *Men of the Lightship;* fifth, but now getting very mixed reactions, a comedy called, *Eating Out with Tommy Trinder;* sixth, *Home Guard.*

I have not the time to go into all the sort of things said about this, but let me skip quickly through a few individual films with some points on them. We found that films about the sea and the Navy always got a very good reaction – *Ships With Wings,* for instance, was tremendous. This is coming well into 1941. On the whole, from our material, the Navy came well out of the whole war, which was very important to them and actually important to me too, because by this time I was also working for the Director of Naval Intelligence, an extremely intelligent man, Admiral John Godfrey who was keen on modern survey methods years before his time. We paid special attention to naval things and we did one rather interesting survey when Admiral Godfrey asked us to do a proper statistical sample interviewing, which we did not normally do. *Ships With Wings* received a general 80 per cent approval and liking, very high. But in seaports – we did special samples of women because the Admiralty were worried about the morale of sailors' wives and we interviewed sailors' wives and others in seaport towns – it received 96 per cent approval, which is about the highest we ever had for anything. It is difficult to get 96 per cent of the British even to give an opinion, for that matter.

Newspaper Train was another interesting film with Len Lye's animated cartoons. This sort of film, we discovered, was liked, even though there was a little bit of disappointment; his was said to over-emphasise commentary. *War in the Pacific* was an interesting film, because it almost entirely relied on maps. It did not have too much talk, though again, it might have done with even less; it did not try to get any particular message across, except that the war was very difficult with Japan. It showed it on maps. And this was one of the few times when we could really say that there was a measurable *effect* from the film: it informed some people. So far I have been talking mostly about liking and disliking; now we come to the much more difficult subject of what such films really *did* to people. *War in the Pacific* made some people feel that they understood something they had not really understood before. Of course, in these days of television that sort of information is put across constantly; but it was not then.

I am surprised, in hindsight, that a lot more films were not made in that way – instead of talking and having those pastoral situations with Bernard Miles and so on. You are patronising ordinary people by giving them that sort of thing. I mention this because John Boulting in a recent television interview had claimed that Bernard Miles in *Dawn Guard* had made a major contribution to the war effort, to peace ideals and so on. I would say exactly the contrary – and we have a report on it; many thought it cheap and stupid.[1] I have to say – and being one myself it is rather easy for me to say it – that the mistake came from a sort of upper middle-class intellectualism out of which group the very clever and nice people who then made films were primarily recruited. We had the greatest difficulty in those days in really looking at working-class and ordinary situations without doing something to them in that way, without thinking that they had better be pastoralised, patronised, whatever you like to call it. That in fact was one of the reasons we started Mass-Observation – to try to get over that difficulty. This was an aspect in which Humphrey Jennings himself was always absorbed.

There was another interesting, much liked film by Paul Rotha, called *An Ounce a Day*, in which he used diagrams entirely. These types of films were very important; there were a few of them. Incidentally, I cannot resist telling you something else rather amusing. We have heard a lot about Jack Beddington and his good nature – and what a liberal man he was. I got a different impression of Jack Beddington. Perhaps he did not like my reports? I liked Jack Beddington, but he was a tough egg in a certain way. That was his great power. This is our Report No. 639 of 5 April 1941, on the film *You're Telling Me*, made by Paul Rotha in March 1941. I got this back from Mary Adams, who has given her war papers to our archive in Sussex University, and very valuable they are, too. There is a note by me to her sending her the carbon of 639, saying, 'This is a report done for Paul Rotha. Strictly Private and Confidential. He is *afraid* of Beddington.' Maybe our reports were just torn up when they arrived and nobody saw them, but that one survived in that form!

I have taken up enough time now, trying too quickly to give my impressions from a mass of observation. I should like to end by summarising. Our observations of films in general showed that Ministry of Information shorts were liked generally. They were usually treated with respect; they were never automatically put in a bad category; people were ready to love the good ones. But whenever we tried to measure them – say, a specific film on savings, waste, gas masks or something like that – we could only conclude that it had practically no lasting *effect*. That would not apply to the sort of films Helen Forman was talking about – the specialist films and the films made to do something for a certain group. I am talking about the general theatre public, which we studied. That was our brief: we were not concerned with anything else.

When it comes to more *general* films, to morale boosting and so on, I do not think that there was any significant effect either.

Morale is not, in my view – and I spent years studying it in those days – affected by things like films. Pints of beer affect morale; being healthy and all kinds of other things affect morale. But official films never really came into it in people's own estimate of what affected them in the crunch. Morale was completely unanalysed and basically misunderstood. From the beginning we were supposed to be dealing with a disease, or an illness, or a wellness – but nobody knew what it was. Was it like schizophrenia, hypochondria, arterio-sclerosis, tertiary syphilis? We just gave war medicines; no one diagnosed. In my view, looking back, it was events and experiences and people's own innate feelings that determined morale. Not only that – there were about 45 million morales in England, not just one. People did not really change at all in the war; they just had to do different things because there was a war.

Helen Forman said that in the Ministry of Information we were not given any directions from above and that anyway we were not plagued by theories about morale. She was not plagued by theories about morale because there were not any theories about morale to be plagued by. I have been trying every way to find out whether anybody ever really sat down and worked out what morale was. I even had a letter from Dick Crossman this morning about it, he was highly mixed up in all that.[2] Like everybody else, he says nobody managed to work out a definition of morale. The 'propaganda' and commentary was mis-directed at nothing, at no-one, so to speak.

I think films made a much more important contribution in just giving people a wholesome, liberal, democratic – or whatever you like – attitude to life. They did develop a style: the Ministry style, which was absolutely British and quite stylish. People appreciated that, and it had a long-term influence. It also led directly to the good style of BBC, Granada and other television which has enlarged people's outlooks since.

But, looked at in the short term, on the spot, in the war, neither films nor posters, nor leaflets, nor any other form of *deliberate* propaganda directed on the home front really mattered at all. The war, morale and all that was going on at another level. That is all I can conclude, and you can shoot me down.

NOTES. (Answers to questions from the floor.)

1 There was a sort of self-intoxication in films among film-makers. There was a great deal of expressed satisfaction and little self-criticism in public. A very good example of that was *Documentary Newsletter*, a splendid magazine. But here is what they said about *Dawn Guard*, which as far as I can see nearly everyone here thinks lousy: 'This is one of the best of the five minute films because it so sincerely and simply tells something deep in our hearts.'

2 I was actually on a thing called the Morale Committee. I was a sort of observer. It consisted, as I recall it, of Julian Huxley, Dick Crossman, Lady Grigg, Tom Hopkinson (Editor of *Picture Post*), Edward Glover (then a top psychiatrist) and Lord Horder, the King's Surgeon. We used to sit for hours at a time arguing as to whether we could ever get a definition of morale. We never did. (Answers to questions from the floor.)

PART IV
The projection of the Soviet Union

12 Soviet documentary film, 1917–40

SERGEI DROBASHENKO

Documentary cinema as an aesthetic phenomenon has played a noteworthy and in certain periods a decisive role in the history of culture. The Great October Socialist Revolution of 1917, the Civil War battles, the early successes of the young socialist republic, the heroic work of the people, the first signs of a new way of life – all these were recorded on celluloid film long before the first Soviet live-action pictures were shot. Topicality, close connection with the problems of the day, vivid depiction of social and political changes determined the important place occupied by newsreels and documentary films in the history not only of cinematic art but also of Soviet culture in general. But, what is the measure of 'true-to-lifeness' that is necessary to make a shot or a whole picture a piece of historical evidence? Are there any specific properties or peculiarities in documentary cinema that transform reality and affect the historical value of the material used in a documentary film? The answers are not as simple as it may seem at first glance.

The problem is complicated, and to a certain extent paradoxical. Even such a devoted proponent of documentary cinema as Dziga Vertov, who saw in it a 'mirror of the epoch', at the same time stated in most definite terms that facts on the screen are not catalogued, but analysed and synthesised, and this does not diminish their historical authenticity. A fleeting moment of life captured by the camera, said Vertov, is already a document, whether or not it bears a registration number. A dog trotting along a street will remain a visible fact even if we do not run after it and read what is written on its collar.[1] For Vertov montage was a means for evolving a generalising poetical meaning from facts.

A documentary shot, in his opinion, did not necessarily have to provide answers to a whole questionnaire: when? where? why? etc. But is it not precisely this that makes a documentary film a document, that makes it possible to treat it as authentic historical material?

This was the point on which Victor Shklovsky disagreed with Dziga Vertov. Shklovsky said he would like to have known the number of the locomotive that he saw lying on its side in a Vertov film. In his article 'Where Is Dziga Vertov Going?' Shklovsky wrote: 'Film chronicle must contain a caption, a date . . . Dziga Vertov cuts his material. His work in this respect is not progressive artistically.'[2]

It is also of interest that Sergei Eisenstein, who made many of the shots in his own films look as if they were documentary, and who valued highly the role of documentary film in the overall development of film art, was intransigent in his polemics with Vertov and refused to admit the positive influence of 'kinopravda' methods on live-action cinema. Eisenstein's article 'On the Problem of the Materialist Approach to Form' (1925) described the Vertov group's methodology as 'primitive impressionism' and insisted that 'kinoglaz' (film eye) could not carry out the task, set by the revolution, of 'ploughing' the public's psychology 'in accordance with the requirements of the class struggle'.[3] Vertov, in his turn, considered Eisenstein's films to be 'intermediate cinema' and called them 'fiction pictures in documentary trousers' which were denied the virtues of both pure fiction and pure documentary.

Another outstanding director of the first post-revolutionary years, Lev Kuleshov, strongly doubted the right of a documentary film maker to interpret facts. 'A news film', he wrote in his article 'Today's Screen', 'must show events as they happen, and the montage in this case is determined not by the author but solely by the material itself'.[4] A clear-cut attitude bordering on absurdity was taken by the writer Sergei Tretyakov who, following in Kuleshov's wake, advised documentary film director Esfir Shub to put her camera into a wall, which would, in his opinion, prevent possible 'distortion' of facts.[5]

All these most complicated problems could not help but result in a multitude of often contradictory methods in practical film-making. In the first years after the revolution the new aesthetics in many ways moved forward as if blindfolded. They had to deal with a new kind of material, the reflection of reality on the screen. There were also at least two circumstances that made the task still harder: this complex problem had to be tackled in the conditions of the rapid development of a new society and the progress of film art, which was itself equally impetuous. No wonder then that the ideas born in that difficult period, on the one hand, had an undoubtedly significant impact on the subsequent development of cinematic art and, on the other hand were, at that early stage, in many cases only sketched, or outlined, and required serious and profound elaboration at a later date.

Thus we are going to dwell on the relationships between film and reality, on the possibility of treating a documentary picture as part of the historical evidence.

The first films produced in Soviet Russia after the revolution in October 1917 were newsreels. Very soon after Soviet power was established in Petrograd, attempts were made to use the cinema as a medium of political information. On the night of 26 October (8 November by the calender now in use), 1917, the Second All-Russian Congress of Soviets completed its work. It proclaimed the establishment of Soviet power and confirmed the composition of the first Soviet Government. The delegates went home to different towns and villages of Russia with Lenin's words still in their ears. In his book *Ten Days that Shook the World* John Reed quotes Lenin as saying to the delegates: 'We have no time to lose . . . Tomorrow morning all Russia must hear the news of colossal significance'.[6] At the same time People's Commissar of Education, Anatoly Lunacharsky signed P. Novitsky's and G. Boltyansky's credentials that gave them the right to photograph in and around Petrograd, the capital of the Revolution. On Lunacharsky's recommendation the two cameramen shot the sites of the major events in Petrograd: the headquarters of the revolution at Smolny, the cruiser *Aurora* on the Neva, the last refuge of the Provisional Government at the Winter Palace. Then Novitsky went to Gatchina outside Petrograd where revolutionary forces were getting ready to fight the cossacks of General Krasnov.

The first newsreel produced in Soviet Russia soon after the revolution was *Kinonedelya* (Film Week). It was made and released by the Moscow Film Committee's News Department in 1918 and 1919. During these two years 43 issues of the newsreel appeared. *Kinonedelya*, supervised first by journalist Mikhail Koltsov and then by film director Dziga Vertov, came out four

times a month. The newsreel was half the 100–150 metres length
of today's *Novosti Dnya* (News of the Day). It usually contained
five or six, sometimes seven, episodes on various subjects.
Kinonedelya retained, in most of its episodes, the time-proven
style of pre-revolutionary newsreels with a dose of sensationalism
and entertainment: 'People Merry-Making in Devichy Field' (no.
1), 'Procession on St Nicholas' Day' (no. 2), 'A Tremendous
Catastrophe in the Zoological Garden' (no. 13), 'Fire at Kursk
Railway Workshops' (no. 31), etc. Often there was information
connected with the after-effects of the World War from which
Russia had withdrawn only several months before: 'Orsha. People
Returning to Formerly German-Occupied Territories' (no. 5),
'Crippled Soldiers Returning from Austrian Prison Camps' (no.
6), 'Russian Prisoners of War Returning from Germany' (no. 43).[7]
   Nevertheless even in these earliest newsreels one can trace what
most definitely dominated the social scene: revolutionary demon-
strations and parades, Civil War battles, portraits of political
figures, the emergence of a new way of life. The captions began
to carry a political appreciation of events: 'Moscow. June 21.
Workers'   Appeal   to   Defend   the   Socialist   Motherland'
(*Kinonedelya*, no. 4), 'Funeral of Red Army Communists Killed
in Yaroslavl in Fight Against White Guards' (no. 10), 'Fierce
Fighting Continues on the Soviet Republic's Frontlines, the
Enemy Forces Are on the Alert, and We Have to Keep a Watch-
ful Eye on Them' (no. 28), 'Sacrifice for the Revolution's Sake'
(no. 34), etc. Unqualified representation of events was giving way
to ideological judgment of them, directed, as all other means of
propaganda, at consolidating and strengthening the forces of the
revolution.
   Of special interest for the student of the history of culture are
the episodes in *Kinonedelya* that reflect the artistic life of the
period. Few people know, for instance, that in *Kinonedelya* one
can see documentary shots of Fyodor Shalyapin's concert for the
workers of Orekhovo-Zuyevo in August 1918 (no. 12), one of the
few shots of the poet Sergei Yesenin (no. 25), and the film star
Vera Kholodnaya's funeral in Odessa on 3 February 1919 (no.
40). Another newsreel, *Kinopravda*, featured in its sixteenth issue
an episode called 'Springtime Smiles of the Proletkult' which
contained *Glumov's Diary*, the first film directed by Sergei
Eisenstein, a short he made with Ivan Pyryev, Grigory
Alexandrov, Maxim Shtraukh and several other future stars of

Soviet film art for his stage production of Ostrovsky's classical play.

Kinopravda in comparison with *Kinonedelya* meant a big step forward; it offered a much more profound and meaningful representation of life. Its twenty-first and twenty-second issues were the ideological peak of the film journal. These were two issues about Lenin where Vertov for the first time made use of retrospective montage that linked the present with the past, and retraced the road of the country's history. What was qualitatively new was not only a greater amount and stricter selection of facts, but also the way these facts were put together in accordance with the author's concept. Some of the issues of *Kinopravda* were more than a collection of visibly unrelated information of the what's-going-on kind, they presented the material so that thematically an issue appeared as one whole, which is characteristic of a more sophisticated cinematic genre, the publicistic film. Dziga Vertov's work in the thirteenth issue of the newsreel dealing with the fifth anniversary of the Revolution (*October Kinopravda*, 1923) is believed to be the turning point in the development of Soviet documentary film in general, which signified the beginning of a new stage in its history. Organised as chronological narration (yesterday–today–tomorrow), *October Kinopravda* scanned the major events over the five years since the revolution, clearly showing the disposition of forces in the class struggle. In *Kinopravda* the author's attitudes and sympathies were more outspoken than in *Kinonedelya*, and expressed in more vivid forms. Dziga Vertov's captions, executed by Alexander Rodchenko, the famous artist, echoed the directness of political slogans, they appealed to the audience: 'See What's Going On in Red Moscow Today!', 'Watch the Red Troops Marching through this Square', etc. Shots of 'politicians from the other camp', put together in one sequence, were prefixed with a scathing one-word caption: 'Junk!'.

These few examples suffice to prove that the documentary cinema of the period was always in the midst of the historic battle of classes and ideas, always focused on the most important elements in the development of society.

With still greater force this comes through in such films which, due to their specific subject-matter, sought more convincing and intense means of social analysis. A major field of film makers' activity lay in the conflicts between the new and the old in all spheres of life: politics, everday life of the people, their ideological views and psychology. Documentary films started exploring these themes, along with that of the transformation of social consciousness, long before the first fiction pictures on similar themes were produced.

In November 1918 a film was released that determined one of the most important trends in Soviet documentary cinema. It was the first historic epic of the revolution *The Anniversary of the Revolution*. In it Dziga Vertov attempted, using archive material, to show on the screen the revolutionary transformation of Tsarist Russia into Socialist Russia. No film maker before him had worked with old footage that lay forgotten on archive shelves, no one could imagine at that time that discarded newsreels which were no longer screened and presumably uninteresting once their news was not new any more, could be used for a big film portraying an important part of the country's history, a whole epoch.

The original version of this picture has not survived. It is only known that it consisted of five episodes and spanned the period from the time tsarist rule was overthrown to the first victories of the young Soviet republic on the Civil War fronts. Although the old film material was employed by Vertov largely to illustrate certain well-known events, *The Anniversary of the Revolution* had, in its time, tremendous social significance.

Along with newsreels and news films a number of filmed war reports were also produced and screened between 1918 and 1920. Among them were A. Lemberg's *The Defence of Tsaritsin* (edited by D. Vertov), P. Yermolov's *Soviet Troops Capture Odessa*, E. Tisse's *The Front and a Glimpse of Soviet Latvia.*

With the beginning of the reconstruction period, documentary film makers started taking an active part in so-called 'production propaganda'. They took their cameras to railway stations and factories being rebuilt from ruins, to the sites of Red Saturdays (voluntary work on Saturday or, sometimes, Sunday), reported on the construction of the first power stations, popularised progressive methods and technology such as water-cannons on peat fields, or showed to the country the first Soviet-made tractors and cars. E. Tisse, A. Lemberg and A. Ryllo went to the Urals on a special assignment to shoot a film about the resurrection of that important industrial region.

With a wider range of subjects the artist was naturally on the look-out for new means of expression. New genres in documentary cinema developed, among them shorts, which featured various enterprises and establishments, and films portraying outstanding personalities. The former was ushered in in 1920 with A. Levitsky's *Gifted Children's Club*; the first specimen of the latter kind was P. Novitsky's picture on Mikhail Kalinin, the first President of Soviet Russia, made in 1919. Two films that appeared in 1923, *The Krasnyi Vyborzhets Factory* and *The Ericson Factory*, were later followed by many others about the country's industrial enterprises.

The Veterans of the Russian Revolution was an example of interesting experiments which sometimes, as in this case, departed from purely documentary cinema. This film was devoted to a meeting of former political prisoners that took place in Moscow in 1924. In the final shots of the live reportage of the meeting itself, the authors managed to capture the emotion-charged atmosphere and impressively portray some of the veteran Bolsheviks. But the story preceding the finale was the history of the Russian Revolution beginning as early as the Decembrists and Herzen. It was here that the director ventured a risky experiment. Authentic documents (for example, the text of the indictment in the Decembrists' trial), still pictures of people and the scenes of action (a drawing of a Siberian convict prison, etc.) were combined with undisguised play-acting that made it possible for the audience to 'witness' the historic events of the pre-film era, for instance to see Karakozov firing a shot at the tsar. The public could also see a political prisoner in his cell, a revolutionary meeting in a village, a serf-peasant punished on his master's orders, Nechayev's execution and finally 'live' Herzen – everything re-enacted in the film for their benefit.

Employment of fiction film techniques in such a way however did not help to solve the specific tasks set for documentary and news film makers. Such tasks necessitated the evolution of specific methods of imaginative publicistic documentary cinema. These were discovered, and a great tribute here is due to the outstanding artist and innovator of Soviet film art, Dziga Vertov.

The group of documentary film makers, led and inspired by Vertov, the people that he called 'kinoks' (from contracted Russian 'kino oko', that is 'film eye', the cinecamera), came into being towards the end of 1919. It included editor E. Svilova (who soon became Vertov's wife), cameramen and 'film scouts' M. Kaufman, A. Lemberg, I. Belyakov, P. Zotov, Ye. Barantsevich,

A. Kagarlitsky, B. Kudinov, V. Komarov and was later joined by I. Kopalin and several others.

Soon after the last issue of *Kinonedelya* was made, Vertov became the editor and director of *Kinopravda* which was the first film magazine, not only in Soviet Russia but also in world cinema, that went beyond impassionate recording of events and was characterised by an actively imaginative approach to the reality which it reflected. *Kinopravda* laid the basis for the poetical cinema in the Soviet Union and that is why the importance of its contribution to the art is by no means limited to documentary film alone (which is equally true of Vertov's other work).

A most interesting creative experiment, in the early stages of his career, was Dziga Vertov's innovative work *Kinoglaz* (1924) that brought the director a prize at the Paris International Exhibition. The film was conceived as a broad panorama of Soviet life, mainly of life that was shot 'unawares'. The separate episodes were sewn together with a semblance of a plot: two groups of Young Pioneers, one in town, the other in the countryside, engage in their daily activities, and as they march through the streets or deliver letters or explore a market-place the audience follow them and see what the children meet on their way. Many of the episodes in this picture can be regarded as Vertov's brilliant artistic discoveries and achievements. Exceptionally vivid, revolutionary at that time was, for example, the sequence that showed the hoisting of the flag at the children's summer camp, a combination of brief shots cut with a perfect sense of rhythm. The children in the film look quite natural and true to life, so do the sequences in the market-place showing the struggle between the new and the old, the shots of Young Pioneers working in a village barber's shop, a blacksmith's workshop, etc. All these episodes anticipate the methods of today's 'direct cinema'. In some parts of the film such important social themes as the establishment of co-operative farming are introduced or the new relationships between town and countryside. The public was also impressed with many a true observation of everyday life that captured the spirit of the people and of the time.

However, as a whole, *Kinoglaz* proved to be rather chaotic, compositionally. Not infrequently one can feel the lack of logic in the course of events. Certain scenes appear redundant, introduced into the film merely because they contained unexpected or spectacular observations. This is how the lunatics got in, the elephant walking through Moscow streets, the Chinese conjurer, and the ambulance sequence.

In the late twenties Vertov made a number of documentaries in which he continued his search for imaginative publicistic cinema. In this period he put together four pictures: *March, Soviet!* (1926), *One-Sixth of the World* (1926), *The Eleventh* (1928) and *Man with a Camera* (1929).

March, Soviet! was commissioned by the Moscow City Soviet and originally was to survey the work done by its Executive Committee. However, when the shooting had already begun, the director went beyond the bounds of the original idea, discovered a new artistic approach to his subject and finally made a strikingly poetic, image-bearing film that depicted the historic changes in the life of the young Land of the Soviets, the great achievements of the Revolution.

The original conception behind *One-Sixth of the World* underwent a similar transformation, so that what was initially commissioned by a state department as a publicity film became a cinematic poem about the Soviet Republic. The first travel pictures had appeared in the country as early as the Civil War years. In most cases these were informative short films on various provinces of the country *Soviet Armenia, Soviet Azerbaijan, In the Soviet Republics*, etc. Then, films carrying economic news came into prominence, pushing the travel film aside. But in the late twenties with the launching of the nationwide campaign against illiteracy, with the masses of the people hungry for knowledge, there was a boom in the production of travel films in view of their considerable informative and educational potential.

At that time film studios began to send numerous teams of film workers on assignments to the lesser-known parts of the country and abroad. For example, in 1925 the young film director V. Shneiderov and cameraman G. Blyum took part in a flight from Moscow to Peking; director V. Semenov-Tianshansky and cameraman V. Yefremov travelled by boat from Leningrad to Astrakhan, shooting on the way the villages and towns on the Volga. In the same year N. Konstantinov made a film about the Soviet ships going to Asian ports, and N. Lebedev, news film director and later film historian, travelled with cameramen A. Lagorio around Germany and Italy. Between 1925 and 1929 Sovkino cameramen shot in Novaya Zemlya, the Altai, Kamchatka, the Far East and the Buryat Region, as well as in

Afghanistan, Turkey, Norway and other countries of the world.

In early 1927 the Sovkino management instructed two young film makers, M. Kaufman and I. Kopalin, to make together with P. Zotov and I. Belyakov a picture showing the sights of the Soviet capital. It was the second film on Moscow: a year earlier the same cameramen had shot the documentary film *March, Soviet!*, directed by Dziga Vertov. The composition of *Moscow* was reminiscent of the German director W. Ruttmann's *Berlin, a Symphony of a Big City*. Still, where Ruttmann had captivated his audience with a visualised, graphically precise analysis of city life dynamics, with spectacular contrasts and inventive montage, Kaufman and Kopalin sought in the first place to make the public think once again of the tremendous changes in the life of the city and in the fate of the country brought about by the October Revolution. With this objective in view, they contrast the city's appearance, hardly different from 10 years before, with its new life, its new people. In this they strike on a felicitous device that to a great extent predetermined the success of the picture and imbued it with serious elements of historical truth and the dynamics of social development.

Take a closer look, the authors suggest, and behind the old facades you will see new reality. Here is the posh mansion that belonged to the rich manufacturer Morozov – now there is a signboard on it that reads: 'All-Russian and Moscow Proletkult'; this palatial building belonged to Prince Shcherbakov – today it houses the Administrative Department of the Moscow Soviet; and here, in what many Muscovites remember as the Hermitage restaurant, you can see country people dine and relax – it is now called the Peasants' House.

In the same period another artistically important trend emerged in Soviet documentary film ushered in by director Esfir Shub's work. Her first documentary film, made in 1927, was *The Fall of the Romanov Dynasty*. This picture, that signified the beginning of a new stage in publicistic cinema, was entirely made from old footage, mostly pre-revolutionary newsreels. No Soviet film-maker before Shub had used such material. One imagined that the revolution had for ever buried the news films of tsarist Russia, and had left them behind with the rest of the old system in its march towards the future. But the young film director managed to look at the archive film documents in a new light and put them to use serving the interests of the new age.

This novel interpretation of the old shots was effected in two ways. Sometimes it was achieved through the author's captions commenting on the shots. These were usually ironic or sarcastic, caustic and biting. For example, the picture shows courtiers dancing a lively mazurka on board a ship during a sea cruise. The caption after it reads: 'By the sweat of one's brow ...' Then a picture of peasants slaving in the fields. And the same caption: 'By the sweat of one's brow ...' which made the two shots a socially meaningful contrast. In other cases the desired effect was achieved by merely juxtaposing the shots, without any verbal comment. Shub's montage clashed together scenes from the life of the upper classes and scenes from the life of common people, thus exposing the profoundest contradictions in tsarist Russia's society. With every image, with the logic of its composition *The Fall of the Romanov Dynasty* laid bare the collapse in the social and political life of Russia prior to the revolution and made it clear that the Russian Revolution was inevitable.

The same device, juxtaposition of contrasting film documents, was employed by Shub in her historical documentary picture *The Great Path* which commemorated the tenth anniversary of Red October. However, this film was essentially different from *The Fall of the Romanov Dynasty* in that a lot of the material was specially shot by two news-film cameramen following the director's instructions. But the main difference was that in *The Great Path* the idea was to show the contrast not between the life of the rich and that of the poor, as seen in pre-revolutionary film material, but between the various stages in the development of the young Soviet state, and through it, to demonstrate in visual images the triumph of the revolution.

What Esfir Shub contributed to documentary film art was a new way of interpreting archive material, which gave rise to a new genre, the historical documentary film, or as it is often called, the montage film. But she made another not less valuable contribution. Unlike Dziga Vertov she invariably tried to preserve the 'wholeness' of reality, to present an event in its 'real-life entity'. Film director Vsevolod Pudovkin aptly defined this peculiarity of her style as 'the right choice of uncut pieces' of newsreels that made it possible to recreate on the screen an atmosphere of special, convincing reality.[8]

After *The Fall of the Romanov Dynasty* and *The Great Path*, Esfir Shub in 1928 made another film from archive material, *The*

Russia of Nicholas II and Leo Tolstoy, in which one could feel considerable influence from current vulgar social theories, and in 1930 she made *Today*, a film on 'labour and capital'.

In the late twenties and early thirties, the country's economic development became a major subject of the Soviet documentary cinema. The first documentary film maker to attempt to create a generalised poetical image of the country of workers was Dziga Vertov. In *Kinopravda*, in his films *March, Soviet!* and *One-Sixth of the World*, using dynamic montage, symbols and allegories, through imaginative visual interpretation of production processes, Vertov sought to express his poet's view of the historic industrialisation of once economically backward, virtually illiterate Russia. In his poetical symbols, in his images of the working class, in the image of the country as one big forging shop, there was a lot in common with the political posters of the Civil War, with Vladimir Mayakovsky's politically minded poetry. From political posters Vertov (and later other film makers) borrowed, for example, the generalised portrayal of people as representatives of certain social groups, certain classes.

This was a hitherto unknown method of representing an individual on the screen, similar, if one looks for comparisons in western cinema, to what John Grierson did. The appearance in films of close-ups of the worker and the peasant, the common people, even if they only represented generalised social types, signified a new stage in aesthetic perception of reality.

Yet another film featuring the socialist transformation of the country, V. Turin's *Turksib* (1929) was distinguished by convincing historical authenticity. The picture was shot by experienced cameramen Ye. Slavinsky and B. Frantsisson on the basis of a script by Ye. Aron, A. Macheret, V. Turin and V. Shklovsky. The script played in this case a special role, as it determined the virtues of the composition and, in part, the expressively pictorial quality of imagery that distinguish this film as a work of art.

The construction of a railway between Turkestan and Siberia (hence its name Turksib) as the subject around which the film was built, was treated dialectically as a struggle between destructive nature and human intelligence and perseverance, a continuing conflict between reciprocally exclusive, though coexisting, forces. The first 'conflict' emerges in the introductory sequence showing 'the disposition of forces before the decisive battle': arid Turkestan, a land of sunshine and the scorching sand of its deserts, and Siberia, a country of snow and long cold winters. It was these regions, separated by enormous distances, situated in so different climatic zones, so unlike each other in many respects, that a thread of railway track was to bring together. The Turkestan–Siberia railway, the film stressed, was very important for the country's economy, it would make it easier to bring grain and industrial goods to the south and transport the southern cotton to the processing factories further north.

After the preliminary exploration of the region, filmed against the impressive, colourful background of Turkestan, the construction of the railway line begins. An army of builders set out from each end of the line. This is how it really worked, the film makers did not have to think anything up. But they cleverly used the real life circumstances to turn them into a striking, emotion-charged story of the struggle of two forces speeding ahead towards a meeting place. These two forces become a kind of dramatis personae of the film: each is peopled with a team of builders, each has its own tasks to fulfil, its own obstacles to overcome. The construction of the railroad is transformed on the screen into a dramatic dialogue of two geographically distant areas, two construction teams whose progress is governed by all-conquering human will. The construction of the Turksib, presented as two building teams moving from the opposite ends of the line, each day diminishing the gap between them, until finally they meet at some point in the desert, this is the dramatic collision at the centre of the picture which, towards the end, resolves into a vivid expression of man's triumph over the forces of nature.

The same period, the late twenties – early thirties, saw the emergence of yet another promising trend in documentary cinema. Following the example of writers and journalists, documentary film makers set up permanent teams at the key economic projects.

In the early summer of 1931 such teams went from Moscow to the Donbass in the Ukraine, to Kuznetsk in Siberia and to other industrial centres. In the coal-mining region of the Donbass, for instance, a team led by film director S. Gurov (cameraman G. Savenko) made four issues of the film journal *Donbass*. Another group of film workers from Moscow, headed by directors Ya. Bliokh and S. Bubrik (cameramen B. Makaseyev and N.

Khmelev) from July to September 1931 shot at Kuznetsk the films *Shock-Work at the Central Power Station, Bridging the Gap, For Rationalisation*, etc. Film workers from Leningrad made six special newsreels on the Svir project and their colleagues from Novosibirsk worked on a film about the young builders at Kuznetsk *The Komsomol at the Kuznetsk Project*.

At the end of 1931, on film director Alexander Medvedkin's initiative, a specially equipped 'film train' was organised. On 15 January 1932 it started on its maiden trip. The crew, numbering over fifty, consisted of directors, cameramen, journalists, lecturers, etc. The coaches of the train housed photography laboratories, an editing studio, an animation studio, a printing shop, an office for the editorial staff, and a power plant. Arriving at the site of a construction project, the film makers usually got in touch with the Party leaders, the cameramen began shooting and soon the builders could see a film on their project. To show how quickly the train teams worked it is enough to cite one example. On the day the Dnieper Hydropower Station was opened (10 October 1932) the film *The Dnieper Station is Ready* was seen by the builders of the power station and factory workers from nearby Dnepropetrovsk, and the next day it was screened in Moscow and Kharkov.

Of special interest are the genres of documentary satirical film pamphlet and documentary comedy film, very popular with the Medvedkin train film makers and other special assignment teams. In the case of Alexander Medvedkin this liking for satire was later developed in his fiction films, for example, his comedy *Happiness*, and satirical comedy always remained a major genre of his work.

Unlike the newsreels and documentary films of the twenties, with their main emphasis on the class characteristics of people and their treatment of individuals as types, the newsreels and films of later periods begin to display interest in the individual, in the psychology of contemporary Soviet people. Evidence of this can be found in Dziga Vertov's *Three Songs about Lenin* (the concrete-mixer, Byelik) and in Esfir Shub's *K.Sh.E.* (the factory meeting sequence), etc.

Many convincing examples of this kind are provided by the work of director and cameraman Roman Karmen. In the mid-twenties Karmen had worked as a photographer for the leading Soviet newspapers and magazines. In 1929 he started his film career. His experience as a newspaper photographer equipped him with some valuable qualities and skills useful to a documentary film cameraman: keen reaction, ability to take his cue in a complicated and fast-changing situation or to keep pace with developments on the scene of action, perfect technical professionalism. In 1930 Roman Karmen, together with M. Slutsky and A. Samsonov, made in the Ukraine a short film *The Kitchen as Big as a Factory*, and the following year took part, with cameraman G. Blyum, in a larger-scale travel picture *Far Away in Asia* directed by V. Yerofeyev. His very first one-man work an episode on the launching of a new blast-furnace at Kosogorsk for *Soyuzkinozhurnal* (Film Journal) in 1932, and a short film *Anna Masonova's Report* in 1934, proved successful. Thus began the long artistic life of an original master of documentary cinema who later won recognition as one of the pioneers of Soviet political publicistic film.

In 1930 Dziga Vertov's first sound film was released, *The Donbass Symphony* (or *Enthusiasm*) shot, like its predecessors *The Eleventh* and *Man with a Camera*, in the Ukraine. The photography was by B. Tseitlin and the montage by D. Vertov and his usual co-director E. Svilova.

The Donbass Symphony was a new experiment in line with Dziga Vertov's constant search for specific cinematic idiom. This time he experimented with the possibilities that the sound cinema provided. But it was also a film by a mature artist, with perfect montage, exposing an important problem that commanded general interest in those days. The picture showed the work of a large industrial enterprise, the heroic effort of the workers striving to bridge the gap between the plan and actual production in the Donbass coal mines. Vertov and his team again opted for a poetic film form that allowed them to go beyond the limits of the immediate story, to open up for the audience a broader panorama of real-life events.

The content of the picture was not confined to showing the Donbass. Slowly, gradually, Vertov came to the central idea of his film, examining interrelations of phenomena, comparing the old (a religious holiday, drunks in a town square) and the new, embodied in the sounds of a Komsomol march clashing with the church bell chimes, in a symbolic episode of a church converted into a workers' club. Just as Moscow's Bolshoi Theatre, in an earlier picture broke into pieces (*Man with a Camera*), so now with the help of special effects the audience saw an icon cracking in front of their eyes or a red flag soaring up to fly on the church dome, with white clouds speeding by high above.

In 1932 Shub's first sound documentary film was produced. Her *K.Sh.E.* (the Russian abbreviation for 'Komsomol, leader of electrification') was an unexpected picture. It looked as if Shub had given up her usual role as a historian, a student of the past. There was no archive material, no generalisations or metaphors based on juxtaposition of contrasting shots. Yet the master remained true to her major principles. Shub's film became a document of the time.

The story was quite typical of that period. Young communists try to find out what disrupts the normal work at their enterprise and, towards the end, manage to overcome the difficulties and boost production. Shub's film ends with shots of the triumphant launching of a hydropower station in Transcaucasia. Nevertheless, *K.Sh.E.* went beyond perfunctory ascertainment of facts and events that already belonged to the past. In film art periodicals, in discussions about the contemporary hero, the critics of the thirties compare *K.Sh.E.* with Alexander Dovzhenko's *Ivan* and Sergei Yutkevich and Friedrich Ermler's *Counter-Plan*, an unusual example, considering that Shub's film was a documentary.

Esfir Shub believes in her material as she takes her camera from one site to another. A young boy who has come from the construction site of the Dnieper Power Station speaks at a factory meeting. He speaks with real ardour, with unaffected passion, without choosing his words. The image of this Komsomol leader, clad in simple shirt and leather jacket, so remarkably corresponds with our idea of the youth of the thirties! His speech was shot in such a way that it did not leave the slightest trace of doubt that this was how it really happened. As seen in this film, Shub was not afraid to show people looking into the camera, frowning at the bright lights, or faltering because the camera bothered them. And their reaction to the camera and the film makers behind it helps to enhance the credibility that the author sought to achieve. The film shows but a single episode in the huge country's construction effort, and Shub does not try to gloss over the sharp angles, to beautify reality – she reaches out for facts and views them at close quarters. The author's belief in her material results in the audience's belief in the authenticity of the film. These are the qualities that not only make *K.Sh.E.* an outstanding documentary picture but provide tangible opportunities for discussing the cinema and the time, for comparing documentary and fiction films on the same subject.

Yet in Shub's film there is another subject – the sound cinema itself. *K.Sh.E.* begins with a parade of cinematographic equipment. The director invites the public to a sound recording studio, displays the possibilities of film technology. And later, the picture is punctuated with shots where one can see the film team at work. This secondary line in the film undoubtedly reflected the film workers' enthusiasm for the new means of expression that appeared with the advent of the soundtrack. Still here (perhaps unknowingly) Esfir Shub made another artistic discovery. Similar devices (the camera taking in the film team with all their paraphernalia, as if saying 'this is all for the show') as we know, are not uncommon in films produced today by various directors who look for effective, spectacular and even shocking forms of influencing their audiences.

The consummate achievement in the Soviet documentary cinema of the thirties was Dziga Vertov's *Three Songs about Lenin* (1934). It summed up the development of the poetical film, the methods and forms of which the director had been perfecting for many years. In the effectiveness of its message, in the presentation of its noble idea it surpassed everything that had been done in Soviet documentary cinema before it. The film was photographed by cameraman D. Surensky, M. Magidson, B. Monastyrsky; it was co-directed by E. Svilova and P. Shtro worked on the soundtrack.

As the title indicates, the authors turned for inspiration to the folk-song tradition, and Vertov most certainly took his cue from oriental poetry. The Orient had already been featured in his earlier work, for example in *Kinopravda* and *One-Sixth of the World*. This theme was well known and spiritually close to the film director. Besides, it was there, in the distant eastern outskirts of the country that one could show with graphic vividness what the revolution had given to the peoples who had had no laws to protect them in tsarist Russia and had suffered from a dual oppression. His trips to the republics of Central Asia, his meetings with folk singers, the songs, proverbs, and tunes that he took down there amply provided the director with poetic material and determined the emotional colouring of his narrative.

In 1932 the young film director M. Slutsky made a short picture *Named After Lenin* about the commissioning of the Dnieper Power Station, which outlined yet another way towards the poetic documentary film. While working on this picture M. Slutsky selected every shot most carefully, striving for the complete realization of his idea. In his earlier film *The Last Cubic Metre*, made from practically the same real-life material, he had shown in detail the ceremony on the occasion of the opening of the power station. But in the poetic song *Named After Lenin* Slutsky departed from the precision of the record and through vivid images showed instead the general jubilation. Slutsky managed to see beyond the official ceremony and understand the significance of the occasion for the people who had built the power station with their own hands. Like R. Karmen in *The Launching of the Blast-Furnace at Kosogorsk*, Slutsky made the audience rejoice, together with the builders, at the fruit of their labour. We hear only one speaker at the meeting, an old Ukrainian construction worker. His colourful, simultaneously recorded speech is partly recollections of the past, of a poor peasant's meditations and partly a story, illustrated by appropriate shots, of how they dammed the Dnieper, of how happy and proud a builder feels. Along with Vertov's *The Donbass Symphony* and Shub's *K.Sh.E.*, Slutsky's documentary film-poem/film-song was an artistic discovery, in the sound cinema, that blazed new trails in the art of film making.

A notable event in the film life of those years was *The Mighty Stream* (1939), of B. Nebylitsky and L. Varlamov. It told how in the summer of 1939 hundreds of thousands of volunteers, collective farmers of Uzbekistan and Tadzhikstan, helped out by the entire country, built in an incredibly short time a 270-kilometre canal in the arid Fergana valley. This film also went beyond the usual impassionate information that registers events in logical order. Nebylitsky and Varlamov sought to preserve the precision of historical facts and, at the same time, to show the event through the eyes of various people. That is why the film was structurally conceived as a poem about the people's exploit. In the introduction the audience hear the voice of an old man singing of human sorrow and hope. Such a beginning demanded, no doubt, that through the rest of the film the story of the canal construction should be told in an appropriate epic style. But, the film makers failed to develop this and the picture is frequently nothing more than newsreel episodes, undiluted information. The commentator talks away giving lots of factual data: how many people volunteered to build the canal, what republics and regions they came from, how much work they did in one day, how much earth had been excavated, etc. The audience could see collective farmers setting off for the construction site, collecting spades and barrows, and cauldrons for cooking, and loading provisions on to arbas, two-wheel bullock-drawn carts. These shots were static and sluggish. There was no movement in them, and any idea that could make them meaningful was replaced with simple enumeration of the things the people took with them. Again, breaking the stylistic unity, there came a large-scale sequence of thousands of people moving across the steppe, and followed by a dull montage of unco-ordinated, unrelated shots that were supposed to illustrate various aspects of the canal builders' life.

In conclusion it is appropriate to note that the documentary cinema of the thirties gave quite a comprehensive picture of the important processes in the life of Soviet society: the country's economic growth and industrialisation. It vividly displayed the enthusiasm of the people translating into reality the target-figures of the first 5-year plans, and the new attitudes towards labour. In certain cases documentary films focused on the same problems as fiction films, like Dovzhenko's *Ivan* or Yutkevich and Ermler's *Counter-Plan*, and like numerous works of literature devoted to the working class.

In the twenties the hero in documentary pictures had represented the revolutionary masses, bound to them by a common fate and class solidarity. He had represented a social type, he was the man who had made the revolution. A symbol, a capacious image that could take in all the features common to a whole class appealed to the film maker, not only in documentary but also in fiction cinema.

The thirties made an important contribution to film art with a realistic portrait of the hero of the time. The search for the new look took place not exclusively in the realm of art. Life itself acted as a guide: a generation of people brought up in the spirit of revolutionary ideas had matured; the notion of 'the Soviet people' came into use in that period and the essence of these 'Soviet people' reflected the major achievements of the revolution. That is why there was such open and avid interest in the individual features, in the psychology of the hero, an interest that dominated not only the Soviet cinema of the thirties but all Soviet art of the period.

D. Vertov, R. Karmen, I. Kopalin, E. Shub, M. Slutsky, A. Ovanesova, O. Podgoretskaya, S. Bubrik, L. Varlamov, B. Nebylitsky, S. Gurov, M. Kaufman, V. Yeshurin and many other documentary film makers tried to recreate on the screen the true image of their contemporaries, they looked for methods and techniques to do this most effectively. They did it in different ways, but there was a common denominator in their search: in their generalisations they all strove to reveal the unique individuality of their heroes. The artistic merging of the individual and the common, the typical and the unique meant that documentary film had passed on to a new stage of its development.

This brief analysis thus leads us to the conclusion that in some cases the Soviet documentary cinema of the twenties and thirties blazed the trail for film art as a whole. It recorded a wealth of facts related to a most important period in the history of Soviet society. Newsreels and documentary films, developed to the level of sophisticated publicistic writing, equipped with an arsenal of means of expression, managed to record for posterity history in the making, the establishment of a socialist state. They showed man and his work, they captured the spirit of the time and expressed it with convincing emotion. All this makes it possible to consider a documentary film not only preliminary raw material, but also fully-fledged historical evidence.

At the same time one should never forget the special qualities of this evidence. In the first place, a fact is used in a film within a certain aesthetic system and is interpreted by the film maker, in comparison with other facts and phenomena. A fact tends to be generalised; an idea is supplemented with feeling. The reality in documentary film is always the fact plus a reaction to it, the event plus a judgment of it. And, of course, it is always a wealth of natural images, the true colours of the world. In other words, historical truth coexists here with emotional truth.

All this, in our opinion, does not diminish the value of a documentary film as historical evidence but, on the contrary, increases it. Not only 'naked facts' can help us better understand the essence of things; aesthetic categories of appreciation can do it just as well.

The documentary film is an instrument of learning the truth. It is an invaluable assistant of the historian. At the same time it is an effective means of moral education, unique in its emotional power. When not limited to pure information, the documentary film can effectively voice social problems, express the basic values of life, accumulate the spiritual energy of the time, and of the epoch.

NOTES

1 D. Vertov, *Stat'i, Dnevniki, Zamysly* (Moscow, 1966) p. 87.
2 *Sovetskiĭ Ekran* (1926) no. 32.
3 S. Eisenstein, *Sobranie Sochinenii v Shesti Tomax*, vol. 1 (Moscow, 1964) pp. 113–15.
4 *Novyi LEF* (1927) no. 4.
5 *Novyi LEF* (1927) nos. 11–12.
6 John Reed, *Ten Days that Shook the World* (London, 1928) p. 112.
7 The wordings of the captions here and elsewhere are given from the author's notes direct from the films.
8 *Kino i Kul'tura*, 1929, nos. 7–8.

13 Soviet newsreel and the Great Patriotic War

D. W. SPRING

Soviet newsreel film forms an important part of the production of the various Soviet publicity media during the Soviet–German war, the co-ordinated aim of which was to mobilise the Soviet people and their resources most effectively to the war effort for the defeat of Nazi Germany.

Joseph Stalin, at the victory banquet in Moscow, 24 May 1945, raised his glass in a toast to the health of the Russian people, 'because they are the most outstanding of all the nations which compose the Soviet Union . . .'. He continued with the following remarkable statement:

> Our government made quite a number of mistakes. We had some desperate moments in 1941/2, when our army was retreating and abandoning our native villages and towns . . . because there was no other alternative. Another people might have said to its government: you have not justified our expectations, you must go. We will install another government that will make peace with Germany and assure our safety. But the Russian people did not take that step . . . and this trust of the Russian people in the Soviet government was the decisive force that ensured the heroic victory over the enemy of mankind, over fascism.[1]

The consequences of these 'mistakes' were apparent in the first six months of the war when a substantial part of the Soviet air force and thousands of tanks were lost, together with up to two million prisoners in the vast encirclements of Belostok (June), Kiev (September) and Vyazma (October 1941). By the end of

August, German troops were approaching Leningrad and by mid-October were close to Moscow. The industrial power needed for victory was significantly reduced: 60 per cent of coal had come from the occupied Donbass; the output of steel was cut by two-thirds and total industrial output fell by 50 per cent by December 1941. The capacity to provide the basic necessities of life was also reduced: the area occupied by the Germans by the end of 1941 produced 38 per cent of Soviet cereals, 38 per cent of the cattle, 84 per cent of the sugar and 60 per cent of the pigs. Agricultural production fell to 30 million tons in 1942/3, only 40 per cent of the 1913 figure, and even in 1945 only reached 84 per cent of 1913 production for a population increased from 160 to 200 million.[2]

The result of the war depended on the existence of the necessary material resources, but also on the will to fight and on the capacity to organise and inspire the population in these conditions of severe privation. N. A. Voznesensky, Director of the State Planning Commission later wrote, after listing the appalling human and material losses in the first six months of the war: 'Russia's resistance, especially in the first year of the war, was a triumph of her superior determination and spirit'.[3] In contrast to its predecessor, the Soviet regime appreciated the importance of propaganda, and of a coherent and positive effort to mobilise the commitment of the population to the goals set by the regime.[4] In this task the film had a notable role, Lenin having pronounced, according to Lunacharsky, that 'of all art, the cinema is for us the most important'. Newsreel as a propaganda instrument had also been singled out by the highest authority: 'If you have a good newsreel, serious and illuminating photos', Lenin had told Lunacharsky in 1922, 'then it is of no importance if in order to attract the public, you also show some useless film of a more or less popular type'.[5] While the desperate war situation increased the importance of effective propaganda, the newsreel, in which the vast majority of cameramen were involved, became a unique medium for bringing the visual reality of the war directly to the civilian population.

An analysis of any aspect of the media, such as the newsreels, in the Soviet Union must begin with an examination of the contemporary political and ideological line of the Communist Party, which was the only body responsible for controlling and directing the dissemination of ideas, the interpretation of events and the selection of news. The Directorate of Propaganda and Agitation of the Central Committee, led by A. S. Shcherbakov until 1945, gave definite tasks to the editors of the press, recommended the themes to be dealt with and gave advice on the reporting of military actions as well as local life and economic problems. In the wartime context the aim of Agitprop was 'to get to everyone and to show them their role in the war'. For the peasantry it was important to emphasise that the struggle for grain was also the struggle for victory over Germany. Amongst the youth of the country, on whom much of the work in transport, building, agriculture and in the factories lay during the war, it was important to emphasise the responsibility on their shoulders in the absence of their elders. It was vital to encourage women to adapt themselves to play a more demanding role in mechanised industry and agriculture. The non-Russian peoples, particularly in the far rear, demanded special attention: propaganda work must link them with their compatriots at the front and emphasise 'the friendship of the various nationalities of the Soviet state in the common struggle against fascism'. For literature and the various arts including the cinema, the Party newspaper *Pravda* on 26 December 1941 defined their aims as

> . . . to educate in all our people the feeling of whole-hearted and self-sacrificing love for their country, a feeling of holy hate for the villainous enemy, a feeling of fearlessness and contempt towards death . . . They should reflect the greatness of our historic days in works worthy of heroes and the heroism of the Patriotic War.[6]

But while the importance and reality of these propaganda aims which the Party set the media and the arts were evident, yet the problem of bringing the message to the people was complicated by the war. For instance in 1942 only 4561 newspaper titles could be published compared with 8806 in 1940; the total print in 1940 amounted to 38 million, whereas in 1942 it was only 18 million. This must have been partly due to the reduced territory in which the Soviet authorities operated in 1942, but nevertheless by 1945 the print of the newspaper press had only risen to 23 million to compare with the 38 million of 1940. In order to get the Party's message across in this critical situation, many more 'newspaper windows' were set up in public places, and a greater use was made of local radio for the broadcasting of official documents and articles. Efforts were also made to establish radio 'listening posts' more widely in the countryside amongst the peasantry.[7]

The cinema also suffered from the impact of the war. In 1940 there were 28,000 cinemas in the USSR; of these 15,500 were fixed and 12,500 mobile. In that year there were 883 million visits to the cinema, an average weekly audience of 17 million. But the cinema-going habit was unevenly spread and did not penetrate very effectively into the rural areas. Although 19,500 out of 28,000 projection facilities were situated in the countryside, as well as the 131 million majority of the population, the average weekly audience in the rural areas was only 3.7 million. In the urban areas however the weekly audience was 13.5 million for a population of 63 million. In the towns the potential viewing public, say from age 10 to 70, must have been no more than 50 million in 1940.[8] But as a result of the German occupation, from June 1941 to mid-1943 the potential urban audience for Soviet films was reduced by about one-third, to perhaps not much more than thirty million, and nearly half the projection facilities in the USSR were lost.[9] If the same proportion of the urban public as in 1940 went to the cinema during the war, the actual weekly audience must have been about 7.8 million.

The urban concentration of the viewing public was also further intensified during the war. The Central Committee reviewing the propaganda work of the Party in 1944/5 drew attention to the fact that in the Bashkir and Tatar Autonomous Republics and in Ulyanovsk province, for instance, 'a significant part' of the cinemas were inactive or the equipment out of order and the cinema had not visited many collective farms for the whole duration of the war.[10] Some issues of the main newsreel the Union Film Journal betray an awareness that their audience was largely more cultivated than could be expected in the rural areas. For instance issue no. 28 (April 1943) records the funeral of Nemirovich-Danchenko, the founder of the Moscow Art Theatre, without mentioning his name, and assuming knowledge of his identity. And in no. 29 (May 1943) the story on the Czech Legion of Col. Svoboda leaves the audience to recognise their national origin only by playing Smetana's 'Vltava'. Issue no. 84 (30 August 1941) was almost entirely concerned with the Jewish Congress in Moscow, at which Ehrenburg gives his speech in Russian, Eisenstein in English and the poet, Pertz Markish in Yiddish without sub-titles or translation!

The small weekly audience in the countryside does not allow us to consider the film and in particular the newsreel on its own, as a significant influence on the rural majority of the population during the war. In the towns where cinema-going was a frequent habit in 1940, it is not possible to say exactly what impact the war had in the absence of statistics. Did attendance increase in the search for entertainment and distraction, or for encouragement to bear the privations of the war effort? Or did it fall as a result of the heavy burdens of over-work and difficult conditions of the war? The evidence above, however, enables us to define the audience as essentially the urban minority of the population, and to conclude that this concentration was increased during the war.

Despite the fact that the newsreel, together with the film in general, was largely limited to the urban minority, the newsreel acquired, in the view of the Party, a particular and predominant importance in Soviet film production during the Great Patriotic War. The directness and immediacy of the newsreel was able to bring the war to distant rear parts of the country in a more universally accessible and less obviously intellectualised form than the press. With the transfer of Lenfilm and Mosfilm to Central Asia in September 1941, the cancelling of some feature films in the course of production and with the closing of the newsreel studios in Kiev and Leningrad, the Moscow newsreel studio remained as the most important and prolific producer of films in the Soviet Union. The newsreel studio expanded and a large number of cameramen went over to newsreel work. Between June 1941 and September 1945, 435 separate newsreels were issued. These included 276 issues of *Soyuzkinozhurnal* (Union Film Journal) by the Central Newsreel Studio in Moscow and of *Novosti Dyna* (News of the Day) after June 1944 by the Central Studio for Documentary Film.

Of particular importance to the newsreels was the filming of front, advanced with the troops, filmed from tanks and bombers on mission, from blockaded Leningrad under appalling conditions, from the heat of the street and house to house battles front, advanced with the troops, filmed from tanks and bombers on mission, from blockaded Leningrad under appalling conditions, from the heat of the street and house to house battles of Stalingrad and from the partisan units in the rear of the German forces. Forty of these front cameramen were killed filming the war. Their work was much appreciated by the authorities, as many were decorated and on 15 April 1944 the

Central Newsreel Studio itself was awarded the Order of the Red Banner.[11]

The film sent from the front was rapidly transmitted to the Moscow studio. The edited newsreel issues appeared when their themes were fairly topical and alive. For the first two months of the war an average of more than two issues per week was maintained. From September 1941 to December 1942, the average was slightly below two per week, and it fell slowly but steadily from just over one per week in 1943 to one per fortnight in 1945. Three-quarters of the war newsreels up to June 1944 were edited by only four individuals. These were I. Setkina (64 issues), M. Fideleva (54 issues), S. Gurov (33 issues) and N. Karmazinsky (20 issues) out of a total of 232 up to June 1944. The musical direction for almost all the wartime newsreels was by D. Shtil'man. As a result of the reorganisation of the newsreel and documentary cinema in mid-1944, the individual editors varied more in the last year of the war. In that year we note that six issues were edited by Dziga Vertov (who had also done two in 1941), four by Esfir Shub and one by Pudovkin.

Newsreel film was also used to produce full-length, large-scale documentaries during the war. These in their immediacy are somewhat akin to the newsreels and sometimes also concerned phases of the military campaign which had not yet been brought to a conclusion. Notable amongst these are Valarmov and Kopalin's *Rout of the German Forces Near Moscow* (February 1942) and *Stalingrad* (1943), Karmen's *Leningrad in Battle* (1942), Dovzhenko's *Battle for the Soviet Ukraine* (1943) and Raizman's *Berlin* (1945). But they are in general in a different category from the newsreels as, while using newsreel footage, they allowed for a more coherent presentation, more generalised and set in the context of longer-term developments. In this way they were probably more effective instruments of propaganda than the isolated incidents recorded in the day to day newsreels, edited in the heat of the moment, often before the significance of the actions they showed could be appreciated.

The first phase of the war from 22 June 1941 to the stabilisation of the front in early 1942, showed the newsreel at a testing time.[12] Production opens with no. 59 including an almost complete recording of Molotov's radio speech at mid-day on 22 June, the first announcement to the Soviet people that the war had begun. This is an important historical document in its own right, confirming the published text. The dull delivery emphasises the personal weaknesses of the Soviet leaders as propagandists, rarely attempting to project themselves on film, even through sound alone. Molotov emphasised that the war was against fascism and not against the German people (also see no. 68, 16 July 1941 and no. 80, 20 August 1941) a theme evident from time to time throughout the war. He displayed his confidence in final victory – 'Victory will be ours!' – referring to the conflict already as the 'Patriotic War', thus relating it from the beginning with the first Patriotic War of 1812 and suggesting its ultimate inevitable outcome.

The impression from many of the newsreels of the first weeks of the war is that propaganda only adjusted slowly to the new situation. Propaganda against Germany specifically had certainly been considerably muted in 1939–41. But the theme of patriotic defence in the Russian and pre-revolutionary past and of unity against all possible external threats had been built up in previous years by the cinema in films like *Alexander Nevsky* (1938), *Peter the First* (1937–9) and *Suvorov* (January 1941).[13] In the war newsreels already no. 61 made reference at length to the Russians in Berlin in 1760 and to Napoleon's campaign. Before the war the film *If There Should be War Tomorrow* (1939) for instance reflected Voroshilov's bombastic view that any attack on the Soviet Union would be speedily repulsed. Likewise Molotov's brave statement that the Soviet army should throw the Germans back over the frontier, broadcast in the first war newsreel, reflected Stalin's instructions to mount an attack and move into the enemy's territory, a view which failed to take into account the real situation at the front even in the first hours of the war.[14]

The newsreels in the first two weeks of the war naturally concentrated on the rear and gave no picture of the critical situation developing at the front: their task was to mobilise people's minds for the war. The 'Hurrah' commentary, fierce slogans and arrogant and brutal speeches and recitations for instance by the actor Buchma (no. 60, 27 June 1941) and the poet Surkov (no. 62, 2 July) were typical of these first days. His face contorted with anger at the treacherous attack, Buchma spat out his challenge:

Our rage is mighty and terrible. For the blood we shed we will pay back in crushing blows without mercy . . . the German fascist gangs do not have the means to overcome the unconquerable, freedom-loving Soviet people. All our help, our feelings, blood and life itself are dedicated to the orders of our wise government, to great Stalin in defence of our dear country. By this and this alone will we live. The Soviet army, workers, intelligentsia, all are committed to smash the fascist brigands and robbers.

But there was no film of the armed forces in the newsreels until 2 July and then it was clearly stock footage of air training using somewhat obsolete biplanes. During the first hours of the war, four teams of cameramen had been sent off to the front by the newsreel studios, but 'Film Report from the Front of the Patriotic War' appeared for the first time only in issue no. 66–7 (14 July 1941), although there had been eight issues since 22 June.

Most of the footage shown in the first two months 'from the front' was about the war in the air: Soviet planes loading up and taking off; German planes shot down by Soviet AA. These actions probably took place some distance behind the land front, although in no. 85 (2 Sept 1941) there was film of Soviet bombing on the South-west front taken from the Soviet bomber itself. Roman Karmen's first pictures were from Velikiye Luki, 250 miles south of Leningrad early in July and depict an air battle rather than ground fighting, which was still about 60 miles away at this date.[15] The cameramen do not appear to have been able to reach the most critical areas of the land front. Little was shown in the newsreels in the first two months of the war which had the genuine air of conflict. There was film of Soviet tanks 'ready for the attack' and occasionally the results of battles – German and Rumanian prisoners, captured or destroyed vehicles. One story which purported to show an attack on a German lorry column (no. 76, 8 August 1941) is suspect as some of the shots are taken from the cab of one of the German lorries as it supposedly moved into the Soviet ambush! The first film claiming to show partisan detachments in the German rear appeared as early as mid-July (no. 68, 16 July and no. 83, 20 August). The newsreels were neither able to give Soviet viewers in this period any idea of the often bitter and tenacious Soviet defence, nor of the extent of the defeats. No maps were used; the source of the front material was merely 'north-west front' or 'south-west front', and only at the end of August did the commentary and a recitation by the poet

Lebedev-Kumach suddenly reveal that Moscow and Leningrad were threatened:

> It is 1917 again. O.K. . . . Come on . . . Just try us. Dozens of brave and honest hands are ready to defend us no worse than yesterday. Moscow is not sleeping. Moscow is ready for battle. You hordes of barbarians and murderers, compounds of loathsome qualities, you could not comprehend the mighty heroism and fierce valour of Muscovites. For every Moscow wound we will repay with shells and bayonets by the million . . . (no. 83, 28 August 1941)

The limited material from the front in these early months of the war was by no means solely a result of disorganisation, but also of the unsuitability of what was available. One cameraman has recently written how difficult it was to film in the conditions of retreat and evacuation of supplies, technology and even cattle: 'When we tried to film these moments, it aroused suspicion amongst the population – aren't these spies if they are filming this unhappiness which has befallen our country?' There was also a psychological barrier to be overcome: the cameraman had no military preparation and yet had to make up his mind whether he would go into the attack with the military detachments. Appropriate material to boost the morale of the public was so lacking, that for some of the short documentaries of this period, the producers resorted to reconstructions and simulations. Soviet newsreel cameramen certainly became bolder as the war progressed. But it is probably also true that the army political authorities were at first very cautious about what they would allow to be filmed. Only later were front groups organised attached to each army, under the control of an experienced cameraman or director and under the general authority of the Army Political Administration. The Political Commissars would decide where the cameramen should position themselves and the themes appropriate for filming. The attachment of groups to each army ensured that the cameras available related to the concentration of Soviet troops and so more filming was possible where there was most likelihood of offensive action.[16]

A few other characteristics of the newsreels of the first two months of war are worth comment. In the first few editions up to mid-July, Stalin's role was more strongly propagandised. His 'cult of personality' was not often expressed in personal appearances on the film (apart from the November anniversaries), but there was a special newsreel issue for his speech of 2 July, his first word to the nation since the war began. Again, in issue no. 71 (23 July 1941) the camera suddenly confronted Stalin, Kalinin, Voroshilov, Mikoyan and others walking together in the Kremlin, while the commentary emphasised Stalin's role in the civil war and his importance in the current situation – 'with the name of Stalin, forward!' But after this little episode the cult of Stalin was remarkably muted in the newsreels and his name was hardly mentioned in the following issues up to the beginning of September 1941.

For the period of the newsreels from September 1941 to the end of February 1942 encompassing the German advance in the Ukraine and to the gates of Moscow and the Soviet winter offensive, there was more substantial material from the front. From 28 November a series of special issues was begun 'In Defence of Our Moscow'. Six were issued before the end of the year. At the same time the general newsreel issues were less frequent as a result of the critical military situation and seven issues were produced from Kuibyshev and Novosibirsk in December in a partial evacuation of the newsreel studios. The material from the home front emphasised the need for production and the involvement of everybody of all nationalities in the Soviet war effort. Nevertheless at the height of the battle of Moscow two editions devoted entirely to the entry of Soviet troops into Iran emphasised that even in adversity Soviet power could be exercised beyond its borders.

In January and February 1942 a pattern becomes clearer. With the success of Soviet troops at Tikhvin, re-establishing connections with Lake Ladoga, and hence with Leningrad, with the recapture of Rostov, as well as the results of the Moscow battle and liberation of most of Moscow province, there was much more positive material for the newsreels. Indeed in these months while the theme of the rear is not entirely forgotten (there are several stories on military production) yet the reporting from the front dominates all other items.

The next period for the newsreels naturally follows the course of the war from the stabilisation of the front in March April 1942, through the Germans' summer offensive reaching Stalingrad in September, the encirclement of Paulus's Sixth Army (23

November) and his final capitulation (31 January 1943). In this period, the average newsreel consisted of a lengthy report 'from the front of the Patriotic War', a story or stories from the home front and, from time to time, a story 'from abroad' or concerned with relations with foreign powers. In March and April 1942 stories from the rear were directly related to the war: the training of troops, treating the wounded and awarding medals to heroes. Apart from military action, the front stories also included visits of delegations, particularly from the non-Russian areas, to emphasise the unity of front and rear. Such stories as the delivery of presents from Ryazan province to the Bryansk front and the troops returning a letter with thanks to the collective farmers (no. 25, 24 March 1942), or gifts from Daghestan in the Caucasus to soldiers on the Karelian front (no. 39, 6 May 1942) and from the Tuva republic on the Soviet–Mongolian border (no. 40, 10 May 1942) emphasising the 'international' role of the Red Army and the commitment of the non-Russian rear to the war.

For the first year of the war there was no coverage of events abroad in the newsreels. The only references to foreign affairs were by film of the arrivals and accreditations of ambassadors and foreign emissaries. Noteworthy were Hopkins' arrival at the end of July 1941 (nos 74–5), the new Czech ambassador at the end of August (no. 82), Harriman and Beaverbrook (September) and Eden (December 1941). These reports merely established the facts of contact. No attempt was made to make any particular propaganda point out of them, but it is significant that it was felt necessary to draw attention to these episodes by including them in the newsreels at certain times and neglecting others. For instance although their American and British allies were already at war with Japan, the Soviet public was reassured in April 1942 by film recording the arrival and reception of the new Japanese ambassador Naotake Sato. Only in June 1942 did the first stories entitled *Za rubezhom* (From abroad) appear illustrating the war outside the Soviet Union and using newsreel film exchanged with Britain and the United States.[17]

The summer and early autumn of 1942 were months of great pressure on the south-west front, as the Germans retook Rostov and advanced towards Stalingrad and the Caucasus. As in every summer several issues were devoted to agriculture and the harvest: 'the harvest is the same as the battle at the front' (nos 56, 58, 61, 62, 63, 66, 71–2, 74, July–October 1942). This is a reminder that the urban population was often drafted to help bring in the harvest. The tone of the reportage from the front increasingly reflected the crisis on the Don towards the end of August with Stalin's call for 'not a step backwards' after Rostov (nos 58, 59, August 1942). The ferocity of the commentary and slogans of the newsreels revealed the intensity of the crisis: 'So that the swine don't creep any further, stick a bayonet in the German's throat' (no. 58); 'the Don will be costly to the enemy . . . defend every metre, fulfil the order of the motherland; only selfless sacrifice will defeat the hated Germans', the commentary recited. And in no. 59 (August): 'the motherland demands that we should die but not retreat . . .' In this, however, the newsreels only presented a rather paler reflection of that intensified propaganda in the press for the 'patrie en danger' initiated by the fall of Rostov and Stalin's order of 30 July.

The retreat to Stalingrad was put over in the newsreels more fully, more frankly and more confidently than the disasters of the previous year. The film from the rear was able to present a more powerful picture of the production of planes and tanks, and of the participation of women in arms production and mining than in the previous year; the economy was now more firmly on a war footing and the drastic reductions of war production, resulting from the occupation, were being overcome. The newsreels in their stories of heroic episodes at the front displayed more confidence in the morale of the army: even if they are retreating, the army will not break. While interspersed with ferocious slogans from time to time, the tone of the commentary in this period was not hysterical. The pictures of the house to house battles in Stalingrad (nos 76–7, November 1942) were largely left to speak for themselves of the unrelenting heroism and activity of the individual Soviet soldier. Only an occasional, quietly confident comment was needed to put over the message of this 'finest hour'.

Throughout December and January 1942/3 the newsreels were able to exploit the extent of the German defeat at Stalingrad with unending lines of dejected German prisoners, German cemeteries and destroyed and captured equipment (nos 83, 86, 88, 89, December 1942). This period culminated in the January 1943 issues (nos 1–8), which now in more detail and with the use of maps explained the Soviet counter-attack and encirclement of Paulus's army. It also coincided with an important advance and liberation of towns on the central front and the re-establishment of land communications with Leningrad (nos 6 and 7, January 1943, again making use of maps). Finally, no. 8 (January 1943) was devoted entirely to the German capitulation at Stalingrad and established the decisive significance of the battle. The pictures themselves were expressive enough in putting over the message of Soviet superiority, and they concluded with Stalin's order significantly thanking only the local commanders, Voronov and Rokossovsky, without mention of the staff, Zhukov and Vassilevsky. As a result of the changed conditions the newsreel footage from the front became more dynamic and daring after Stalingrad. The Germans on the run, the liberation of towns, the crimes of the Germans in occupation, all these demanded to be fully exposed and could be used most effectively now there was such rich actuality film footage.

In 1943 the newsreels reflected the more positive attitude towards certain aspects of the imperial Russian past and the attempts to raise the prestige and standing of Soviet officers, which had begun before Stalingrad. In October 1942 epaulettes, condemned since the revolution, were reintroduced and in issue no. 9 (February 1943) a substantial section was devoted to officers, in particular, displaying their new markings. Much was made also by the newsreels of the new medals for officers only, the Orders of Suvorov and Kutuzov, named after generals of the imperial period (nos 11, 12, February and no. 31, May 1943). Zhukov and Vasilevski were presented with the Order of Suvorov by Kalinin and soldiers were seen visiting Suvorov's grave, the camera lingering on the inscription while the commentary emphasised: 'Maintain the purity of the traditions of Russian arms'. The newsreel commentaries and selection of material cannot, nevertheless, be said to reveal so strongly that streak of Great Russian nationalism and emphasis on the role of the Russian people in the defeat of Germany, which were evident in the written propaganda, particularly of the later period of the war.[18] This theme was, in the newsreels at least, continually balanced with stories about the unity of the front with the non-Russian rear and the commitment of the non-Russian nationalities of Central Asia and the Caucasus in the struggle at the front. In 1943/4 the theme of the non-Russians in the war was a frequent one, in spite of the predominance of stories from the front.[19]

The newsreels did not exploit excessively antipathy towards the

Germans, Ehrenburg's 'holy hate', even when the first large-scale atrocities were being revealed as towns were liberated in the first half of 1943.[20] After the first weeks of the war, distinctions were less frequently made between the German people and their Nazi leaders, between 'good' and 'bad' Germans. Occasionally over film of German war crimes in 1943/4 the commentator promised: 'We will avenge the enemy's actions' or 'We will never forget'; 'Hitler's swine will not escape the reckoning'; 'There is nothing better than death for the German leaders; death to the Hitlerites' (no. 23, April, nos 57, 58–9, September 1943). But even the stories concerned directly with atrocities contained rather few sequences directly revealing the human suffering and calculated to arouse emotions. For instance no. 23 (April 1943) with a story on this theme was limited to a statement by Kalinin and film of a visit by N. M. Shvernik and the Metropolitan Nikolai of the investigation commission to some of the ruined villages, and in particular to desecrated churches. This was incidentally also evidence of preparation for the formal reconciliation between the Russian Orthodox Church and the state with the election of a Patriarch in September 1943. At the same time as atrocity stories were becoming more frequent in the newsreels, they were nevertheless balanced by a remarkable film of German prisoners of war as possible 'good' Germans. This story showing them being encouraged by their compatriots to oppose Hitler and his regime in the Committee of Free Germans 'for a free and independent Germany' was significant immediately after the Soviet victory at Kursk (no. 50, August 1943).

During 1943 in the period after Stalingrad, notably in the lull before Kursk (July), the newsreel commentaries were strikingly low-key and long sequences from the front were left almost or entirely without commentary (nos 22, 23, April; nos 29, 31, May; nos 38, 39, June). After Kursk however there is a more coherent and energetic presentation based on the liberation of particular towns, signposting the campaign and coinciding with the introduction of Moscow salutes by Stalin for each significant town liberated, which concluded each of these newsreels. Notable examples were the liberation of Bryansk and of Novorossiysk (nos 61, 62, September 1943).[21] The commentary also became more robust towards the end of the year and a fiercer tone was evident in the revelation of atrocities (nos 70, 71, November, liberation of Kiev; no. 78, December, Smolensk). These changes must certainly be related to the increased attention by the Party to film propaganda in the second half of 1943. In July and September the Central Committee discussed the problems of the cinema. In September a new sub-department for cinematography was formed in the Party's Directorate of Propaganda and Agitation and in November the leaders of front cine groups met in the Council of Peoples Commissars' Committee for Cinema Affairs to consider the successes and 'a few weaknesses' of the year's work.[22]

The theme of Soviet relations with the outside world appeared more frequently in the newsreels from mid-1942. Several stories in 1943 were devoted to Eastern Europe, in particular to the Poles and the Czechs. In June the Polish Patriots Congress was publicised with its leaders Colonel Berling and Wanda Wassilewskaya, a Pole, but also a deputy of the Supreme Soviet. In August 1943 the newsreels issued a story (nos 51–2) on the newly formed Kosciusko division of Poles on Soviet territory which included a Roman Catholic service and the taking of the oath to free Poland from the Germans and maintain the alliance with the USSR. This was a sign of things to come. In March 1944 (no. 19) again the new Polish armed forces were publicised: the Poles were encouraged to wreak vengeance on the Germans for Katyn and all other evils. For the negotiations with the Poles in Moscow in the summer of 1944, inevitably the Lublin Poles were well publicised by the newsreels and the London Poles forgotten even for the visit of Mikolaicyck in July/August 1944 (News of the Day, nos 3–4, July/August 1944). The Czechs were treated less deviously. Svoboda's Czech division was given two newsreel stories in April/May 1943 (nos 28, 29) and Benes visit to Moscow in December 1943 was given full coverage (nos 77, 78).[23]

Soviet newsreels of 1942–43 inevitably concentrated on the Soviet front. But from mid-1942 the exchange of film material with Britain enabled them to present more fully the war outside Russia. From October 1942 almost every issue to the end of the year included foreign newsreel footage, mainly from Britain, and in particular showing the Mediterranean and north African fronts (nos 72, 75, 79, 81, 87, October–December 1942; nos 3, 5, January 1943). Even at the height of the Stalingrad battle they did not neglect the allies contribution. In 1943 there were more varied stories using allied film: the bombing of Essen (no. 25), north Africa (no. 30), the bombing of Naples (no. 32), the capture of Tunis (nos 40–1), the Pantellaria campaign (nos

47–8), bombing of Italy (no. 49), the north Atlantic (no. 50), Malta (no. 50), allied forces in Italy (nos 58–9) and the St Nazaire operation (no. 60, September 1943). There were numerous other items from America and Britain and some from the British dominions in the Soviet newsreels for 1943. In the previous year there had been special newsreel issues on the signing of the Anglo-Soviet treaty (May), on the Churchill-Stalin meeting (July) and three issues of a series based on British newsreels, 'Great Britain in the Days of the War'.[24] These latter did not however continue into 1943. In the regular editions of the *Union Film Journal* for 1942/3, given the relative importance of the north African and Soviet fronts and the fact that the newsreels were for a Soviet audience, it cannot be said that there was a significant imbalance between the Soviet and Allied war efforts. In Britain, where the German threat was no longer so immediate and direct as in the Soviet Union in 1942/3, the newsreels gave wide coverage to the Soviet war effort, but the public and the film companies only showed limited interest in the longer documentaries of the Soviet front such as *The Battle of Orel, Battle for the Ukraine* and *The People's Avengers*, the latter on the partisan movement.[25]

Neither side in this partnership had full confidence in the other as is perhaps suggested by the fact that from June 1942 to September 1943 the stories 'from abroad' based on British newsreel footage were carefully cut out of the Soviet newsreels before they were sent to London. The foreign stories certainly appeared in the original Soviet editions shown in the Soviet Union, as the British Films Officer in Kuibyshev (and his opposite number in London) kept a close eye on what was shown and commented on any lack of balance.[26] It may simply have been thought not worth sending the British material in the Soviet newsreels back to London. But that there was some other motivation is suggested by the fact that there was a sharp change of policy from September 1943. From this time virtually every story based on allied footage was retained in the Soviet newsreels sent to London, up to and including the last *Union Film Journal* issue no. 29, June 1944 on the Normandy landings.[27]

This change of tactic coincided, as we have seen above, with the increased interest of the Party in the cinema and in the effectiveness of its impact from mid-1943. The omission of British stories from the Soviet newsreels sent to London in 1942/3 perhaps resulted from an exaggerated defensiveness over the

Soviet treatment of the Allied war effort. After Stalingrad this was less appropriate. Yet this still remains a puzzle. The stories 'from abroad' in the newsreels, particularly for the second half of 1943 seem to be fair both in content and commentary. There was for instance no attempt to make propaganda out of the delay in opening a second front in France. But in the first half of 1944 in the 29 issues of the *Union Film Journal* there was a significant reduction in footage on the allied war effort. Only no. 20 (April) and no. 29 (June) included allied stories on Italy and the Normandy landings. In the new *News of the Day* (18 issues in the second half of 1944) the only substantial stories on the allied land forces in Europe were no. 1 ('Advance of Allied Forces into Rome') and no. 12 ('The Liberation of Belgium'). Thus the space devoted to the Allied war effort declined as that effort became greater in terms of land forces concentrated in Europe.

In 1945 only three issues included material on the allied war effort (no. 8 on allied bombing; no. 9 on the attack on the Rhine; no. 24, 'The Allies Bomb Japan'). Certainly both in 1944 and 1945 the various inter-allied meetings were fully filmed. There were special documentaries on Yalta and Potsdam and on the visits of various allied leaders to Moscow, and also stories on developments in the allied countries (the death of President Roosevelt, 'A Great American President', and the election campaign in the United States), but the decrease in footage on the Allies fighting role in the war, as that role became greater in 1944/5 was evident. It had obvious implications in a system in which such matters were not left to chance.

On 15 May 1944 a special statement was issued by the Central Committee of the Soviet Communist Party, 'On the Production of Newsreels and Documentary Films'.[28] This statement marked a turning point for these productions during the war. Serious criticisms were made of the recent camera work, editing and commentary particularly in the documentary *Battle of Orel* (September 1943) on the struggle for the Kursk salient in the summer of 1943, and in the Union Film Journal newsreel nos 23–4 on the Crimean campaign in the spring of 1944. The editing was unoriginal, it was said. The commentary merely echoed what the picture showed and the films as a whole had no ideological educative value. The newsreels of the first months of 1944 as the Soviet armies began to reach the frontiers of their territory and move into Eastern Europe, were 'not a convincing reflection of the growing power of technological competence of the Soviet army'. The circle of questions dealt with by the newsreels had narrowed and their treatment lacked depth. The newsreel producers had also failed to use effectively writers who had experienced the front line in the war. Professor Drobashenko has written that these weaknesses resulted from the fact that the editors and writers had got into a rut and were producing stereotyped, standardised productions, without considering new approaches.[29]

As a result of the Party's criticisms certain measures were taken in the summer of 1944. The *Union Film Journal* newsreels were discontinued. The new *News of the Day* appeared less frequently and did not deal with the military campaign, for which a series of 'Special Front Issues' was begun. These brought together a more substantial body of material than it had been possible to use in a single newsreel and concentrated on a single phase of the campaign, giving a coherent and completed coverage. For the full length documentary productions, following Dovzhenko's example, a group of feature film directors was drawn in – Heifitz, Raizman, Zarkhi and Yutkevich. The Union Newsreel Studio now became the Union Documentary Studio with a feature film director, S. Gerassimov at its head in September 1944. At the studio was established an Artistic Council of directors, cameramen, musicians and writers to consider all questions of production.[30]

This period in 1944/5 sees the decline of the newsreels, strictly interpreted. In 1941 there had been over a hundred issues; in 1942–88; in 1943–67. In 1944, however, there were only 41 separate issues and 11 separate 'front issues'; in 1945 there were only 26 newsreels and seven 'front issues'. The reason for the decline of the newsreels in the last year of the war, at least as a series of short topical stories, cannot be understood merely by a consideration of the artistic and technical weaknesses of the reporting about the front. It must be seen in a wider context. In 1944 with the conclusion of the war with Hitler on the horizon and with the advance of Soviet troops into Eastern Europe, the Party began to consider its future ideological and propaganda work. Most of the current members of the Party had joined during the war, two and a half million new members in 1944 alone. It was necessary to take measures against complacency and carelessness, against dangerous 'bourgeois influences' and against 'bourgeois nationalism', which appeared to be reasserting itself in some of the non-Russian republics: 'The hour of retribution was near against the Nazi invaders when the Red Army reached the Soviet frontiers (April 1944); but not even a hint of complacency could be allowed'.[31]

More intensive political work was called for amongst the troops as they moved into Eastern Europe. In the non-Soviet lands it was necessary to help those nations to learn the truth about the Soviet Union and to show the advantages of socialism over capitalism. It was also important for the propaganda media to change into a new gear at this stage because of the large number of Soviet citizens who had been in German occupied territory or taken as prisoners of war or directed labour to Germany. In the projection of the East European countries to the Soviet people it was important to distinguish between the ruling classes and the working masses, particularly in those countries which had fought on Germany's side, and in Germany itself. As Soviet troops moved into the more developed countries of Eastern and Central Europe, they should, it was considered by the Communist Party, find fresh confirmation of the advantages of socialism over capitalism. Propaganda should emphasise the might of Soviet weapons, the skill and heroism of officers and men, the support of the rear for the army and the liberating mission of the Red Army.[32]

Soviet newsreel cameramen had in a vivid way reflected many sides of the heroic period of the nation at war, when every picture of front line action and destruction from places deep in Soviet territory evoked the imperative of selfless defensive struggle against the invader. But by mid-1944 the rather haphazard, short, fragmentary treatment of the military campaigns by the newsreels was inadequate. A more selective judgement, a more propagandistic attention to the role of Soviet forces in Eastern Europe was necessary to put over the desired message once the homeland was no longer under threat and the prospect of victory allowed a relaxation of attention and the raising of questions with less obvious answers than at the height of the war.

It is significant that it is precisely at this time, when the propaganda machine changed into a new gear, that the supply of Soviet newsreels to their British ally dried up. For the first half of 1944 almost all issues reached London, but of the 18 issues of *News of the Day* from September 1944 only three arrived, and none of the 'Special Front Issues'. In 1945 only one newsreel (nos

1–2) arrived. The new atmosphere, influenced by the new tasks and perspectives, rapidly affected even cultural exchanges as the war drew to a close.

NOTES

1 S. M. Shtemenko, *The Soviet General Staff at War, 1941–5* (Moscow, 1970) pp. 378–9.
2 A. Werth, *Russian at War* (London, 1964) pp. 222–3. For the war-time domestic and military context of this paper, apart from Werth, I have used the following: A. Seaton, *The Russo-German War, 1941–5* (London, 1971); J. Erickson, *The Road to Stalingrad* (London, 1975); S.P.Platonov, *Vtoraya Mirovaya Voina, 1939–45. Voenno-istoricheskii Ocherk* (Moscow, 1958); A. M. Samsonov, *Stalingradskaya Bitva* (Moscow, 1960); M. M. Minasyan *et al.* (eds.), *The Great Patriotic War of the Soviet Union. A General Outline* (Moscow, 1974).
3 Quoted in I. Deutscher, *Stalin. A Political Biography*, rev. edn (London, 1966) p. 460.
4 General Denikin wrote of the tsarist government's attitude towards propaganda in the army: '. . . an Imperial Order was issued shortly before the war, strictly prohibiting any discussion amongst the soldiers on the subject of the political issues of the moment . . . the authorities persistently refrained from awakening wholesome patriotism by explaining the causes and aims of the war . . .', A. I. Denikin, *The Russian Turmoil* (London, n.d.) p. 28.
5 Tamara Deutscher (ed.), *Not by Politics Alone . . . The Other Lenin* (London, 1973) pp. 204–5.
6 *Istoriya Kommunisticheskoi Partii Sovetskogo Soyuza*, vol. V (i), (1938–58) (Moscow, 1970) pp. 405, 413, 418–20.
7 Ibid., pp. 413–15.
8 Statistics from *Narodnoye Khozyaistvo SSSR v 1958 godu* (Moscow, 1959) pp. 867–9; *SSSR v tsifrakh. 1973* (Moscow, 1974) pp. 216–17. Figures are not available for the war years. In the whole population in 1939, 25.1 per cent were under 10 or over 69 years old. There was however a much higher proportion of the very old and very young in the countryside. My estimate is based on a very young and very old urban population of about 20 per cent. See P. G. Pod'yachikh, *Naselenie SSSR* (Moscow, 1961) pp. 29–34.
9 *Istoriya KPSS, op. cit.*, vol. V (i), p. 426. A rough estimate from statistics for the urban population for 1939 suggests that between 18 and 24 million of the urban population were cut off by occupation: *Narodnoye Khozyaistvo SSSR v 1958 godu*, op. cit., pp. 20–30.
10 *KPSS v rezolyutsiyakh i resheniyakh s'ezdov, konferentsii i plenumov Ts.K.* (Moscow, 1971) vol. VI (1941–54) pp. 13–14, 130–1; *Istoriya KPSS*, op. cit., vol. V (i), p. 426.
11 V. Smirnov, *Dokumental'nye filmy o Velikoi Otechestvennoi Voiny* (Moscow, 1947) pp. 7–10, 264; Y. S. Kalashnikov *et al.* (eds), *Ocherki Istorii Sovetskogo Kino*, vol. II (Moscow, 1956) pp. 548–9, 559–62; M. P. Kim *et al.*

(eds), *Sovetskaya Kul'tura v gody Velikoi Otechestvennoi Voiny* (Moscow, 1976) pp. 255–60. Smirnov gives numerous examples of the exploits of Soviet cameramen in the war and some references to their diaries and reminiscences.

12 I am indebted to the Imperial War Museum for permission to use their collection of Soviet war-time newsreels on which this analysis is based. The collection consists of 152 issues of *Union Film Journal* (out of 232 issued) from 22 June 1941 to June 1944 and four out of the 44 issues of *News of the Day* for September 1944 to September 1945. It does not include any of the 'Special Issues' on for instance the inter-allied conferences or Stalin's November anniversary speeches. Nor does it include the thematic 'Special Front Issues' (19 issues) which became the main form for material from the front in the last year of the war. The collection is however extensive enough to provide a basis for judgements on Soviet war newsreel up to June 1944, when there was a change of policy in the whole field of propaganda. Up to June 1944 the main gaps are from 2 September 1941 to 28 February 1942 and a dozen issues for May/June 1942. I have been able to check the contents of the missing newsreels from the full filmography of Soviet documentary film in the Soviet–German war in Y. S. Kalashnikov, op. cit., pp. 790–837. The Imperial War Museum reference numbers are RNA for 1941, RNB for 1942 etc., together with the Soviet newsreel number.

13 I have not been able to view Soviet newsreel for the first half of 1941 to consider the impact of the outbreak of the war on newsreel coverage and there is no substantial treatment of Soviet documentary cinema from the mid-1930s to 1941. The relevant volume of the standard history (Y. S. Kalashnikov, vol. II (1935–45), op. cit.) includes a separate chapter and detailed filmography on documentary and newsreel film in the war years, but strictly from 22 June 1941. There is no full discussion of documentary film in the years immediately preceding the war (ibid., pp. 20–30). There is however a full discussion of feature film and a filmography for 1935–41. This reticence about Soviet documentary cinema of the late 1930s is also reflected in Professor Drobashenko's paper in this volume.'

14 Y. S. Kalashnikov, vol. II, op. cit., pp. 143–6; A. A. Grechko *et al.* (eds), *Istoriya Vtoroi Mirovoi Voiny* (Moscow, 1974–   ) vol, III, pp. 398–9.

15 J. Leyda, *Kino* (London, 1960) pp. 367–9; N. Kolesnikova *et al,*, *Roman Karmen* (Moscow, 1959) pp. 73–4. Karmen's first war pictures from Velikiye Luki appeared in issue no. 69 (July 19). The German forces reached Velikiye Luki towards the beginning of August.

16 A. A. Lebedev, 'Frontovaya kinokhronika' in M. P. Kim, op. cit., pp. 255–60, 236–7.

17 The British exchange took place through Cairo and Tehran and films took up to four months to arrive. The first Soviet newsreels (for February 1942) arrived in London at the end of June. The issues for 22 June to September 1941 were also probably not delivered to London before 1942. It is not clear why the issues for September 1941 to February 1942 were not sent, but in December 1941 the Ministry of Information was still complaining that they had nothing more than still photographs to distribute in their efforts to propagandise Anglo–Soviet co-operation against Hitler. It was noted that Stalin's 'gift to Beaverbrook did not include film' (on his visit to Moscow at

the end of September 1941). Public Record Office, INF/1/676. The Foreign
   Office files on diplomatic communications for 1941/2, which made
   reference to the problems of transport of these films, have been entirely
   destroyed.
18 See Werth, op. cit., pp. 738–40.
19 Issues 11–12, 14, 15, 16, 44, 49, 50, 55, 57, 79 (1943) and nos 17, 20, 28
   (1944) include non-Russian, mainly Caucasian and Central Asian stories.
   References to some of the non-Russian nationalities are also of interest in
   showing the suddenness of the change of policy towards them during the
   war. In July 1941 the Volga-Germans were chosen (no. 62, 2 July 1941) to
   make the usual points about bringing in the harvest. This positive reference
   to Soviet–Germans was hardly fortuitous, given the outbreak of the war only
   a few days before. In August the Volga-Germans were deported *en masse* for
   disloyalty. One of the last positive references to the Kalmycks (deported in
   late 1943) is in the newsreel no. 5 (January 1943) concerning the liberation of
   Elista, 'capital of the Kalmyck ASSR'. In March 1944 (no. 17) a story is
   devoted to reconstruction in the tiny Kabardin-Balkar ASSR in the north
   Caucasus. This area had already been freed from German occupation for
   many months. In April the Balkars were deported for collaboration with the
   Germans and all references to them were prohibited until their rehabilitation
   in 1956. Unfortunately the copy in the Imperial War Museum collection of
   the controversial issue nos 23–4 (April 1944) on the liberation of the Crimea
   is a mute print. It is not therefore possible to determine whether the
   reception by the local population is referred to. The Crimean Tartars were
   deported in May/June 1944. See R. Conquest, *The Nation-Killers. The
   Soviet Deportation of Nationalities* (London, 1970) pp. 54. 62–3, 100–1,
   105–6.
20 The strident and all-embracing propaganda against the Germans was an
   important feature of Ehrenburg's popular patriotic writings during the war,
   which helped to strengthen morale. It recurred strongly towards the end of
   the war as Soviet troops entered Germany, but in February 1945 the Party
   authorities condemned it as an incorrect approach (Werth, op. cit., pp.
   411–14, 965–7). I am unable to say how far this tone was reflected in the
   newsreels in late 1944 and 1945 when the 'Special Front Issues' were able to
   reveal the destruction of German cities.
21 Smirnov, *op. cit.,* pp. 114–18.
22 Ibid., pp. 118; *Istoriya KPSS*, op. cit., vol. V (i), pp. 425–6; A. A. Grechko
   et al., op. cit., vol. VII, p. 360.
23 See Werth, op. cit., pp. 760–1 for this visit.
24 Smirnov, op. cit., p. 56.
25 INF/1/631, *Films. Monthly Report,* Jan. 1944.
26 Ibid., *Films. No. 22 Monthly Report*, July 1943.
27 The only omissions are no. 68 (Oct. 1943) with a story on the allied attack on
   Salerno and no. 80 (Dec. 1943) which was not sent for obvious reasons as its
   theme was the Cairo and Tehran conferences, entirely based on British
   footage.
28 Unfortunately this document does not appear to have been published.
   Istoriya Velikoi Otechestvennoi Voiny Sovetskogo Soyuza (Moscow, 1962)
   vol. IV, pp. 650–1 gives a reference to the archive of the Institute of

Marxism–Leninism. Also see *Istoriya KPSS*, op. cit., vol. V (i), p. 425.

29 Kalashnikov, op. cit., vol. II, pp. 547, 567, 592–3; A. A. Grechko *et al.* (eds), op. cit., vol. VIII, p. 347; *Short History . . .*, op. cit., pp. 344–7. The film *Battle of Orel* had, however, received very favourable reviews in the Soviet press, including *Pravda* when it first appeared in September 1943. Smirnov, writing in 1947, still refered to the film as 'a great event in the life of Soviet cinematography' (pp. 91–2). The criticisms of newsreel nos 23–4 on the liberation of the Crimea were also a little surprising as this was the first of the few issues of *Union Film Journal* to have a military consultant, Major-General S. P. Platonov, later known for his history of the Second World War.

30 Kalashnikov, op. cit., vol. II, pp. 592–3; Leyda, op. cit., pp. 385–6.

31 *Short History . . .*, op. cit., p. 345.

32 Ibid., pp. 344–7.

Index